Exchange Rate Dynamics

A Modern Analysis of Exchange Rate Theory
and Evidence

Eric J. Pentecost

Department of Economics
Loughborough University
Leicestershire, UK

Edward Elgar

Published by
Edward Elgar Publishing Limited
8 Lansdown Place
Cheltenham
Glos GL50 2HU
UK

Edward Elgar Publishing Company
Old Post Road
Brookfield
Vermont 05036
US

Reprinted 1996

A CIP catalogue record for this book is available from the British Library

Library of Congress Cataloging-in-Publication Data
Pentecost, Eric J.
    Exchange rate dynamics: a modern analysis of exchange rate theory and evidence/by Eric J. Pentecost.
        p.   cm.
    Includes bibliographical references and indexes.
    1. Foreign exchange rates. 2. Foreign exchange rates—Econometric models.
        I. Title.
HG3851.P46 1993
332.4'56—dc20   92–28723
                                                                      CIP

ISBN 1 85278 138 6
    1 85278 903 4 (paperback)

Printed in Great Britain at the University Press, Cambridge

Contents

Figures

Tables

Preface

From the end of the Second World War until the early 1970s the international monetary system based on the agreement reached at Bretton Woods in 1944 functioned according to a fixed exchange rate system. Over these three decades, although the debate over the relative merits of fixed and floating exchange rates continued, the determinants of the equilibrium exchange rate, under floating rates, were not extensively considered. With the collapse of the Bretton Woods fixed exchange rate system in the early 1970s, and the move to generalized floating on the part of the major industrial nations by the spring of 1973, economists had to rediscover the pre-war and inter-war literature on floating exchange rates. The first clutch of papers on the determinants of floating exchange rates appeared in 1976 in the *Scandinavian Journal of Economics*. In the same year Dornbusch's classic paper on exchange rate overshooting appeared in the *Journal of Political Economy* and the rediscovery was under way.

From 1976 to date the literature on exchange rate determination has exhibited exponential growth. The early work remained faithful to the concept of purchasing power parity developed in the inter-war years, and the monetary approach to the balance of payments, which was the state-of-the-art fixed exchange rate model in the early 1970s. By the end of the decade the portfolio balance model had been developed from the earlier work of Mundell, Fleming and Tobin. To the present time these two types of model dominate the exchange rate literature, although they have been extended in a number of directions during the 1980s, in an attempt to better represent the movement of actual exchange rates, particularly following Meese and Rogoff's seminal paper in 1983 which suggested that the state-of-the-art exchange rate models could not outperform a simple random walk model out-of-sample. It is not unfair to say that into the 1990s the determinants of the equilibrium exchange rate are still only very imperfectly understood. An appraisal of the competing models of exchange rate determination is the theme of this book, although this will necessarily take us beyond international monetary economics into recent econometric methods and the mathematics of non-linear dynamic models.

This monograph is written for advanced undergraduates and post-graduate students of economics. The reader will therefore require an understanding of intermediate macroeconomic and microeconomic principles as well as more than a passing acquaintance with econometric and mathematical methods. To facilitate understanding of some of the more technical aspects required by this text, several appendices to chapters have been included where more than what may be regarded as 'standard techniques' are required. The book is organised in three parts. Chapters 2 and 3 consider the historical foundations of exchange rate theory, in Classical and Keynesian monetary theory respectively, without international capital flows. Chapters 4 and 5 focus on Monetary and Keynesian models with perfect capital mobility. Chapters 6 and 7 consider models which permit interaction between capital flows and trade balance flows and so represent the most general classes of exchange rate model. Chapter 8 considers recent developments in exchange rate modelling, including models with chaotic dynamics. Throughout the book empirical evidence is presented adjacent to the respective theoretical models. This helps not only to highlight the problems involved in empirically testing the particular theory in question but also to assess its ability in explaining sample data and implications for exchange rate policy.

Nearly every chapter makes use of theories and concepts developed in the early chapters and cross-references are frequently given. Nevertheless, the reader need not read straight through the book from page one to the end. Different reading patterns can be followed according to the reader's main interest or structure of the lecture course. The chapters have been written to stand, in most cases, as independent of the whole so that the reader can just dip into the book to read a specific chapter or to understand a particular model, without having to read all the preceding chapters. For example, a reader interested only in the monetary approach to exchange rate determination should read Chapters 2, 4 and 6; a reader interested in monetary history should read Chapters 2 and 3; recent extensions to the Mundell–Fleming model of a floating exchange rate are covered in Chapter 5 and lead on to the portfolio balance models covered in Chapter 7.

This book has emerged, somewhat belatedly, from my PhD thesis on 'Exchange Rate Determination and Macroeconomic Policy' (London University, 1984), although it is no longer recognisable as having any similarity with my thesis. I remain grateful to David Currie for supervising my thesis and other members of the Economics Department at QMC for encouragement and support during this period, in particular to Bernard Corry. In writing this book I have benefitted from helpful comments on individual chapters and sections from Ron MacDonald, Chris Milner, Andy Osbaldestin and John Presley. I am especially grateful to Stephen Hall and Paul Mizen who each read the entire manuscript and saved me from making several slips as well as suggesting many improvements to the text. Unfortunately, none of the above can reasonably be held accountable for any errors that remain all of which are my responsibility. I am also grateful to Edward Elgar for his forbearance as this project has taken rather longer to complete than first envisaged. Finally, my biggest debt is to my wife, Gillian, for so ably coping with the pressures of rearing two boisterous young children, John and Anne, to allow me the time to complete this manuscript. Unlike the case of many authors this will not be my first and last book, so perhaps I should apologise in advance for the continuing neglect of my fatherly duties, and promise to dedicate my next work to them.

Eric Pentecost
Loughborough University

1 Introduction

1.1 Exchange and rates of exchange

The notion of exchange is central to economics. It is through the exchange of goods that societies can move away from subsistence agriculture toward an economy where the members can enjoy the advantages of the division of labour and the resulting specialization in production. Individuals are not equally endowed with strength and skills, nor do they have the same needs or desires. It is by concentrating on the things which the individual can do best, and exchanging the product of his labour for those things that his neighbour can produce, that man in society makes material progress. The activity of exchanging goods and services is therefore at the heart of economic and social advancement.

To understand the importance of this process consider a simple example of two individuals, A and B, each producing two goods, cloth and wine, exclusively for their own use. In Figure 1.1 each individual is assumed to produce amounts of cloth and wine according to a constant marginal rate of transformation, given by the AA locus for A and the BB line for individual B. In otherwords if A spends all his time producing cloth he is able to produce 12 units, whereas if he only produces wine he can produce 6 units. That is to say the opportunity cost of producing 1 unit of wine is 2 units of cloth. Similarly, individual B can produce either 4 units of cloth or 12 units of wine, giving B's opportunity cost of 1 unit of cloth as 3 units of wine. Both individuals are assumed to have the same consumption preferences, given by the indifference curves I_0 and I_1 so that in the absence of trade between A and B, A produces (and consumes) 6 units of cloth and 3 units of wine (at point A^*) and B produces and consumes 1 unit of cloth and 9 units of wine (at point B^*). In these initial equilibrium positions both individuals have utility equal to I_0.

Suppose now that the individuals become specialized in production and undertake trade in cloth and wine. Individual A will specialize in the production of cloth since he can produce cloth more cheaply than B, and B will specialize in the production of wine, since he can produce this more cheaply than A. To see this, the opportunity cost to A of producing 1 unit of wine is 2 units of cloth; that is, the relative price of cloth to wine is 2:1. The opportunity cost to B of producing 1 unit of wine is only 0.33 units of cloth, and so the relative price of cloth to wine is 1:3. Individual B therefore specializes in wine production. By a similar analysis it can be shown that individual *A* will specialize in cloth production, since the opportunity cost of 1 unit of cloth is 0.5 units of wine for *A* and 3 units of wine for *B*. With trade between the two parties, *B* is now able to obtain cloth at the cost of 1 unit of wine (rather than at 3 units without trade) and *A* is able to obtain wine at the cost of 1 unit of cloth (rather than at 2 units without trade). With exchange, therefore, both individuals are better off than before, as indicated in Figure 1.1, by a move to point *E* on the higher indifference curve I_1.

The exchange that takes place between individuals *A* and *B* does not depend upon the existence of money. Relative prices, in this case the relative price of wine to cloth, reflect the opportunity costs of producing one good rather than the other and exist in barter economies where there is a direct exchange of goods. Barter economies, however, are not very efficient because they require a double coincidence of wants. That is, individual *A* not only has to find a buyer for his surplus product, but a buyer who will exchange for *A*'s product the good which *A* wants to obtain. To alleviate the need for this double coincidence of wants

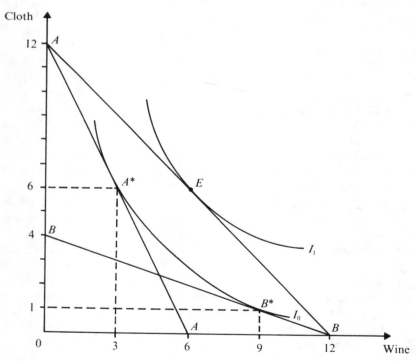

Figure 1.1   The gains from exchange

mediums of exchange emerged very early in the development of human societies. To see this, suppose there are three individuals, *A*, *B* and *C* and that *B* wants *A*'s product but that *A* wants *C*'s product and not *B*'s product in exchange. In this case *B*'s good can serve as the vehicle, or medium, of exchange if *C* will accept *B*'s product in return for his own. *A* can exchange his good with *B*, and then exchange *B*'s unwanted product with *C*. Such a web of exchanges is extremely limiting on trade. For example, the goods must be perceived to be of equal value or in some way divisible, they must be storable, in the sense that they are not perishable and hold their value, if they are used as a medium of exchange rather than for immediate consumption. For these reasons and many others[1] money emerged very early in the development of human societies to facilitate exchange. Each good, therefore, is usually priced in terms of units of money. In the example used above, at *A** the relative cost of cloth to wine was 2:1, hence the price of cloth could be £5 per unit and wine £2.50 per unit. The relative price would still reflect the relative cost of 2:1, as cloth is twice the price of wine. This example shows that the existence of money does not affect relative prices, it serves merely to facilitate exchange.

The problem with money (or any commodity that is used as a medium of exchange) is that the quantities supplied and demanded of that good may fluctuate and so the value of the medium of exchange may also fluctuate. The price of money, in terms of the commodities it will buy, is generally regarded as the reciprocal of the general level of prices $(1/P)$. A rise in the price level will therefore be equivalent to a fall in the value of money, since as the money prices of all commodities have risen by an equal amount a given quantity of money will now buy less goods and services than before.[2] Note, however, that relative prices will remain unchanged.

The analysis of exchange and exchange ratios suggests that there are three kinds of prices: relative prices, which reflect the exchange of goods for other goods and which exist in both barter and monetary economies; money prices, which reflect the exchange of money for other goods, and which can obviously only exist in a monetary economy; and thirdly, the general level of prices, which reflects the average price of all commodities and which again can only exist in an economy with money. There is, however, a fourth kind of price, which is the subject-matter of this book. This is the price of one money (or medium of exchange) in terms of another money (or medium of exchange). Hence, rather than exchanging money for goods or services, money can be exchanged for another money. All the while different national, or even area currencies exist, then to buy goods or services or acquire assets from a different currency area may require that the potential purchaser pay in the local medium of exchange.

Domestic residents need therefore to acquire foreign currency before buying foreign goods or services and foreign residents similarly need to acquire domestic currency before purchasing home goods and services. The exchange rate as used in all that follows is the relative price of one currency in terms of another. Without different national or area currencies, it would not be necessary to exchange one money for another and exchange rates as subsequently used in this book would not exist.

1.2   Types of exchange rate

The exchange rate may be defined as the domestic price of foreign currency or, as its reciprocal, the foreign price of domestic currency. Helmers (1988) reports that, of the 137 countries whose exchange rates are given in the IMF's International Financial Statistics, 114 report their exchange rates as the domestic price of foreign currency, including the USA, Germany, France and Japan, while the other 23 countries report them as the foreign currency price of domestic currency, including Australia, New Zealand, Switzerland and the UK. In this book, the former definition is employed, so that the exchange rate, denoted E, is the domestic price of foreign currency. A rise in E is a rise in the domestic price of foreign currency and therefore, by definition, a fall in the foreign price of the domestic currency, denoted as E^*.

To define 'the' exchange rate as simply the price of a unit of a foreign currency in terms of domestic currency is, however, rather naive. There are very many complications stemming from the large number of 'foreign currencies', each of which has its own spot markets. In addition, the major trading countries' currencies also have forward markets, that is, markets where prices are agreed today for future delivery or purchase. Since the exchange rate is a money price there is also the problem, at least for the economist, as to whether the exchange rate is to be measured in real or money terms. This section concentrates on the spot exchange rate, with the next section looking at the linkages between the spot and forward exchange markets.

For any country there are as many spot exchange rates (that is, foreign exchange for immediate delivery or purchase) as there are trading partners with independent currencies. These exchange rates are called the *bilateral* exchange rates and take the form of the dollar–franc rate, the dollar–pound rate, the dollar–mark rate and so on. In practice, it is usually sufficient to speak in terms of a single exchange rate because *cross-rates* of exchange are always closely aligned through arbitrage. Thus, if the dollar–mark and dollar–pound rates are known, then the mark–pound cross-rate can easily be computed, at least within very narrow limits, as the cost of exchanging currencies is generally very small. Furthermore, with the domestic currency floating against all the other major currencies it is difficult to establish 'the' exchange rate. For example, a depreciation of the home currency against one foreign currency may correspond to an appreciation against another. To ascertain the average value of the home currency an average of the bilateral rates is needed. The *effective exchange rate* index is a geometric, trade-weighted index which is used to assess the average value of the home currency in terms of the foreign currencies of the home country's major trading partners. The weights used in this calculation may be either bilateral trade weights or multilateral trade weights. The bilateral weights measure each trading country's share of total domestic exports plus imports, whereas the multilateral weights, in contrast, are the shares of each country in the combined total trade of all the foreign countries included in the index. The difference between these two indices is that the former does not allow for competition in third markets, whereas the multilateral exchange rate index does.

The bilateral, cross and effective exchange rates are measured in money terms. That is, they do not allow for the effect of inflation on the real purchasing power of the currencies concerned. To adjust for inflation it is necessary to deflate the nominal exchange rate by the domestic price level and multiply by the foreign price level. The *real bilateral exchange rate* between the home and the foreign country for example, would be: $R = EP^*/P$, where R is the real exchange rate, E is the nominal exchange rate, P is some measure of the domestic price level and P^* is some equivalent measure of the foreign price level. Hence, if the price level rises faster in the home country than in the foreign country, then for a given value of E, the real price of the domestic currency will be falling and foreign price-competitiveness improving against the home country. Note that movements in the real exchange rate will only be the same as those of the bilateral rate if price movements between the home and foreign countries are identical. A more widely used measure is the *real effective exchange rate index* which measures the average level of competitiveness against all the major trading partners. This is defined as the effective exchange rate index multiplied by the price index of the home country and deflated by an average foreign price level index, with identical country weights as in the effective exchange rate index.

There are, of course, many different measures of the real exchange rate, depending upon what price indices are used. These various measures of the real exchange rate reflect the different purposes for which the exchange rate index may be used. Helmers (1988) for example, cites six different measures. An index which uses the domestic consumer price index (CPI) and the foreign wholesale price index (WPI*) for example, would show how domestic prices compare with traded goods prices (since wholesale price indices contain a high proportion of traded goods). Alternatively, the real exchange rate index could attempt to measure the ratio of traded goods prices to home goods prices, where the foreign price index would consist of the prices of home imports and exports, compared to some domestic price index. A third measure could be of the competitiveness of home production. In this case the domestic price index could be replaced by an index of domestic wage costs.

These definitions cover most of the theoretical exchange rate concepts, but they do not correspond directly to the way in which exchange rates are measured in practice. Consider a bilateral exchange rate. For this particular rate of exchange there will always be two prices: the higher price is the selling price and the lower price is the buying price. The difference between the two prices represents the dealer's margin. Hence the price of foreign exchange depends upon whether you are a buyer or a seller. Statisticians and economists take the average of the buying and selling prices to compute the bilateral, nominal exchange rate. There is a further problem: at what time is this average taken? Since the exchange rate fluctuates continuously during the day, the time of day at which the average is calculated could be important. Frequently, exchange rates are measured at midday or when the market closes for the day. Most econometric studies of the exchange rate, however, are concerned with monthly or quarterly values of the exchange rate rather than daily or even weekly frequencies, which give rise to two alternative measures: the period average measure or the end of period measure. Which measure to use poses a problem for the economist, since to use end of period rates increases the probability of choosing an outlier, whereas the use of a period average has the effect of smoothing the data. Both kinds of measure have been widely used in empirical work and there seems to be no obvious statistical or economic reason for preferring one to the other in all circumstances.

1.3   The relationship between spot and forward rates
The spot market for foreign exchange is closely linked in practice to the forward market. The forward market is simply the market where foreign exchange is traded for delivery or purchase at some point in the future. These markets are linked by three kinds of activity: arbitrage, hedging and speculation. These activities are frequently undertaken by the same agents in the markets, although it may be useful, at least for expositional purposes, to think of the three activities as being undertaken by different agents.

Arbitrageurs seek to maximize the return on a given portfolio of investments and hence invest this portfolio in assets with different currency denominations. For this group of agents, therefore, interest rate differentials are important. Hedging activity is generally linked to real trade flows. Because of the difference between the payment date for the goods and the actual delivery of the goods companies may seek to cover their foreign exchange receipts and payments by using the forward market. Indeed, in most cases arbitrageurs are also hedgers in the forward markets. Both of these parties generally opt for 'closed' positions in foreign currency; that is, they cover in the forward markets and do not bear the exchange rate risk. Speculators, on the other hand, do take 'open' positions in foreign currency and hence speculate about movements in the spot exchange rate. From these definitions it should be clear that the same party may actually be simultaneously arbitraging, hedging and speculating in the markets.

Consider the following simple example of interest rate arbitrage. Suppose a UK resident has £100 to invest for twelve months and can chose to invest in a UK bond at 8 per cent per annum or a US government bond at 12 per cent per annum. If the risk of default is the same and the pound–US dollar exchange rates are fixed, then, ignoring transactions costs, the individual would prefer to invest in the US bond since the return would be greater. If, however, exchange rates are liable to change over the year, then the relative return on the two assets will also depend upon the direction and magnitude of these exchange rate changes. Suppose the spot, pound–dollar exchange rate appreciates over the year from £0.50 to £0.55. The total value of the US investment will now be £124, giving a total return of 24 per cent compared with an unchanged return on the sterling investment of 8 per cent, hence the dollar investment is still preferred. Of course, had the sterling price of the dollar fallen from £0.50 to say, £0.45, the value of the dollar investment would have fallen to just £101.81 and the sterling investment, worth £108, would now be preferred.

As the above example shows, movements in the exchange rate are critical in the evaluation of rates of return on foreign assets. The actual movements in the spot exchange rate, however, are not known at the start of the year when the investment is made. Thus an investor will bear all the exchange rate risk if he holds an open position in foreign currency, which is, of course, equivalent to speculating on exchange rate movements. More commonly the trader or arbitrageur will avoid the exchange risk by covering in the forward market. Hence, when the UK resident is choosing which investment to make, the forward exchange rate will enter into the calculation, since he will want to sell all his dollar earnings forward at a rate of exchange agreed now – the twelve-month forward rate. Hence if the current twelve-month forward rate is £0.53 then the sterling value of the dollar investment at 12 per cent will gross £124 and will exceed the value of the sterling investment. Moreover, this return is certain as the $224 dollars are sold forward today, for delivery in one year's time at an agreed rate of \$1.90 per pound (that is, £0.53 per dollar). If, however, the forward rate is £0.476, then the sterling investment is the most profitable, yielding 8 per cent rather than just under 7 per cent on the dollar investment.

The trader or interest arbitrageur, by hedging his investment, does not bear the exchange rate risk. For either party to be able to sell his dollars forward for pounds at \$1.90 per pound, however, requires that some other party in the market must be prepared to sell pounds forward at \$1.90 each. In order to persuade other foreign exchange market participants to sell pounds forward (that is, to buy dollars forward) the pounds have to be sold at a premium relative to the spot rate. This premium or discount is the price paid to compensate the speculators for the risk involved in holding forward dollars. Thus, in terms of our example, interest arbitrage will only be profitable provided that the interest differential in favour of the US is not more than offset by the forward discount on the dollar. The covered interest rate parity condition may be written more succinctly as follows:

$$(F/E)(1 + i^{us}) = (1 + i^{uk}) \tag{1.1}$$

where F is the forward exchange rate (£/\$), E is the spot exchange rate (£/\$) and i^{us} and i^{uk} are the domestic and foreign rates of interest. Taking logarithms of equation (1.1) gives:

$$f - e = r^{uk} - r^{us} \tag{1.2}$$

where lower-case letters denote natural logarithms, $r^{uk} \simeq ln(1 + i^{uk})$ and $r^{us} \simeq ln(1 + i^{us})$. If condition (1.2) holds then there will be no incentive to move money across the exchanges, because any interest gain on the dollar asset is wiped out by a forward discount on the dollar. Equations (1.1) and (1.2) show that the spot and forward exchange rates are closely linked through the activities of arbitrageurs, hedgers and speculators, where speculators typically hold open positions in foreign currency that the other transactors are not prepared to carry.

The relationship between spot and forward foreign exchange markets can also be given diagrammatic treatment, drawing on the seminal paper of Tsiang (1959). Assuming that speculation only takes place in the forward market and that there is initially covered interest parity, so that there is no interest arbitrage, the demand and supply schedules for spot dollars represent the demands and supplies of commodity traders. In Panel A of Figure 1.2 the demand for spot dollars schedule, denoted by SD^c, slopes down to the right since as the sterling price of the dollar falls (dollar appreciation) UK exports become more competitive in the USA and so demand for them increases, which raises the demand for dollars along SD^c. Similarly, a depreciation of the dollar will make US exports more competitive in foreign markets and hence the supply of dollars will rise and the SS^c schedule will have a positive slope. The market for spot dollars clears at e_0 in Figure 1.2. The forward market consists of two elements. There is the demand and supply of forward dollars emanating from the hedging activities of the commodity traders, depicted in panel B of Figure 1.2 by the FD^c and FS^c curves respectively. The second element in the forward market is the activity of speculators. If the forward rate is equal to their expectation of the future spot rate, as at f_2, then they will have a zero excess demand for forward dollars. Alternatively, if the forward rate is lower than their expected future spot rate they will have a positive excess demand for forward dollars, which will increase as the actual forward rate declines relative to the expected future spot rate. The line XFD^s is the excess demand for forward dollars from speculators in the market. The line FD^{c+s} is the horizontal sum of the demand curves for hedgers and speculators. The forward market is assumed to clear at f_0 because, by assumption, there is no arbitrage activity, so that $e_0 = f_0$, and US and UK interest rates must be equal.

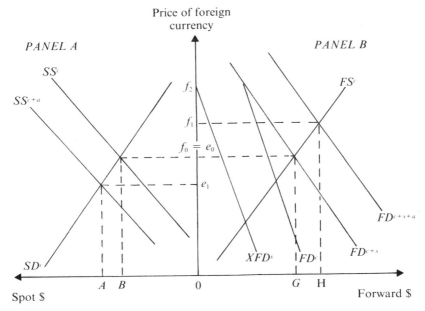

Figure 1.2 Spot and forward markets for foreign exchange

Consider now a rise in the UK rate of interest. Arbitrageurs will now enter both the spot and forward markets. Arbitrageurs will sell dollars in the spot market, in order to buy pounds with which to buy sterling assets, and buy dollars in the forward market to cover the exchange risk. Thus the supply schedule for spot dollars will shift to the right, to SS^{c+a}, and the demand for forward dollars will simultaneously shift to the right, to FD^{c+s+a}. Thus the spot price will fall and the forward price of dollars will rise until the forward premium on the dollar exactly matches the interest rate differential. The interest rate differential will be $f_1 - e_1$. In this new equilibrium the distance AB represents the arbitrageurs' sales of spot dollars which is exactly matched by their purchases of forward dollars given by the distance GH.

In the analysis above it was the uncertainty about the future spot exchange rate which forced commodity traders and arbitragers to enter the forward market. If, in contrast, it is assumed that arbitrageurs are certain about the time path of the future spot rate then they will not enter the forward market and the arbitrage position would be uncovered. In this case the equilibrium condition would be:

$$\varepsilon_t e_{t+1} - e_t = r_t^{UK} - r_t^{US} \tag{1.3}$$

where $\varepsilon_t e_{t+1}$ is the expected spot exchange rate in period $t+1$ based on information available at the end of period t. This condition is known as the uncovered interest rate parity condition (UIP). In a certain world $\varepsilon_t e_{t+1} = f_t$ and equations (1.2) and (1.3) would be identical. With uncertainty, $\varepsilon_t e_{t+1}$ and f_t differ by an amount equal to the risk premium required to persuade speculators to fulfil forward contracts. The equilibrium condition given by equation (1.3) is important because it represents a situation of perfect capital mobility. Perfect capital mobility is taken to be the joint hypothesis that bonds, identical in all respects apart from their currency of denomination, are perfect substitutes and that international portfolios are adjusted instantaneously. This assumption will be widely used in Chapters 4 to 8 of this book.

1.4   Dynamics, equilibrium and stability

There is probably little need to dwell too long on these concepts which are an integral part of the economists' vocabulary. Some comment is necessary, however, given the debate over these matters in the inter-war and early post-war years (see, for example, Frisch, 1936; Hicks, 1939, 1967; Samuelson, 1947; Harrod, 1948; Machlup, 1959; and Baumol, 1970) and because of their extensive use in this book. In recent years the term 'dynamics' has taken on a more precise usage, referring to 'the type of analysis in which the object is either to trace and study the specific time paths of the variables or to determine whether, given sufficient time, these variables will converge to certain (equilibrium) values' Chiang (1974, p. 427). Thus dynamics are concerned with the *method of analysis*, rather than with the subject under study. These methods attempt to answer two questions: first, will the model return to equilibrium following a disturbance, and second, what will the time path of the endogenous variables look like between two such equilibria? The techniques employed to address these questions are primarily those of linear, constant coefficient difference and differential equations, although very recently some non-linear dynamic methods have started to appear in the exchange rate literature.[3] This section is confined to a non-technical analysis of the use of linear dynamic methods in the sense defined above.

Consider the simplest case of the foreign exchange market where the spot planned demand and planned supply functions are only dependent upon the current spot exchange rate and other currently dated exogenous variables. The equilibrium exchange rate is given by the intersection of these two schedules. This model is in equilibrium in that it will not move from this position unless there is a change in one of the parameters of the system. If, however, the exchange rate is away from this equilibrium will it return to this equilibrium position? This is an inherently dynamic question, although the model is generally regarded as static. The usual hypothesis in the context of the market model is that price varies directly with excess demand. In Figure 1.3 if the supply and demand curves are respectively S and D, then at E_1 an excess supply prevails and E will fall to E_0. Similarly if the demand curve has a positive slope like D' then there will still be an excess supply equivalent to cd in Figure 1.3 and the equilibrium will stable. In the case where the supply and demand curves are given by S' and D' respectively, there is an excess demand of bc at E_1 and so the exchange rate will rise, thereby moving away from the equilibrium position. The intersection of the D' and S' lines in this case is still an equilibrium, in the sense that if the model finds itself at this position there will be no tendency to depart from it, but, on the other hand, if the model is away from this equilibrium position there will be no tendency to return to it. Thus the standard result is established that the slope of the supply curve must be less than that of the demand curve to ensure stability of the model; that is, to ensure a tendency towards equilibrium. The important point here is that to ascertain the stability of equilibrium requires the explicit formulation of a dynamic adjustment process.

The second purpose of dynamic analysis is to study the evolution of the exchange rate over time. Suppose that the static model above yielded the same value for the equilibrium exchange rate at all time periods. In this

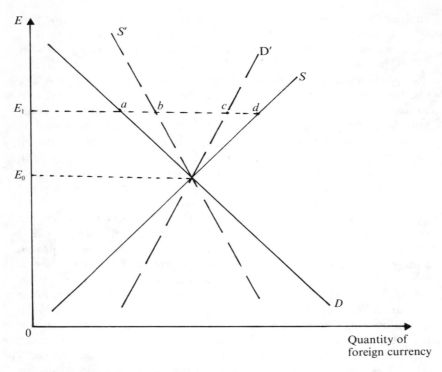

Figure 1.3   Stability in the foreign exchange market

case the equilibrium exchange rate would be stationary (constant) over time, as indicated in Figure 1.4 by the AB locus. This is not a dynamic model, however, since the exchange rate at time period t is independent of the exchange rate in past and all future time periods. Suppose now, however, that the equilibrium exchange rate generated by the model is not the same in all time periods. Although the foreign exchange market clears in each period it clears at a different exchange rate. The model now exhibits a moving equilibrium, with the exchange rate in Figure 1.4, for example, falling over time as along the line AC. This kind of model is again classified as a static model since the exchange rate at time t is not linked by theory to any variable other than those dated at t. The dynamic method employed in this volume necessitates the linkage of the exchange rate at any period to economic variables dated at a different time period as in a linear difference or differential equation. Suppose there is a shift out in the demand schedule for foreign currency; then the equilibrium exchange rate will rise, as from E_0 to E_1 in Figure 1.5. The dynamic path of the

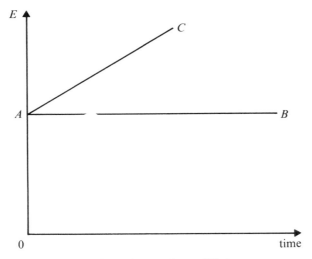

Figure 1.4 Stationary and moving static equilibria

exchange rate between the two static equilibria can now be determined from the model. Figure 1.5, for example, shows three alternative dynamic time paths for the exchange rate. Path 1 shows monotonic adjustment, whereby the exchange rate rises steadily at a declining rate over time; path 2 also shows monotonic adjustment, but after the exchange rate has initially overshot its final equilibrium; finally, path 3 shows a non-convergent time path. These are the main dynamic patterns that the exchange rate models expounded in this book generate.

It is important to note that these time paths for the exchange rate refer to 'model time' and not to 'calendar time'. That is to say, although the path of the exchange rate is clearly identified this path could be representative of one day, one week, one month, one year or five years in terms of calendar time. In other words the short-run adjustment path from one equilibrium position to another has no real time equivalent. This problem leads to considerable diversity in the interpretation of dynamic exchange rate time paths. At the macroeconomic level, where data are available only at a monthly or quarterly frequency, deviations from the long-run equilibrium are usually attributed to sluggish adjustment of actual to desired asset stocks, or to the fact that asset markets clear much faster than goods markets, which can give rise to temporary exchange rate overshooting. At data frequencies greater than monthly, say weekly or daily, it is believed that short-run movements are heavily dependent upon speculators' expectations as to future short-term and long-term levels of the exchange rate.

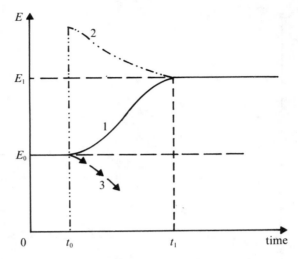

Figure 1.5   Dynamic exchange rate time paths

Because expectations are generally modelled, for technical reasons, by general rules of thumb, it is not usually possible to capture changes in the way these beliefs are formed or, of course, of seemingly irrational beliefs. The literature has adopted the term 'speculative bubble' or just 'bubble' to explain short-run exchange rate movements which are not consistent with the long-run path of the exchange rate as given by the underlying fundamentals, but which are consistent given agents' expectations of the time path of the exchange rate in the very short run. In the very short run, that is at intra-daily exchange rate frequencies, it is unlikely that the simple dynamic paths generated by linear differential equations will be in any way adequate to capture exchange rate movements. For this reason economists have recently started using non-linear, 'chaotic' dynamic methods, which provide for a very much greater diversity of time paths. In particular this kind of technique can explain why the exchange rate can show little movement for a long time and then suddenly jump, and why temporary shocks may have permanent effects on the equilibrium exchange rate.

1.5   Outline of the book

The very rapid and sustained growth in the exchange rate determination literature since the mid-1970s means that it is probably now impossible to survey the whole field in a single volume. Hence all authors have to be selective and neglect some aspects of the subject which could legitimately be included. This volume is no different from others in the field in this respect, although what has been omitted has been partly determined by what already exists. For instance, the area of exchange market efficiency is almost entirely omitted partly because it is so well-covered by MacDonald (1988) and Baillie and McMahon (1989). There is also little discussion in this volume of the arguments for and against floating, as compared to fixed, exchange rates for which the reader is referred to MacDonald (1988) and Williamson and Milner (1991).

The thrust of this book is to consider the determinants of the equilibrium exchange rate, the stability of this equilibrium rate and the adjustment path of the exchange rate back towards this equilibrium following a disturbance, in the context of specific models of exchange rate determination. Throughout the book empirical evidence will be integrated with the theoretical analysis to provide an adjacent appraisal of the theory in question. These objectives motivate each of the following chapters and form the content of the rest of this book, which divides into three parts, with each part containing two chapters, as demonstrated in Table 1.1. The parts of the book correspond to the sophistication assumed about international asset markets and the chapters to the assumptions made about the supply-side of the economy. Chapters with even numbers correspond to the development of the Classical, or flexi-price approach to the exchange rate, with a constant real exchange rate, and the odd-numbered chapters correspond to the Keynesian, fixed- or sticky-price approach, with fixed or sticky aggregate prices and a changing real exchange rate.

Part I of this volume, in contrast to most of the other recent contributions to the literature, examines exchange rate dynamics in models without international capital flows. Although this analysis may seem a little dated it is important to remember that, if capital flows are indeed transitory phenomena, then the long-run, stationary state equilibrium exchange rate is determined exclusively by the *ex ante* current balance and hence its long-run movement is similarly determined by current balance developments. The two chapters which make up Part I each consider a different approach to modelling the trade balance. Chapter 2 examines the tradi-

Table 1.1   Plan of the book

	I *Trade balance models*	II. *Capital flows models*	III. *Stock–flow interaction models*
Flexi-price approach	Chapter 2	Chapter 4	Chapter 6
Fixed-price approach	Chapter 3	Chapter 5	Chapter 7

tional (Classical) monetary approach to the exchange rate when there are no capital flows and output is supply-constrained. In this simple model the equilibrium exchange rate is determined by the ratio of the domestic to the foreign price level (purchasing power parity) and its dynamics are determined by the speed of adjustment of the domestic and foreign money markets. Chapter 3 considers the (Keynesian) income-expenditure approach to the exchange rate. In this model it is the price level that is fixed and output determined by aggregate demand. The equilibrium exchange rate is therefore determined by relative aggregate demands in the home and foreign countries, and its dynamic time path by the speed of adjustment of the exchange rate to current account disequilibrium. This chapter also shows the importance of the price elasticities of import and exports to exchange market stability in the absence of capital flows.

Part II of the book introduces international capital flows as the key determinant of the exchange rate, where these flows are regarded as part of an international stock-adjustment process and hence consistent with modern portfolio theory (Markowitz, 1952; Tobin, 1958). The emphasis in this part of the book is therefore on the short-run dynamics of the exchange rate and, in particular, the role of exchange rate expectations. The enormous variety of models in this category bears witness to the interest in the area since the mid-1970s. Chapter 4 examines the monetary approach to exchange rate determination, with perfect asset substitutability between domestic and foreign bonds, The equilibrium exchange rate now depends not only on current relative prices but on all expected future relative prices, if expectations are assumed to be model-consistent, so that continuous purchasing power parity and a constant real exchange rate are maintained. Chapter 5 also assumes perfect asset substitutability, but considers models in which the price level is fixed, or sticky in the short run, hence allowing fluctuations in the real exchange rate and exchange rate overshooting of the long-run equilibrium in the short run.

Part III of this book considers stock-flow interaction models of the exchange rate. These models are more general in that they allow for interaction between current account and capital account influences largely, although not necessarily, through wealth effects. Chapter 6 considers a class of models known as currency substitution models since domestic and foreign monies are the only assets in them (as in the Classical approach). A large number of dynamic paths are possible for the exchange rate and again long-run equilibrium is determined by the speed of the adjustment of the domestic and foreign money markets. Chapter 7 extends the range of assets from domestic and foreign money to include domestic and foreign bonds which may or may not be perfect substitutes. This class of models is the most general, although tractable results are not always easily found. The equilibrium exchange rate is driven by current account balance, although short-run overshooting may occur if asset markets adjust faster than goods markets.

The final chapter (Chapter 8) provides a summary of the main conclusions from the previous chapters and considers four aspects of current research in this area: firstly, the use of survey data on exchange rate expectations to test the rational expectations hypothesis in the context of the foreign exchange market and the use made of technical analysis by market participants to forecast the exchange rate in the very short run; secondly, the growing interest in chaotic dynamics to capture complex exchange rate dynamics in both theoretical models and in high frequency exchange rate data; thirdly, the dynamic behaviour of the exchange rate in target zone models; and finally two suggestions for improving the structural modelling of the long-run equilibrium exchange rate.

Notes

1. Among these reasons are that the existence of money reduces transactions costs and uncertainty. See Harris (1981) and Goodhart (1989) for a discussion of these issues.
2. For this reason some monetary theorists are again advocating the notion of competing currencies, which are independent of state control. See, for example, Hayek (1976, 1978), Vaubel (1984) and Visser (1991) for a brief survey.
3. These so-called 'chaotic dynamics' are briefly considered in Chapter 8.

2   The classical monetary approach

2.1   Introduction

The Classical approach to exchange rate determination is based upon two, often controversial, propositions. The first proposition is that of purchasing power parity (PPP), whereby national aggregate price levels are linked through the nominal exchange rate. Since the price of each national money is the reciprocal of the average price level, the exchange rate is sometimes referred to as the relative price of domestic money in terms of foreign money, that is the purchasing power of domestic currency, compared to foreign currency. The second is that the Quantity Theory of Money is a valid description of the aggregate economy. This is taken to imply that all prices, including wage rates, are perfectly flexible, thereby establishing automatic full employment of resources, and that the velocity of circulation of money is constant, so that money is neutral in its effect on the real economy.

Both of these propositions are controversial and their somewhat crude representation above obscures the richness of much of the Classical and Neoclassical writers on the subject. With regard to the notion of PPP, many of the controversies surrounding this principle are concerned with the choice of the appropriate price indices. There have been those who advocated the use of traded goods price indices to emphasize the role of international commodity arbitrage (*inter alia*, Pigou, 1920; Viner, 1937) and those who have argued for the broadest possible price index, including both traded and non-traded goods, thereby emphasizing the role of equilibrium in the money markets (*inter alia*, Hawtrey, 1919; Cassel, 1928). It is this latter view which has dominated, with the modern monetary approach to the exchange rate based on this foundation. As far as the Quantity Theory is concerned, it is clear that most of the Neoclassical writers believed neither in permanent full employment nor in the constancy of the velocity of circulation. Both of these propositions are therefore best interpreted as propositions about the long-run, steady-state equilibrium, rather than propositions which are valid at all points in time (Harris, 1981). The link between the determination of the price level, via the Quantity Theory of Money, and the exchange rate by PPP can be found in Ricardo (1821) and was reformulated in its modern guise by Cassel (1916).

It is not the purpose of this chapter to set out the historical record on

Classical monetary theory, which is treated extensively elsewhere.[1] Rather it is to set out a simple version of the Classical approach to the exchange rate under the assumption of no international capital flows. This chapter is referred to as 'Classical' not because it represents a particular model which can be attributed to the classical economists, but because it emphasizes the stock adjustment process which is characteristic of Classical monetary theory since at least the early eighteenth century. In this sense, at least, the treatment of the adjustment process ignores explicit consideration of some of the features of monetary disequilibria to be found in Neoclassical economics. For example, the role of interest rates and inflation expectations are excluded, although Marshall (1923) gives these factors considerable weight in determining the short-run velocity of circulation. Similarly, exchange rate expectations are excluded from the analysis in this chapter, although they appear in the work of Cassel (1928, 1930) and Robertson (1928).[2] These important variables will be introduced in Chapter 4, when discussing the modern monetary approach, although this should not be taken to mean that these factors were completely overlooked by the Neoclassical economists.

This chapter begins with a formal specification of the Classical Monetary Model (CLMM) in Section 2.2, in which all goods are assumed to be costlessly and freely traded goods. The dynamics of exchange rate adjustment are driven by the stock adjustment process whereby the desired demand for transactions balances adjusts slowly to the nominal money supply. The outcome of this process for the time path of the exchange rate is shown to be both convergent and monotonic. Section 2.3 extends the model of Section 2.2 by postulating that the domestic and foreign economies are characterized by two distinct kinds of goods: traded goods and non-traded goods. In this section it is demonstrated that short-run overshooting of the exchange rate may occur if non-traded goods prices are not fully flexible in the short run. This implies that money may not be neutral in its effect upon real output in the short run, although this neutrality is maintained in the long run. Section 2.4 provides a critical appraisal of the empirical evidence appertaining to the validity of the absolute and relative purchasing power parity hypotheses which underlie the models developed in Sections 2.2 and 2.3. There seems to be little evidence to support PPP, although this conclusion must be tempered by the somewhat inadequate empirical methodology used in the majority of studies.

2.2 The basic model

The Classical model of the exchange rate is based firmly in the Quantity Theory tradition of fully flexible prices and wages so that labour markets always clear in long-run equilibrium and that real output is supply-determined. Aggregate demand, on the other hand, only determines the price level and hence money is unable to affect output in the long run. The static equilibrium model is set out below with the dynamics considered in the following sub-section.

2.2.1   The static equilibrium

The model can be represented as consisting of six principal assumptions, set out as follows:

1. There are two countries, the home country and the foreign country, both of which exhibit full employment of the factors of production, due to perfectly flexible factor prices, so that domestic output, Y, and foreign output Y^*, are exogenous. (Note that asterisks will be used to denote foreign country variables throughout.)
2. Both countries produce and consume the same commodity, or bundle of commodities, all of which are traded. Therefore in full equilibrium there are no trade- or terms of trade-related problems.
3. Perfectly competitive goods markets and costless commodity arbitrage ensures that absolute purchasing power parity (PPP) holds, that is:

$$P = EP^* \tag{2.1}$$

where P is the domestic price level, E is the exchange rate, defined as the domestic price of foreign currency, and P^* is the foreign price level.

4. The home and foreign central banks control their own nominal money supply in circulation outside the banking system such that M and M^*, respectively, are exogenously determined.
5. The desired demands for real cash balances by domestic and foreign residents, L and L^* respectively, are exclusively for transactions purposes and hence depend directly upon the levels of domestic and foreign real income respectively. That is:

$$L = L(Y) \text{ and } L^* = L^*(Y^*) \tag{2.2}$$

where Y is the level of real income, L_1, $L^*_1 > 0$ are the partial derivatives of L and L^* with respect to income. Domestic currency is only held by domestic residents and foreign currency is only held by foreign residents.

6. In full equilibrium the desired real demands and actual real supplies for domestic and foreign money are equal, so that

$$M/P = L(Y) \text{ and } M^*/P^* = L^*(Y^*) \tag{2.3}$$

The static equilibrium of the model is obtained by solving equations (2.3) for P and P^* respectively, and then using equation (2.1) to solve for the equilibrium exchange rate using the solutions for P and P^* to give:

$$E = [M/L(Y)][L^*(Y^*)/M^*] = [M/M^*][L(Y^*)/L(Y)] \tag{2.4}$$

Thus the equilibrium exchange rate is given by the ratio of the domestic to the foreign money stock multiplied by the ratio of foreign to domestic demands for real money balances. The equilibrium of the model is represented in Figure 2.1. Quadrants I and III show domestic and foreign

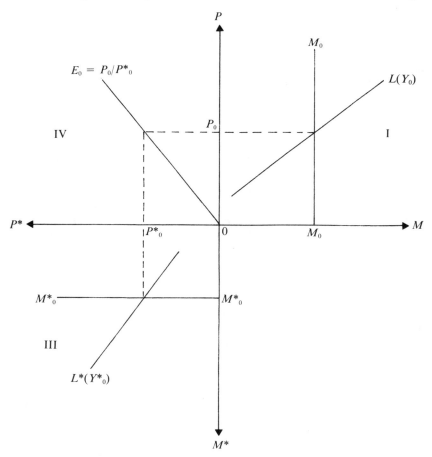

Figure 2.1   Equilibrium in the Classical Monetary Model (CLMM)

money market equilibrium. The nominal money supplies are exogenous and so both M_0M_0 and $M*_0M*_0$ are independent of P and $P*$ respectively. The nominal demand for money functions are positively related to their respective price levels and are each drawn for a given level of real income. Quadrant IV depicts the PPP condition given by equation (2.1) The line E_0 gives the equilibrium exchange rate as the ratio of the home to the foreign price level $(P_0/P*_0)$. This simple diagrammatic framework can be used to examine the comparative static properties of the model following changes in any of the exogenous variables $(M, M*, Y, Y*)$.

Consider an increase in the domestic money supply from M_0 to M_1. In Figure 2.2 at the initial price level there is now an excess supply of money given by the horizontal distance AB. With domestic income fixed at Y_0, the domestic price level, and hence the nominal demand for money, must rise, to force domestic residents to hold the additional money balances. The increase in the domestic price level, with a fixed foreign price level, causes the exchange rate to depreciate (a rise in E) by the same amount as the rise in the price level. When E reaches E_1 and P reaches P_1 a new stock equilibrium will be attained. Note that in this model if the home and the foreign money supplies increase by the same amount, the price levels rise in proportion and the equilibrium exchange rate will be unchanged. This is demonstrated in Figure 2.2 by the point D on the E_0 schedule, where the rise in the domestic money supply is exactly matched by a rise in the foreign money supply, thereby leaving the exchange rate unchanged.

Consider now a rise in domestic output. This will lead to a rise in the demand for money, which, for a given level of nominal balances, will necessitate a fall in the domestic price level until the real money supply has increased sufficiently to satisfy the higher demand. The lower domestic price level, via PPP, results in an appreciation of the exchange rate. In terms of Figure 2.3, the higher income will shift the demand for real balances to the right, to $L(Y_1)$, thus creating an excess demand for money which in this simple model can only be adjusted by a fall in the domestic price level, to P_1 and a consequent rise in the equilibrium exchange rate, to E_1. This model demonstrates the interesting policy result that countries with relatively high rates of economic growth will tend to experience exchange rate appreciation.

2.2.2   Exchange rate dynamics

Within this simple framework there are two ways of representing exchange rate dynamics: first, by slow adjustment of the exchange rate back to PPP following the initial monetary disturbance, or second, by the sluggish adjustment of desired to actual real money balances. The second approach is slightly more general, allowing the domestic and foreign

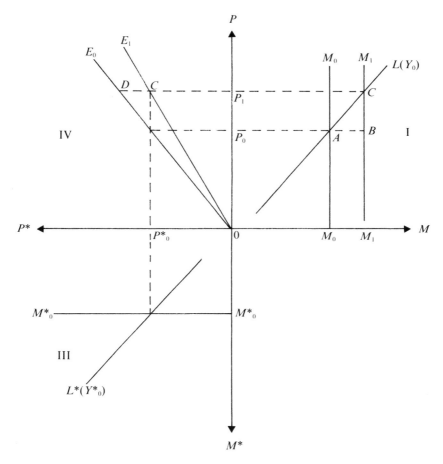

Figure 2.2   An increase in the domestic money supply in the CLMM

money markets to clear at different speeds, but the two approaches give
the same dynamics for the exchange rate, that is, a time path which is both
monotonic and convergent, and identical to that of the general level of
prices.

Consider the more general case where the change in the real money
supply adjusts to the discrepancy between desired real money balances
and the actual real money stock for both countries, as follows:

$$d(M/P)/dt = \pi[L(Y) - M/P] \qquad\qquad 0 < \pi < \infty \qquad\qquad (2.5)$$

$$d(M^*/P^*)/dt = \pi^*[L^*(Y^*) - M^*/P^*] \quad 0 < \pi^* < \infty \qquad (2.5')$$

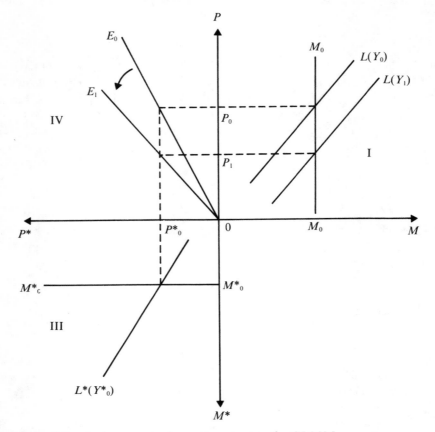

Figure 2.3   An increase in domestic output in the CLMM

These equations show that the two countries are independent. The exchange rate links the two economies without influencing them. Suppose now that the home country experiences an exogenous increase in its money supply. At the given price level, M/P will now exceed L and, according to equation (2.5), real cash balances will start to decline. This decline can only take place through an increase in the domestic price level and the speed of the price rise can be found by rewriting (2.5) for a given level of M; that is:

$$(dP/dt)(1/P) = \pi[1 - PL(Y)/M] \qquad (2.6)$$

If M is exogenously increased, the rate of price increase responds according to:

$$[(dP/dt)(1/P)]/(dM/M) = \pi[PL(Y)/M] = \pi \tag{2.7}$$

where initially it is assumed that the money market clears such that $PL(Y)$ $= M$. The interpretation is that, owing to the adjustment lag in cash balances, the immediate effect of money on prices is only partial, its strength depending on the speed of adjustment, π. Since π must be less than infinity for there to be only partial adjustment, the model is dynamically stable and converges monotonically to the new equilibrium.

The implications for the exchange rate are straightforward: it simply follows the path of prices. To see this, note simply that differentiating (2.1) with respect to time gives

$$(dE/dt)(1/E) = (dP/dt)(1/P) - (dP*/dt)(1/P*) \tag{2.8}$$

and substituting for $(dP/dt)(1/P)$ from (2.7), assuming that there is no change in the foreign price level, gives:

$$(dE/dt)(1/E) = \pi[1 - PL(Y)/M] \tag{2.9}$$

and a rise in the money supply causes the exchange rate to instantly depreciate by

$$(dE/dt)(1/E)/(dM/M) = \pi[PL(Y)/M] = \pi \tag{2.10}$$

which is equivalent to equation (2.7). Clearly, if there is full, instantaneous adjustment the exchange rate depreciates exactly in proportion to the money supply increase.

The CLMM can also be used to analyse the effect of real disturbances on the exchange rate, through their effects on the demand for money. A rise in productivity, for example, would increase real income, raise the demand for money and lead to an appreciation in the exchange rate. From equation (2.9) the extent of exchange rate appreciation will depend upon the money market adjustment parameter π, exactly as for the nominal shock discussed above, that is:

$$(dE/dt)(1/E)/(dL/L) = -\pi \tag{2.10'}$$

This result can be generalized such that the dynamics of the exchange rate are identical in the face of nominal or real shocks. It is important to note that this result occurs only when wage rates and other prices are perfectly flexible. If wages are in some respect sticky, then an increase in the money supply will be accompanied by a depreciation of the exchange rate and temporary over-full employment. Analogously, a decrease in the money supply will give rise to an appreciation of the exchange rate and a rise in unemployment.

2.3   The model with non-traded goods
The analysis of the previous section was limited to the case of traded goods. This section extends the model to include non-traded goods in addition to the two costlessly traded bundles of commodities. This is the case to which Cassel (1916, 1918, 1921, 1922) and later Keynes (1924, 1930) gave the name Purchasing Power Parity (PPP). The model is set up in the next sub-section and the implied exchange rate dynamics examined in the second part of this section.

2.3.1   *The static model with non-traded goods*
For the home country the general level of prices, P, is specified to be a linear homogenous function of traded and non-traded goods prices, P_T and P_N respectively, given by equation (2.11):

$$P = P_T^{1-v}P_N^{v} \tag{2.11}$$

where v is the expenditure share of non-traded goods in home country output. The foreign country also has a traded and a non-traded sector and it is assumed for ease of exposition that the proportion of the traded goods sector to total expenditure in the foreign economy is the same as for the home country. Hence the foreign average price level is also a linearly homogenous function of traded and non-traded goods prices and can be written as:

$$P^* = P^*_T{}^{1-v}P^*_N{}^{v} \tag{2.11'}$$

The relationship between the two economies now depends only upon traded goods price parity, that is:

$$E = P_T/P^*_T \tag{2.12}$$

Using equations (2.11) and (2.11'), equation (2.12) can be rearranged in terms of average price levels, which are still determined by the stock equilibrium in the money market, and non-traded goods prices, to give:

$$E = K[P/P^*] \tag{2.13}$$

where $K = [(P_T/P_N)/(P^*_T/P^*_N)]^v$, which is the relative ratio of traded to non-traded goods prices. This is known as Relative PPP. It differs from Absolute PPP in Section 2.2 by the constant term, K. The absolute version (when $K = 1$) is valid only under very special circumstances, namely when both price indices cover only costlessly traded goods and the same weights are used in both price indices. In this case it is also trivial, reflecting only commodity arbitrage. The absolute version is also unnecessary, since the relevant propositions can be derived from the relative version. The relative version of PPP, developed in this section, recognises that K will generally be different from unity because the two index numbers include non-traded or imperfectly traded goods and because the weights in the construction of P and P^* will, in general, be different. Substituting into equation (2.13) for P and P^* derived from equations (2.3) gives:

$$E = K[(M/M^*)(L^*(Y^*)/L(Y)] \qquad (2.14)$$

If the relative prices of traded to non-traded goods in both countries are assumed to be constant, then the exchange rate is proportionate (but not equal) to the relative purchasing power of the two currencies. There is no reason why one-off changes in the money supply or the demand for real money balances should have any permanent effects on K.

2.3.2   Exchange rate dynamics with non-traded goods

The dynamics of the exchange rate are richer in this more general model. The one case that remains the same is the effect of an increase in the foreign or domestic money supplies: the exchange rate depreciates in proportion with a time profile which is monotonically convergent. In response to real shocks, however, it is possible that the time path of the exchange rate may not be monotonic, although it will still be convergent. This possibility is investigated in this section using the diagrammatic apparatus developed by Clements (1981).

Figure 2.4 illustrates equations (2.11) and (2.11') in quadrant I. Along the curve labelled AA the price level is held constant at P_0. AA gives the various combinations of P_T and P_N which are consistent with P_0. The schedule is negatively sloped because a higher P_T must be offset by a lower level of P_N if P is to remain constant, at P_0. Moreover, because of the linear homogeneity assumption embodied in equations (2.11), if P_T and P_N rise equiproportionately then P also rises in the same proportion. This means that an increase in the price level shifts the AA schedule outwards (for example, from AA to A_1A_1 in Figure 2.4). The proportionate outward shift, as measured along the ray from the origin, is equal to the increase in the price level. Equation (2.13) gives the relative prices of traded to non-traded goods in the home and the foreign countries, which are assumed to

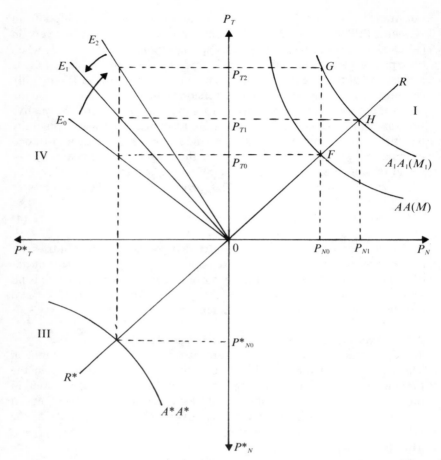

Figure 2.4   A monetary increase in the CLMM with non-traded goods

be determined by the real economy and to be constant. Equation (2.13) is represented by the ray OR from the origin, which gives the various combinations of P_T and P_N consistent with the relative price. In Figure 2.4 the initial equilibrium is at F in quadrant I. Quadrant IV shows the traded goods PPP condition given by equation (2.12) and quadrant III shows the foreign country's AA line, as A^*A^*, and PPP consistent with relative prices, by the ray OR^*.

Consider an increase in the domestic money supply. With real incomes and relative domestic prices fixed, the AA schedule moves out to the right giving a new equilibrium at H. The prices of traded and non-traded goods rise in proportion and the exchange rate correspondingly depreciates from E_0 to E_1, thus preserving the homogeneity result and the neutrality of money. Suppose, however, that in the short run the price of non-traded goods is sticky. The increase in the money supply, say by x per cent, will have to raise the price of tradeables by more than x per cent if the average domestic price level is to rise by x per cent. Hence, in terms of Figure 2.4, the short-run equilibrium is at G and the price of traded goods is P_{T2}. The exchange rate must therefore depreciate to E_2 to maintain the PPP of traded goods. At E_2, however, the structure of the domestic economy is unchanged, and so relative prices are also unchanged. Hence at G there must be an excess supply of traded goods and a corresponding excess demand for non-traded goods. Thus the price of non-tradeables will rise (and the price of tradeables fall) over time, until their relative price is re-established at H: the long-run equilibrium. This results in an appreciation of the exchange rate in the long run following its over-depreciation in the short run. Hence this model exhibits exchange rate overshooting in the short run, because of sticky non-traded goods prices. This result can be generalized in that any rigidities in the economy may produce relative price shifts and hence short-run exchange rate overshooting. This exchange rate overshooting result is independent of capital flows and of expectations about the future level of the exchange rate. It is a result solely of price stickiness in the price of non-traded goods.

2.4   Testing purchasing power parity

The empirical evidence for the Classical approach to exchange rate determination and dynamics hinges in part on the specification of the demand for money function and in part on the purchasing power parity condition. Since the specification of the demand for money functions is extremely simple it is perhaps unlikely that these functions would receive much empirical support. On the other hand, the equilibrium condition of PPP is independent of the demand for money specification and so does provide a way of testing the empirical validity of the underlying equilibrium hypothesis. In this section the empirical evidence for the Classical approach to exchange rate determination therefore concentrates on the PPP hypothesis. If PPP is accepted by the data as a valid equilibrium relationship then the Classical approach is based on an appropriate equilibrium foundation. If, on the other hand, the PPP postulate is rejected by the data then either the testing methodology is inappropriate, or the CLMM is invalid.

This section is sub-divided as follows. Section 2.4.1 considers the theoretical and conceptual problems involved in testing the PPP hypotheses, including data limitations. Section 2.4.2 examines the most appropriate estimation techniques and, in particular, the use of cointegration time series methods. Finally, Section 2.4.3 reviews some of the recent econometric results obtained.

2.4.1   *Theoretical and conceptual difficulties in testing PPP*

This section addresses two important problems: the likely validity of the relative PPP hypothesis from a theoretical perspective, and the data available to test this hypothesis and, in particular, its limitations which may affect the reliability of the empirical results.

From the simple theoretical relationships outlined in Sections 2.2 and 2.3 it should be clear that the absolute PPP hypothesis is a special case of the relative PPP hypothesis. The conditions for absolute PPP are rather restrictive in that it assumes *inter alia*, that all goods are traded goods and that there are no transactions costs incurred as result of trade. Moreover, if all goods are traded goods absolute PPP is a truism, being only an aggregate version of the law of one price. PPP, on the other hand, postulates a relationship between home and foreign aggregate price levels, which include both traded and non-traded goods prices. The more relevant concept for testing is therefore relative PPP.

On theoretical grounds, however, there are also many reasons why relative PPP may not hold. Officer (1976a) notes eight factors, listed as follows:

1. restrictions on trade and capital movements,
2. transfer pricing by multinational companies,
3. autonomous capital flows,
4. speculation in the foreign exchange markets,
5. expectations of different inflation rates at home and abroad,
6. official intervention,
7. cyclical divergences in the real economies, and
8. productivity bias.

The restrictions on trade and capital movements and transfer pricing will both distort the relationship between home and world prices. As far as the former are concerned, the gradual reduction in tariff and non-tariff barriers and the relaxation and abolition of capital controls in the 1970s and 1980s would lessen the problem rather than intensify it. Autonomous capital flows may lead to systematic divergences from PPP, which, like speculative activity and expected differential inflation rates need to be explicitly modelled in a more general model. Official intervention in the foreign exchange markets has been substantial and important, particularly in the short run, over the floating rate period. Bearing in mind that PPP is a long-run equilibrium condition, this intervention may not be important if it is for short-run smoothing purposes, or if it is subsequently reversed within the month (or quarter) depending upon the frequency of the data. The cyclical change in real incomes over the cycle will be partly reflected by changes in broadly-based price indices and so the extent of this problem may be diminished by using appropriate price indices. The final factor, productivity bias, is thought to arise from systematic divergences between countries in the internal price ratio; that is, in the ratio of the price of non-traded goods to traded goods. Balassa (1964) attributed this effect to relatively faster productivity growth in traded output than in non-traded output in the faster-growing industrialized economies. Officer (1974) however, argues that the quality of non-traded output is higher in fast-growing countries . Moreover, some careful empirical work has failed to find any convincing evidence for the existence of the bias (Officer, 1976b). In any case, the impact on relative PPP is likely to be small over the medium term, especially if both countries are subject to similar movements in relative domestic prices.

Despite these qualifications, it would seem that relative PPP is not an unreasonable proposition on which to base an equilibrium model of the exchange rate, especially if the data are selected and applied carefully. In particular, the choice of price index and the length of the time series available are likely to have a large influence on the results.

The relative PPP hypothesis is a long-run equilibrium condition which is only valid after all temporary adjustments have taken place. The length of calendar time required for any short-run deviations from PPP to work themselves out is an often neglected empirical question. Isard (1983) estimates that two to five years are required for PPP to be re-established after a disturbance. Manzur (1990) also identifies the length of the long run as five years, although Frankel (1986), on the other hand, maintains that ten or more years may be required. Early tests by Gailliot (1970), which were supportive of PPP, were based on comparisons of the exchange rate to relative prices on a decade by decade basis (using five-year averages). This implies that it is not the number of observations that is essential, but rather the length of the sample period in terms of calendar time. This point has been forcibly made by Hakkio and Rush (1991), who argue, 'it seems clear that testing a long-run property of the data with 120 monthly observations is no different than testing it with ten annual observations' (p. 972). It is possible therefore that any data set of less than ten years duration may reject relative PPP, not because the hypothesis is empirically invalid, but simply because the exchange rate has not had time to return to equilibrium following a disturbance.

Another data consideration concerns the appropriate measure of aggregate prices. There is no shortage of aggregate indices: export price indices

(XPI), wholesale price indices (WPI), gross domestic product deflators (DPI), consumer price indices (CPI), unit factor costs (UFC), or unit labour costs (ULC), although all raise theoretical problems. Keynes (1930) noted that a PPP calculation from traded goods prices alone is close to a truism. Export prices in domestic currency are likely to adjust fully to changes in exchange rates, at least under perfect competition, but the squeeze on profits that results in the appreciating country may lead to a movement of production out of traded goods and into non-traded goods. Thus, although PPP may be observed, it does not always correspond to a stable equilibrium relationship. Furthermore, a small change in the exchange rate is likely to widen or restrict the group of goods in international trade, thus making the conventionally calculated XPI a less relevant measure. WPI is also rather heavily weighted with internationally traded goods, and therefore suffers from the same problems as the XPI, but to a lesser extent.

Costs, on the other hand, are less liable to adjustment following exchange rate changes and exclude the volatile element of profits. To this extent they may capture the underlying trend of prices better than both the XPI and the WPI. The UFC measure includes interest and rent, as well as wages, adjusted for productivity changes, but because interest and rent are small and difficult to measure the ULC measure is sometimes preferred. Officer (1976a) has demonstrated that, on certain assumptions, absolute UFC parity is equal to an absolute price parity, where the price levels are production-weighted averages of commodity prices; that is, gross domestic product price levels. An alternative is to use cost of living indices, which are consumption-weighted averages of prices (CPI). Hence both DPI and CPI indices are linked to traded goods prices directly, but also take some account of the income adjustments which follow from trade disequilibrium.

There is also a further set of conceptual problems which arise from the statistical difficulties of measuring these price indices. First, all indices are computed from samples of individual prices and are thus imperfect representations of actual prices. Second, statistical definitions and sampling practices differ between countries. Third, the weights used in more general price indices differ between countries, hence, as Yeager (1968) notes, since expenditure in each country will be concentrated on those goods with relatively lower prices, a divergent bias in the computed parity will result. The choice of price index is therefore an essentially empirical question, but the presumption can be made that the more broadly-based indices, such as the CPI or the DPI, are likely to have greater predictive power in exchange rate models.

2.4.2 *Specification and estimation problems in testing PPP*

The specification of an empirical version of the relative PPP hypothesis given in equation (2.13) may seem fairly straightforward but, in fact, several alternative versions are possible.

Expressing (2.13) in logarithms, parameterizing and adding a random error term u_t, gives:

$$e_t = k + \beta p_t + \beta^* p_t^* + u_t \qquad (2.15)$$

where relative PPP requires that $\beta = 1$ and $\beta^* = -1$. (Absolute PPP additionally requires $k = 0$). This is the most general empirical form of equation (2.13) which does not impose homogeneity on the price level terms. As Taylor (1988b) points out β and β^* may differ because of measurement error (see section 2.4.1) or transport costs. If, however, homogeneity is imposed, as in Enders (1988) for example, then (2.15) becomes:

$$e_t = k + \beta(p_t - p_t^*) + v_t \qquad (2.15')$$

and v_t is the error term. Relative PPP now requires $\beta = 1$ and absolute PPP needs both $\beta = 1$ and $k = 0$. A third alternative specification, which also imposes homogeneity, is to define the real exchange rate, q, as $q_t = e_t - p_t + p_t^*$, and test:

$$q_t = \alpha_0 + \alpha_1 q_{t-1} + w_t \qquad (2.15'')$$

where w_t is a white noise error term. Relative PPP now requires $\alpha_1 = 0$, while for absolute PPP α_0 must also equal zero.

Each of these three specifications is consistent with the view that PPP is strictly a long-run equilibrium relationship. Empirically, if long-run PPP exists then time series for the logarithms of the nominal exchange rate and the average price level indices should move together over the long run. That is, the exchange rate and price level series should both be individually integrated of order one, denoted I(1), and combine to be jointly cointegrated, with stationary residuals, denoted I(0). If the estimated residuals from (2.15) are not stationary then it implies that e_t, p_t and p_t^* diverge over time and thus do not constitute a valid empirical equilibrium relationship. Only if a cointegrating relationship can be found between the exchange rate and price levels is long-run relative PPP a valid empirical equilibrium relationship.[3]

A less strict interpretation of PPP would also allow for some short-run deviations from PPP which disappear in the long run. If exchange rates and price levels cointegrate then the residuals from the cointegrating regression, such as (2.15), can be included in an error correction model (Hendry *et al.,* 1984), which enable the short-run disequilibrium dynamics to be investigated. The error correction model for equation (2.15) takes the form:

$$\triangle e_t = \gamma_0 + \gamma_1 \triangle p_t - \gamma^*_1 \triangle p^*_t + \gamma_2 u_{t-1} + \epsilon_t \tag{2.16}$$

where ϵ_t is a white noise error term and u_{t-1} is the estimated residual from equation (2.15). There are three important points to note about this equation. First, if e_t, p_t and p^*_t are I(1) processes, as assumed, then all the variables in equation (2.16) are stationary, that is I(0). Secondly, the coefficient γ_2 gives a measure of the extent of disequilibrium and an indication of the speed of adjustment back to the long-run equilibrium. Thirdly, the error correction model is only valid if a cointegrating vector is found. If e_t, p_t and p^*_t do not cointegrate then there can be no error correction representation.

The empirical results reviewed in the following section mainly rely on the two-stage cointegration methodolgy proposed by Engle and Granger (1987), although this technique is inferior to the Johansen (1988) approach, since the latter provides estimates of all the cointegrating vectors that exist within a vector of variables, rather than just a single, non-unique vector provided by the two-stage method. Furthermore, the Johansen procedure offers a test statistic for the number of cointegrating vectors, which the two-stage regression based methodolgy does not, and therefore the Johansen approach may be viewed as more discerning in its ability to detect a false null hypothesis. Both the two-stage approach of Engle and Granger and the maximum likelihood approach of Johansen to cointegration try to reject the null hypothesis of non-cointegration.

2.4.4   *Recent Econometric Evidence*

Recent econometric tests of PPP have been undertaken for both the recent float and for the floating rate period in the 1920s, using the cointegration econometric technique outlined in section 2.4.3. Earlier tests which do not use the cointegration methodology include, *inter alia*, the studies by Isard (1977), Frenkel (1978, 1981a), Junge (1984) and Edison (1985a, 1985b) are summarized in MacDonald (1988). In this sub-section only recent studies are considered and ordered according to the time period to which they relate.

Evidence for the 1920s   Using the Engle and Granger method and imposing price level homogeneity, Taylor and McMahon (1988) test for PPP in the inter-war period using monthly data from February 1921 to May 1925

Table 2.1   Cointegrating regressions for PPP in the 1920s

Tests for stationarity: null hypothesis is series is I(1)

	Exchange rate	Relative prices
$/£	−1.54	−2.23
Fr/£	−0.71	−0.78
DM/£	2.77	1.85
Fr/$	−1.10	−0.47
DM/$	2.83	1.90
DM/Fr	2.88	1.81

Critical values for ADF test are −3.58, −2.93 and −2.60 at 1%, 5% and 10% respectively, and −3.75, −3.00 and −2.63 at 1%, 5% and 10% for the DM equations where a smaller sample period is used (see Fuller, 1976).

Tests of cointegrability of e and p − p* using: $e_t = \alpha + \beta(p - p^*)_t + u_t$

Exchange rate	α	β	CRDW	ADF
$/£	1.841	0.687	0.303	−2.59
Fr/£	3.272	1.061	0.662	−4.62
DM/£	8.338	1.028	1.944	−4.19
FR/$	1.128	1.330	0.804	−3.89
DM/$	6.308	1.039	1.904	−4.09
DM/Fr	5.047	1.028	1.998	−4.34

Null hypothesis is that u_t is I(1). The null is rejected if computed values exceed the critical values. The critical values for the CRDW test is 0.511 at 1% and 0.386 at 5%; for the ADF test, −3.77 at 1% and −3.00% at 5%.

Source: Taylor and McMahon (1988).

for the US dollar–pound, French franc–dollar and French franc–pound exchange rates and from February 1921 to August 1923 for the US dollar, pound sterling and French franc exchange rates with the German mark. Wholesale price indices were used. The principal results are shown in Table 2.1. The logarithms of all exchange rate and price series are shown to be stationary in first differences. Exchange rates and relative prices also cointegrate, with the exception of the US dollar–sterling exchange rate,[4] indicating the validity of PPP in the 1920s. The fact that PPP is found to hold in the 1920s, for a five-year period is perhaps a little surprising given the discussion in Section 2.4.1 above. Moreover, Cochrane (1991), suggests that for exchange rates unit root tests have low power and may give misleading results unless the calendar time period is at least five to ten years. Taylor and McMahon's sample only spans about four and a half years and so perhaps too much weight should not be placed on these results. If PPP does hold in the 1920s then this can probably be explained by the absence of supply-side shocks, such as productivity growth and resource discoveries and to the predominance of hyperinflation in Germany.

Evidence for the 1970s and 1980s   In contrast to the results of Taylor and McMahon (1988), for the more recent period of floating exchange rates strong support for PPP is not found. Using the Engle and Granger approach, Baillie and Selover (1987) report no evidence of long-run PPP using monthly data from March 1973 to December 1983, on the spot exchange rates for the UK, Japan, West Germany and Canada. Similar results are found by Corbae and Ouliaris (1988) who reject long-run PPP for the Canadian dollar, French franc, Deutsche mark, Italian lira, Japanese yen, and UK pound–US dollar spot exchange rates, using monthly data for consumer prices over the period July 1973 to September 1986. Enders (1988) reports 'mixed' results for PPP over both the Bretton Woods and subsequent floating exchange rate periods and Mark (1990), using monthly observations from June 1973 to February 1988 for eight OECD countries, finds little support for long-run PPP, even though mid-month bilateral exchange rates are used to coincide with the CPI which are sampled in mid-month, with no evidence of cointegration. Layton and Stark (1990) find that PPP is rejected, in that there is little support for the cointegration of the US consumer price inflation rate and an effective exchange rate adjusted CPI series computed from its six major trading partners (the UK, West Germany, Canada, France, Italy and Japan), over the period 1963–87. When comparing the strength of support for PPP across the different exchange rate regimes it is found to be in evidence during the fixed exchange rate period, although the evidence is weak and the data period rather short. Layton and Stark argue that a possible reason for the failure of the PPP hypothesis during the 1970s and 1980s is due to the changing structure of the industrialized countries, in particular to the rise in service production which is largely non-tradeable. Davutyan and Pippenger (1985) and Fisher and Park (1991) also argue that deviations from PPP are dominated by shocks that alter the relative prices for non-tradables and therefore, according to Davutyan and Pippenger, the empirical results are biased against PPP.

In view of these negative results recent tests of the PPP hypothesis have concentrated on larger samples spanning a longer period of calendar time or adopted different (more robust) statistical procedures. For example Kim (1990), using the Engle and Granger method and annual data on Canada, France, Italy, Japan and the UK, tests PPP for the period 1901 to 1987. Kim finds that in most cases the CPI and the WPI are cointegrated with the exchange rate at the five per cent level and that the error correction term is invariably significant, with the estimated coefficients suggesting that between 30 and 50 per cent of the deviations from PPP are corrected by exchange rate movements within the subsequent year. This suggests a two or three-year adjustment process which is consistent with the earlier work of Isard (1983) and with Abauf and Jorion (1990). It is not possible, however, to disentangle the effect of the long time period spanned by the data set from the mixed exchange rate regime effects.

Other authors such as Abauf and Jorion (1990), MacDonald (1991) and Fisher and Park (1991) have argued that the unit root tests used in the two-step procedure are not sufficiently discerning in their ability to reject a false hypothesis and have used alternative tests. MacDonald (1991) tests for PPP on five US dollar bilateral exchange rates using monthly data from January 1974 to June 1990 and the Johansen maximum likelihood procedure. MacDonald finds unique cointegrating vectors for most of the exchange rate and price level combinations, although the homogeneity of prices is tested and rejected in every case. Although MacDonald claims to have found 'strong support' for 'weak-PPP' the reported magnitudes of the coefficients on domestic and foreign prices, β and β^* respectively, look in many cases to be very different from unity,[5] although with the exception of the Canada–US equation, all are correctly signed.

Fisher and Park (1991) use tests based on the variable addition approach descibed in Park (1990) which yield two types of statistics: the J_1 statistic which is based on the null of co-integration and the J_2 statistic which is based on the null of no cointegration, thus series which are cointegrated should not only fail to reject the null under J_1 but also reject the null under J_2. Fisher and Park examine consumer prices, wholesale prices and bilateral exchange rates of the G–10 countries, giving fifty-five different bilateral exchange rates, sampled monthly over the period March 1973 to May 1988. The J_2 statistic rejected the null of a unit root at the 5% level in six of the 55 cases, indicating that in the main exchange rates have a unit root. All price indices were also found to have unit roots. The J_1 statistic was then used to test for cointegration. Fisher and Park found almost no evidence that the US bilateral exchange rates were cointegrated with the relevant price indices, but excluding the US and Canada, the hypothesis of cointegration between exchange rates and prices could not be rejected in 28 of the 36 remaining cases. These results were confirmed using the J_2 test. Furthermore Fisher and Park estimate error correction models for the cointegrating equations and find that the error correction parameter (γ_2 in equation 2.16) is uniformly negative and in the majority of cases statistically significant. The estimates of γ_2 indicate that a 10% real depreciation gives rise to a nominal exchange rate appreciation of about 1–2% in the next month, which is strong evidence that these exchange rates display overshooting characteristics. This set of results is consistent with those of Davutyan and Pippenger (1985), that real economic variables have changed the relative price of traded to non-traded goods in the G–10 countries over the recent floating exchange rate period.

On balance the evidence for PPP, especially over the recent floating exchange rate period, still remains questionable, with the bulk of the results against the hypothesis, but with some of the more robust results finding in favour of PPP.

2.5 Conclusions
The conclusions from this chapter are that the CLMM of exchange rate determination, although limited in its scope, has all the ingredients of the modern approach. It has PPP as a long-run equilibrium condition; it has a stock adjustment process as the principal mechanism by which equilibrium is restored following an exogenous disturbance; and it has exchange rate overshooting if some prices are not fully flexible in the short run. It is limited in its scope by not considering capital flows and exchange rate expectations, both of which are believed to be important determinants of the exchange rate.

The empirical, validity of PPP as a long-run equilibrium has not been settled, at least not for the 1970s and 1980s. To the extent that PPP is not a valid representation of equilibrium then the CLMM is also weakened. This weakness, however, will also be a feature of the modern monetary approach and indeed for some, like Smith and Wickens (1986), it is the main reason for the failure of the modern monetary models. Before the modern monetary approaches are examined it is necessary to consider the early Keynesian fix-price models of the exchange rate which, while continuing to omit exchange rate expectations and capital flows, also eschew stock adjustment for continuous flow equilibrium.

Notes
1. There are many good discussions of this in the literature, for example Schumpeter (1952) and Blaug (1968). In the context of the exchange rate, Myhrman (1976) makes an interesting contribution.
2. Indeed Humphrey (1980) has argued that Robertson in fact had the notion of rational expectations, at least in respect of the foreign exchange markets.
3. See Cuthbertson, Hall and Taylor (1992), Chapter 5.
4. A cointegrating relationship is found if the last year of the sample is excluded. Taylor

and McMahon attribute this to 'non-stationary fundamental factors' affecting the sterling exchange rate immediately before its return to the gold standard.

5. The most satisfactory results are obtained using wholesale prices, but this does not preclude some very large and very small coefficients on the price levels. For example, with the US as the 'foreign' country, in the UK–US normalized cointegrating vector $\beta = 0.403$ and $\beta^* = -1.353$; in the Japan–US case the values are, $\beta = 2.403$ and $\beta^* = -1.753$; and in the German case the values are, $\beta = 65.984$ and $\beta^* = -37.594$!

Appendix: The cointegration method

The essence of the cointegration methodology is to test the existence of equilibrium relationships between economic variables. If two variables, such as the exchange rate and relative prices, are proportional in equilibrium, then over time they should not diverge, but trend up or down together. Cointegration enables this long-run relationship to be tested independently of the short-run dynamics. It can be shown, however, that the error correction methodology (see Alogoskoufis and Smith, 1991; Hendry *et al.*, 1984; Hendry and Mizon, 1978) is closely related to that of cointegration, and indeed if a long-run equilibrium is discovered between two variables then there exists an error correction mechanism. This is known as the Granger Representation Theorem (Granger, 1986).

To test for cointegration is most easily thought of as a two-stage process. The first stage consists of a check of the time series properties of the variables. In particular, the order of integration needs to be established. This is tested by running the following equation for each of the variables in the equilibrium relationship:

$$\triangle X_t = \beta_0 + \beta_1 X_{t-1} + \sum_{i=1} \gamma_i \triangle X_{t-i} + u_t \qquad (A2.1)$$

where $\triangle$ is the first difference operator. If $\beta_1 < 0$ then X is stationary, while, if $\beta_1 = 0$, X_t is non-stationary. The hypothesis that $\beta_1 = 0$ (that is, for non-stationarity) is tested using the t-ratio. This t-ratio is called the Augmented Dickey Fuller test (ADF) if some lags of $\triangle X$ are required on the right-hand side to make the residuals, u_t, white noise, and the Dickey Fuller test (DF) if no lags are required. Under the null hypothesis of non-stationarity the distribution of the ADF and DF statistics is not Student's t, and so the tables in Fuller (1976) must be used. Suppose that the exchange rate, e, and relative prices, $p - p^*$, are both found to be of order one, denoted as I(1); that is, they are stationary in first differences. The fact they they are both integrated of the same order implies that an equilibrium relationship may exist between them. (Note that no equilibrium can exist between variables which are integrated of different orders.)

The second stage is to test for the existence of cointegration. This is done by regressing e_t on $(p - p^*)_t$ and testing that the residuals from this cointegrating vector are I(0), that is, stationary. In this case the null hypothesis of non-stationarity needs to be rejected. This time the appropriate test statistics are not those in Fuller (1976), but the adjusted versions found in Engle and Granger (1987) and Engle and Yoo (1987). An alternative test in this case is to test the cointegrating regression Durbin Watson statistic (CRDW) against a value of zero. If this hypothesis is not rejected then the residuals contain a unit root.

For further details of this procedure and the various refinements to it, such as the three-step procedure, the maximum likelihood method of Johansen (1988) and tests for seasonal cointegration due to Hylleberg *et al.* (1990), see Cuthbertson, Hall and Taylor (1992) or Charemza and Deadman (1992). For an accessible application of the technique see Hall (1986) and Holden and Thompson (1992).

3   The early Keynesian approaches

3.1   Introduction

The early Keynesian approach to exchange rate determination emerged during the Second World War (Metzler, 1942; Lerner, 1944), and was developed during the 1950s and 1960s by Laursen and Metzler (1950), Alexander (1952, 1959) and Machlup (1955, 1956). To a large extent this research programme focused upon extending the income-expenditure model developed from Keynes' *General Theory of Employment, Interest and Money* (Keynes, 1936) to the open economy. These extensions concentrated on the flow demand for goods and services and the extent to which a devaluation may be able to alleviate a balance of trade deficit.

This analysis was in contrast to what had gone before. In particular there were three developments that were striking. First, the general level of prices, which had been the focus of the Classical approach, was now relegated to a side issue by the assumption of a perfectly elastic aggregate supply function, which effectively fixed the price level. Underlying this assumption were the additional postulates that money wages were fixed, or at least rigid downwards, and that the economy possessed a degree of spare capacity. Secondly, along with this relegation of the importance of the price level went the sidelining of the money supply as an important macroeconomic variable in the determination of the exchange rate. The reason for this was that the new Keynesian approach focused on goods market flows, rather than on money market stocks. Hence the exchange rate was to be determined by the demand and supply of foreign currency that passed across the foreign exchange market in response to the demand and supply of exports and imports of goods and services. Thus the emphasis was changed: the exchange rate now depended upon the export and imports of goods and not upon the relative general level of prices. The equilibrium exchange rate would therefore be determined by the trade balance and not by purchasing power parity. This analysis, in turn, led to a third departure from the Classical approach in the development of the importance of the elasticities of demand and supply for exports and imports, and hence the elasticities of the demand and supply of foreign currency. Bickerdike (1920), and later Joan Robinson (1937) had already completed the analysis which became known as the elasticities approach to devaluation and exchange rate stability before Lerner (1944) gave his name to the crucial condition. This approach as typified by Haberler

(1949) showed that a sufficient condition for a devaluation of the exchange rate to improve the trade balance was that the sum of the demand elasticities of exports and imports be greater than unity in absolute value. Much of the work in the later 1950s and 1960s attempted to reconcile these competing views of exchange rate determination. The consensus that emerged (Laursen and Metzler, 1950; Alexander, 1959; Tsiang, 1961) seemed to suggest that the elasticities approach captured the short-run movements in the exchange rate, whereas the multiplier approach was relevant in the medium term, and, moreover, the Bickerdike–Robinson condition was not a necessary condition for foreign exchange market stability.

In this chapter on the early Keynesian models of exchange rate determination the emphasis will be on the multiplier approach, although, as will become apparent in due course, the Marshall–Lerner elasticities condition is crucially important for the stability of the exchange rate in this flow equilibrium approach. The multiplier approach in this chapter is taken to include both the income and absorption approaches to the exchange rate. The income approach focuses exclusively upon the implications of export and import functions depending upon foreign and domestic real income respectively, whereas the absorption approach also includes the exchange rate as an argument in these net export functions. Thus the absorption model is the more general method and it is a version of this approach which is extensively employed in this chapter.

This chapter is divided into three main sections. The elasticities approach to exchange rate determination and stability is considered in Section 3.2, with the more restrictive Marshall–Lerner condition developed as a special case of the general condition espoused by Bickerdike and Robinson. Section 3.3 examines the income-expenditure or absorption model of the exchange rate. This section begins by setting out the general two-country model, before examining the exchange rate dynamics in both the large and small country cases and the long-run comparative statics. Section 3.4 concludes with a consideration of the dynamics of the exchange rate in the general version of the model. Section 3.4 considers the empirical evidence on price and income elasticities of demand, which seems to suggest that the foreign exchange market will be stable. Section 3.5 draws together the arguments developed in this chapter for exchange rate dynamics.

3.2   The elasticities approach

This approach to exchange rate determination is based on the notion that foreign currency is demanded purely to finance purchases of foreign goods (imports) and received solely from the sale of domestic goods to foreigners (exports). It follows, therefore, that the equilibrium price of foreign currency depends on the balance of supply and demand for foreign currency, which is derived from the balance between the value of exports and that of imports. Moreover, with a floating exchange rate system, the exchange rate is expected to appreciate in response to an excess demand for foreign currency and depreciate in response to an excess supply. To obtain the derived demand and supply schedules for foreign currency, the underlying market supply and demand schedules are required for both imports and exports of goods. This is tackled in Section 3.2.1. The stability of the foreign exchange market and the effects of exogenous shocks to the import demand and export supply schedules on the exchange rate are considered in Section 3.2.2.

3.2.1 The export and import markets

The model consists of two goods: an export good and an import good. It is assumed that there are two countries and each country produces both commodities. The markets for both commodities clear so that home demand for the import good (I) equals the foreign supply of the import good (X^*) and that the home supply of the export good (X) equals the foreign demand for the export good (I^*). Furthermore, the law of one price holds for each commodity so that:

$$P_I = EP^*_I \text{ and } P_x = EP^*_x \tag{3.1}$$

where E is the exchange rate, defined as the domestic price of foreign currency, P_I is the price of the import good in the home country, P_x is the price of the export good in the home country and asterisks denote the foreign currency equivalents.

The market for exports Consider the market for the export good. The domestic supply of exports (X) is assumed to be a positive function of the domestic price of exports, as in equation (3.2):

$$X = X(P_x) + \alpha \qquad\qquad X_1 > 0 \tag{3.2}$$

while the foreign demand for domestic exports (I^*) is a negative function of the foreign currency price of exports (defined as the domestic currency price, P_x, deflated by the exchange rate, E, measured as the domestic currency price of a unit of foreign currency) as given by equation (3.3):

$$I^* = I^*(P_x/E) \qquad\qquad I^*_1 < 0 \tag{3.3}$$

where α is an exogenous disturbance to export supply and X_1 and I^*_1

represent the partial derivatives of X and I^* with respect to P_x. If the market for exports clears then $X = I^*$, and equations (3.2) and (3.3) can be solved for the percentage changes in both P_x and X, given by $\hat{P}_x$ and $\hat{X}$, respectively. Setting (3.2) equal to (3.3) and totally differentiating gives:

$$I^*_1 E^{-1} dP_x - I^*_1 (P_x/E^2) dE = X_1 dP_x + d\alpha \tag{3.4}$$

Defining the price elasticities of demand and supply as:

$$\eta_x = -I^*_1 P_x/X \text{ and } \varepsilon_x = X_1 P_x/X \tag{3.5}$$

respectively, substituting equations (3.5) in equation (3.4) for I^*_1 and X_1, and rearranging gives:

$$\hat{P}_x = [\eta_x/(\eta_x + \varepsilon_x)]\hat{E} - [1/(\eta_x + \varepsilon_x)](d\alpha/X) \tag{3.6}$$

where $\hat{P}_x = dP_x/P_x$ and $\hat{E} = dE/E$. Having solved for $\hat{P}_x$, substituting back into the supply equation gives the solution for $\hat{X}$. Hence differentiating equation (3.2) totally, and substituting for $\hat{P}_x$ from (3.6), using equation (3.5) gives, after rearranging:

$$\hat{X} = [\varepsilon_x \eta_x/(\eta_x + \varepsilon_x)]\hat{E} + [1 - (\varepsilon_x/(\eta_x + \varepsilon_x))]d\alpha/X \tag{3.7}$$

where again ^denotes a proportionate change. Hence a rise in E will lead to a rise in both export volume and price, measured in home currency.

These results mean that a depreciation of the exchange rate will give rise to an unambiguous increase in export value, measured in terms of the domestic currency, since $\hat{V}_x = \hat{P}_x + \hat{X}$, and the expression in brackets in equation (3.8) is positive, where it has been assumed that $d\alpha = 0$.

$$dV_x = V_x[\eta_x(\varepsilon_x + 1)/(\eta_x + \varepsilon_x)]dE/E \tag{3.8}$$

This result ensures that the supply of foreign currency schedule can not be negatively sloped.

The market for imports   The domestic demand and foreign supply functions are given by equations (3.9) and (3.10) respectively.

$$I = I(P^*_1 E) + \beta \qquad\qquad I_1 < 0 \tag{3.9}$$

$$X^* = X^*(P_I^*) \qquad\qquad X_1^* > 0 \tag{3.10}$$

Equation (3.10) shows the foreign export supply function is assumed to be an increasing function of the foreign currency price. The domestic demand for the import good is a decreasing function of the home currency price (P_I) and β denotes an exogenous import demand shock. As with the export market, if the market clears, then expressions can be derived for the proportionate change in both prices and volumes in terms of the exchange rate. Setting $X^* = I$ and totally differentiating gives:

$$X_1*dP*_I = I_1E.dP*_I + I_1P*IdE + d\beta \tag{3.11}$$

Defining the import demand and supply elasticities respectively, as

$$\eta_I = -I_1P_I/I \text{ and } \varepsilon_I = X*_1P_I/I \tag{3.12}$$

substituting for $X*_1$ and I_1, using equation (3.12) and rearranging gives:

$$\hat{P}*_I = -[\eta_I/(\eta_I + \varepsilon_I)]\hat{E} + [1/(\eta_I + \varepsilon_I)](d\beta/I) \tag{3.13}$$

$$\hat{I} = -[\varepsilon_I\eta_I/(\eta_I + \varepsilon_I)]\hat{E} + [\varepsilon_I/(\eta_I + \varepsilon_I)](d\beta/I) \tag{3.14}$$

These equations show that a depreciation of the home currency will lower the levels of both domestic import prices and volumes. A depreciation of the exchange rate may, however, lead to a rise or a fall in import value. The proportionate change in import value is given as: $\hat{V}_I = \hat{E} + \hat{P}* + \hat{I}$, so substituting for $\hat{P}*$ and $\hat{I}$ yields:

$$\hat{V}_I = [\varepsilon_I(1 - \eta_I)/(\eta_I + \varepsilon_I)]\hat{E} \tag{3.15}$$

where it has been assumed that $d\beta = 0$. The sign of this expression depends upon the size of the import elasticity of demand. If $\eta_I > 1$, then a depreciation of the exchange rate will cause of fall in import value. On the other hand if $\eta_I < 1$, then a rise in E will lead to a rise in import value. This suggests that the derived demand curve for foreign currency will not necessarily be downward sloping and so the question of market stability is raised. This issue is considered in the following section.

3.2.2   The trade balance and exchange rate dynamics
Under floating exchange rates the trade balance will always be in equilibrium and hence can be written as:

$$T = P_xX - EP*_II = 0 \tag{3.16}$$

where $EP*_I$ is the home currency price of the import good (P_I) and T is the nominal trade balance of the home country, measured in domestic currency.[1] For the foreign exchange market to be stable, in the sense that the exchange rate depreciates (appreciates) to eliminate a potential trade deficit (surplus), then the change in the domestic exchange rate must be related to any excess demand for foreign currency. Hence, if the value of domestic exports exceeds the value of domestic imports, there will be an excess demand for domestic currency and the relative price of domestic currency will rise (that is, E will fall). Therefore the change in the exchange rate over time is given by:

$$\dot{E} = \tau[EP^*{}_II - P_xX] \tag{3.17}$$

where $\dot{E} = (dE/dt)$ is the time derivative of the exchange rate, which is equal to zero if the trade balance is in equilibrium and τ is the speed of adjustment of the exchange rate to an excess supply of foreign currency.

For market stability it is essential that the exchange rate appreciates in response to an excess supply of domestic currency (excess demand for foreign currency). To consider this issue, totally differentiate equation (3.17) and divide both sides by P_xX, which gives, if trade is initially balanced:

$$d\dot{E} = (\tau P_xX)[\hat{I} + \hat{P}^*{}_I + \hat{E} - \hat{X} - \hat{P}_x] \tag{3.18}$$

Replacing each of the right-hand side terms in brackets (except $\hat{E}$) with their equivalents from equations (3.6), (3.7), (3.13) and (3.14) gives, after rearrangement:

$$
\begin{aligned}
d\dot{E} = {} & (\tau P_xX/E)[\{\varepsilon_x\varepsilon_I(1-\eta_I-\eta_x) - \eta_x\eta_I(\varepsilon_x+\varepsilon_I+1)\}/\{(\eta_x+\varepsilon_x)(\eta_I+\varepsilon_I)\}] \\
& dE + (\tau P_xX/E)[\{(\varepsilon_I+1)/(\eta_I+\varepsilon_I)\}(d\beta/I) \\
& - \{(1+\eta_x)/(\eta_x+\varepsilon_x)\}(d\alpha/X)]
\end{aligned} \tag{3.19}
$$

For stability the first term expression within square brackets, call it N (for numerator), must be negative, which means that:

$$N = \{\varepsilon_x\varepsilon_I(1-\eta_I-\eta_x) - \eta_x\eta_I(\varepsilon_x+\varepsilon_I+1)\} < 0 \tag{3.20}$$

This is in fact the Bickerdike–Robinson condition for stability of the foreign exchange market under floating exchange rates. It is a necessary and sufficient condition for stability, if income is held constant (as is assumed here). This formula is rather complicated and for many purposes the simpler Marshall–Lerner condition is used. In the context of Keynesian-type exchange rate models, this is certainly the case, since the aggregate supply schedule is assumed to be flat. Hence, if the supply elasticities are infinite, equation (3.20) reduces to the Marshall–Lerner condition, which is:

$$\eta_x + \eta_I > 1 \qquad\qquad (3.21)$$

Equation (3.21) says that the sum of the elasticities of demand for exports and imports must exceed unity for the foreign exchange market to be stable. This is a sufficient but not a necessary condition since, as the more general formula in (3.20) shows, stability may prevail even if this condition does not hold, if the supply elasticities are sufficiently small. This stability condition will be used extensively in Section 3.3.

Returning to equation (3.19), the effects on the exchange rate of shocks to the import demand and export supply functions can be considered. In equilibrium $dE/dt = 0$, and so rearranging (3.19) gives:

$$dE = N^{-1}\{(1 + \eta_x)/(\eta_x + \varepsilon_x)\}(d\alpha/X) \qquad\qquad (3.22)$$

$$dE = N^{-1}\{(\varepsilon_I + 1)/(\eta_I + \varepsilon_I)\}(d\beta/I) \qquad\qquad (3.23)$$

Equation (3.22) says that an exogenous rise in the supply of domestic exports, $d\alpha$, will lead to an appreciation of the exchange rate since, if the Bickerdike–Robinson condition holds, $N < 0$. On the other hand, a positive shock to import demand, $d\beta$, will give rise to a depreciation of the exchange rate under a floating exchange rate system. Such movements in the exchange rate will continue until trade balance equilibrium is restored. Note, however, that equal autonomous shocks to export supply and import demand functions may not leave the exchange rate unchanged. To see this, set $d\alpha = d\beta = d\gamma$ in the neighbourhood of equilibrium in (3.19) and solve again for dE, which yields:

$$dE = N^{-1}[(1 + \eta_x)/(\eta_x + \varepsilon_x) - (\varepsilon_I + 1)/(\eta_I + \varepsilon_I)]d\gamma/X \qquad\qquad (3.24)$$

which can be positive, negative or zero, depending on the relative magnitudes of the elasticities of demand and supply of imports and exports.

The conclusion from this section is that exchange rate movements from one equilibrium to another will be stable if the Bickerdike–Robinson condition holds. A sufficient condition, however, is that the sum of the demand elasticities exceed unity. In this model the long-run equilibrium exchange rate is determined by the trade balance, with deficits being offset by depreciation of the domestic currency and surpluses by appreciation of the currency. In other words it is a flow equilibrium, between domestic and foreign goods markets, rather than stock equilibrium, between domestic and foreign asset markets, which is important in this model and in the income-expenditure model in the next section.

3.3 The income-expenditure approach

This approach, as the name suggests, focuses on the flow of income and the aggregate demand for goods and services as determinants of the exchange rate. Like the elasticities and Classical approaches it can be developed as a two-country model, in which both economies are assumed to have an identical structure, although a small-country version will also be developed since this makes the model more amenable to graphical treatment. It shows that even with infinite supply elasticities the Marshall–Lerner condition for exchange rate stability has to be modified to allow for changes in real income. Section 3.3.1 introduces the static two-country version of the model, while Section 3.3.2 examines the dynamic implications for the exchange rate. Finally Section 3.3.3 considers the comparative statics of the two-country model.

3.3.1   The two-country model

This model, which, as noted above, develops the Keynesian income-expenditure model (IEKM) in an open economy context, is based upon three main assumptions.

1. The average level of prices is fixed in both countries and normalized to unity for convenience. This reflects the extreme Keynesian assumption of infinitely elastic aggregate supply.
2. The model has no monetary sector or asset markets and so interest rates are omitted from the model. This also implies that there are no international capital movements between the two countries.
3. Finally, there is no government sector so that public sector expenditures are specifically excluded from the model, as are the financing implications.

These assumptions imply that the income-expenditure system for a two-country world can be written as a seven-equation system, consisting of three identities, two national income identities and a trade balance equilibrium equation, and four behavioural equations, an expenditure function and an import function, for each country. The national income identities are given below as equation (3.25):

$$Y = A + X - I \text{ and } Y^* = A^* + X^* - I^* \tag{3.25}$$

where Y is the level of national income, which as in all Keynesian-type models is demand-determined, A is the level of absorption (consumption plus investment expenditures) on locally-produced goods, X denotes exports, I, imports and asterisks denote the foreign country equivalents. The third identity is that for the balance of trade. In a two-country world domestic exports are foreign imports and vice versa. It is assumed that imports are measured in terms of local currency, that is of the importing country, hence domestic exports, X, are equal to foreign imports, I^*, multiplied by the exchange rate, E. Hence the trade balance, measured in domestic currency and with constant prices, is given as:

$$T = EI^* - I \tag{3.26}$$

where $X = EI^*$. Since the exchange rate is assumed to be freely floating, so as to equate export and imports, it follows that (3.26) can also be expressed as $EI^* = I$. Equivalently, measuring the trade balance in terms of foreign currency gives:

$$I^* = I/E \tag{3.27}$$

The first pair of behavioural equations are those for absorption, defined as consumption plus investment demands by the private sector, which are given as equations (3.27) and (3.28):

$$A = A(Y, E) \qquad 1 > A_1 > 0, A_2 > 0 \tag{3.28}$$

$$A^* = A^*(Y^*, 1/E) \qquad 1 > A^*_1 > 0, A^*_2 > 0 \tag{3.28'}$$

A_1 is the usual marginal propensity to consume (absorb) and A_2 is the effect of a depreciation of the exchange rate on domestic expenditure. This effect, first introduced by Laursen and Metzler (1950), is expected to have a positive effect on domestic absorption, so that a depreciation of the exchange rate raises domestic absorption.[2] The argument is that a depreciation of the exchange rate will raise import prices and hence lower the real value of domestic income. Given that the average propensity to consume rises as income falls, lower real domestic income will be associated with a rise in consumption expenditures. Note that in the foreign absorption equation the reciprocal of the domestic exchange rate appears with a positive partial derivative. This reflects the fact that a rise in E represents an appreciation of the foreign currency, and so reduces foreign absorption as foreign import prices fall, raising the level of real income and hence reducing consumption as the average propensity to consume declines. The effect is symmetrically opposite to the effect of the exchange rate on home economy absorption.

The second pair of behavioural equations are those for domestic and foreign imports, given by equations (3.29) and (3.30):

$$I = I(Y, E) \qquad\qquad 1 < I_1 < 0, \qquad I_2 < 0 \qquad\qquad (3.29)$$

$$I^* = I^*(Y^*, 1/E) \qquad\qquad 1 < I^*_1 < 0, \qquad I^*_2 < 0 \qquad\qquad (3.30)$$

Domestic imports are assumed to depend positively on income, with the marginal propensity to import, I_1, strictly less than unity, and negatively on the exchange rate, since a rise in E means the value of the home currency has fallen and imports are relatively more expensive. Foreign imports vary directly with foreign real income and negatively with the reciprocal of the exchange rate.

The complete static two-country model can be reduced to a system in three equations by substituting the behavioural functions into the three identities, to solve for the equilibrium values of Y, Y^* and E. The equations are as follows:

$$Y = A(Y, E) + EI^*(Y^*, 1/E) - I(Y, E) \qquad\qquad (3.31)$$

$$Y^* = A^*(Y^*, E) + I(Y, E)/E - I^*(Y^*, 1/E) \qquad\qquad (3.32)$$

$$I(Y, E)/E - I^*(Y^*, 1/E) = 0 \qquad\qquad (3.33)$$

where equations (3.31) and (3.32) are measured in local currency and equation (3.33) is written in terms of foreign currency.

The next step is to linearize this three-equation system, using Taylor's expansion, ignoring all second and higher order terms, and denoting such deviations from the equilibrium level, Z^e, by $\overline{Z}$, where $\overline{Z} = Z - Z^e$, to give:

$$\overline{Y} = (A_1 - I_1)\overline{Y} + I^*_1 \overline{Y}^* + (A_2 + I^* - I^*_2 - I_2)\overline{E} \qquad\qquad (3.34)$$

$$\overline{Y}^* = (A^*_1 - I^*_1)\overline{Y}^* + I_1\overline{Y} - (A^*_2 + I - I_2 - I^*_2)\overline{E} \qquad\qquad (3.35)$$

$$I_1\overline{Y} - I^*_1\overline{Y}^* - (I - I_2 - I^*_2)\overline{E} = 0 \qquad\qquad (3.36)$$

where it has been assumed that initially $E = 1$. Since $I = Ei$, where i is domestic import volume, and $I^* = i^*/E$, the third term in parentheses in each of the equations above can be written in terms of the demand elasticities for domestic imports and exports. To see this, totally differentiate the expression for I which yields:

$$dI/dE = i + E(di/dE) = i[1 + (E/i)(di/dE)] = i(1 - \eta_I) = I_2$$

where, as before, $\eta_I = -(E/i)(di/dE)$. Similarly, for I^* we obtain:

$$dI^*/d(1/E) = i^*(1 - \eta_x) = I^*_2$$

where $\eta_x = -[(1/Ei^*)(di^*/dE)]$ and substituting for I_2 and I^*_2 in (3.36) gives:

$$I(\eta_x + \eta_I - 1)\overline{E} \tag{3.37}$$

as the final term, where it has been assumed that $i = i^*$ at the equilibrium point.

3.3.2 Exchange rate dynamics

The dynamical system that emerges from the linearized model is represented by equations (3.38) to (3.40) below. It is assumed that the level of national income in both countries varies directly with the level of excess demand, such that a higher level of excess demand leads to a rise in output and a fall in excess demand gives rise to a fall in output. Thus the equations for excess demand are:

$$d\overline{Y}/dt = k_1[(A_1 - I_1)\overline{Y} + I^*_1\overline{Y}^* + (A_2 + I(\eta_x + \eta_I - 1))\overline{E} - \overline{Y}] \tag{3.38}$$

$$d\overline{Y}^*/dt = k_2[(A^*_1 - I^*_1)\overline{Y}^* + I_1\overline{Y} - (A^*_2 + I(\eta_x + \eta_I - 1))\overline{E} - \overline{Y}^*] \tag{3.39}$$

The rate of exchange, which is the domestic price of foreign currency, tends to increase (decrease) if there is excess demand (supply) in the foreign exchange market for foreign currency. If the dominant currency is that of the foreign country, then the demand for such currency emanates from the import demand of the home country and so is $(1/E)I$, while the supply emanates from export revenue of the home country and so is I^*. Using the linearized form, given by (3.36) and substituting for the final term using (3.37) gives equation (3.40):

$$d\overline{E}/dt = k_3[I_1\overline{Y} - I^*_1\overline{Y}^* - I(\eta_x + \eta_I - 1))\overline{E}] \tag{3.40}$$

The stability of this differential equation system can be examined from the characteristic equation, which is:

$$\lambda^3 + c_1\lambda^2 + c_2\lambda + c_3 = 0 \tag{3.41}$$

Expanding the determinant gives:

$$\begin{vmatrix} k_1(A_1 - I_1 - 1) - \lambda & k_1 I^*_1 & k_1[A_2 + I(\eta_x + \eta_I - 1)] \\ k_2 I_1 & k_2(A^*_1 - I^*_1 - 1) - \lambda & -k_2[A^*_2 + I(\eta_x + \eta_I - 1)] \\ k_3 I_1 & k_3 I^*_1 & -k_3[I(\eta_x + \eta_I - 1)] - \lambda \end{vmatrix} = 0$$

where

$$c_1 = k_1(1 - A_1 + I_1) + k_2(1 - A^*_1 + I^*_1) + k_3 I(\eta_x + \eta_I - 1)],$$

$$c_2 = I(\eta_x + \eta_I - 1)[k_2 k_3(1 - A^*_1) + k_1 k_3(1 - A_1)] + k_1 k_2[I_1(1 - A^*_1) \\ + (1 - A_1)(1 + I^*_1 - A^*_1)] - k_1 k_3 I_1 A_1 - k_2 k_3 I^*_2 A^*_2$$

$$c_3 = k_1 k_2 k_3[(1 - A_1)(1 - A^*_1)I(\eta_x + \eta_I - 1) - I_1 A_2(1 - A^*_1) \\ - I^*_1 A^*_2(1 - A_1)].$$

The stability conditions in this case are:

$$c_1 > 0, \; c_3 > 0, \; c_1 c_2 - c_3 > 0$$

Gandolfo (1980) shows that the crucial inequality is the second one, $c_3 > 0$. Taking account of the assumptions made about the various partial derivatives and noting that the ks are positive partial adjustment coefficients, this second inequality requires that

$$[(1 - A_1)(1 - A^*_1)I(\eta_x + \eta_I - 1) - I_1 A_2(1 - A^*_1) - I^*_1 A^*_2(1 - A_1)] > 0 \tag{3.42}$$

Rearranging this expression to facilitate economic interpretation yields:

$$(\eta_x + \eta_I) > 1 + [I_1 A_2(1 - A_1) + I^*_1 A^*_2(1 - A^*_1)]/I \tag{3.43}$$

This condition for stability can be compared with the Marshall–Lerner condition of Section 3.2. It is apparent that the difference between these two conditions is the positive term in brackets on the right-hand side of (3.43). Hence the elasticities of demand for imports and exports have to exceed unity by some constant amount to ensure stability of the model. This more stringent stability condition is due to the effect of exchange rate changes on the level of absorption. If $A_2 = 0$ and $A^*_2 = 0$, then equation (3.43) reduces to the simple Marshall–Lerner condition. The economic intuition behind this result is fairly simple. As the domestic price of foreign currency rises, home exports become cheaper and foreign imports become more expensive, hence the demand for domestic output is stimulated, which raises domestic income and leads to an increase in imports. The increase in imports serves to partly offset the stimulus to domestic demand. It follows from this that the larger are A and A^*, the more significant these offsetting, contractionary effects will be.

To help understand this model, consider the small-country case which is represented graphically in Figure 3.1. In this set-up foreign income is assumed not to be an influence in the domestic export equation, hence $I^*_1 = 0$. The internal balance schedule (*IB*) is upward sloping in (E, Y) space since a rise in E requires a higher level of aggregate supply to meet the higher demand for domestic goods from overseas. Formally, totally differentiating (3.34), with $I^*_1 = 0$, and rearranging gives:

$$d\overline{E}/d\overline{Y} = [(1 - A_1)/A_2] > 0 \tag{3.44}$$

Note that $A_2 > 0$ is essential for *IB* to have a positive slope. All points above the *IB* line are therefore points of excess demand and points below the *IB* line are points of excess supply. At point G, for example, income is too low for the exchange rate E_0 and so income needs to rise to reduce the level of excess demand. At H, on the other hand, income is too high for E_0 and so income needs to fall from H back to Y_0 to restore internal balance. The slope of the external balance line (*EB*) can be negatively or positively sloped, depending on whether or not the Marshall–Lerner condition holds. If the Marshall–Lerner condition is satisfied then the *EB* schedule will also have a positive slope, which is obtained by totally differentiating (3.36), using (3.37), to give

$$d\overline{E}/d\overline{Y} = [I_1/I(\eta_I + \eta_x - 1)] > 0 \tag{3.45}$$

Hence as income rises the home trade balance will deteriorate as imports rise, necessitating a rise in E to expand exports and help to curtail imports to restore external balance. In terms of Figure 3.1, points above the *EB* line, like G, are positions of external surplus, since the exchange rate is higher than required for external balance, and must therefore fall, at a given level of income, to restore external balance. Points below the *EB* line, like H, are therefore points of deficit, necessitating exchange rate depreciation to restore external equilibrium.

Examination of Figure 3.1 shows that stability requires that the *IB* line has a steeper slope than the *EB* line. This condition can be formally stated as:

$$\eta_I + \eta_x > 1 + [I_1 A_2/(1 - A_1)]/I \tag{3.46}$$

This condition is the small-country equivalent of the stability condition

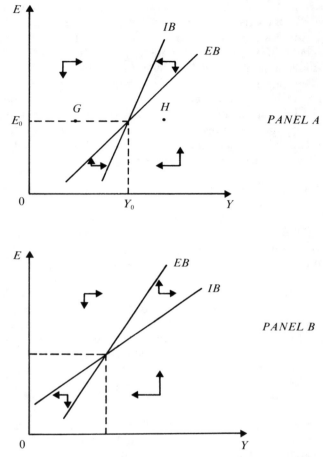

Figure 3.1 Stability in the Income-Expenditure Model (IEKM)

given by equation (3.43).[3] It shows that even in the context of a small country, if income varies with the exchange rate then the Marshall–Lerner condition is not a sufficient condition for exchange market stability.

3.3.3 Comparative statics

Having considered the dynamic stability of the model, some comparative static exercises may also be considered. In particular, consider the effect on the exchange rate and national income of an autonomous shock to domestic demand and an autonomous shock to domestic imports. These exogenous shocks are captured by the addition of the shift parameters δ and β to the absorption and import functions, respectively. First, the intuitive results are considered using the diagrams developed above for the small-country case, and then a formal analysis, in the context of the two-country model, concludes the section.

Consider an exogenous rise in domestic demand, as shown in Figure 3.2. This will lead to a shift in the *IB* line, to the right to IB_1, as for each level of the exchange rate domestic output will rise to meet the higher demand. However, not all of the higher domestic demand will be met from domestic production, and imports will increase, giving rise to a depreciation of the exchange rate. The new equilibrium will be established at point *F*, where the level of output is higher at Y_1 and the exchange rate has depreciated to E_1. Interestingly, domestic output rises by more when the exchange rate is flexible than when it is fixed (given by Y_2), because the subsequent depreciation of the exchange rate gives a secondary boost to domestic demand. Figure 3.3 demonstrates the effect of an autonomous rise in domestic imports, which shift the *EB* line to the left, from EB_0 to EB_1. In this case, for a constant level of exports, the exchange rate will depreciate to clear the foreign exchange market, which in turn will stimulate domestic output as the demand for domestic goods increases from Y_0 to Y_1. Note that in this case, if the exchange rate were fixed at E_0, domestic output would actually fall (to Y_2) rather than rise to Y_1.

In the two-country version of the model, the domestic demand shock is

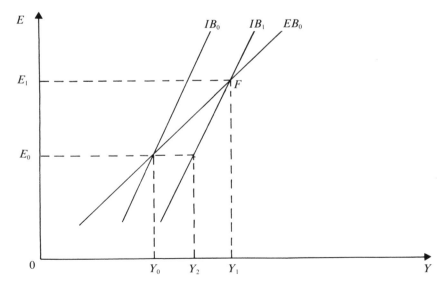

Figure 3.2   A rise in domestic demand in the IEKM

denoted by δ and the import shock by β. The model is represented by equations (3.47) to (3.49):

$$Y - A(Y, E) = \delta \qquad (3.47)$$

$$Y^* - A^*(Y^*,1/E) = 0 \qquad (3.48)$$

$$I(Y, E)/E - I^*(Y^*,1/E) = -\beta \qquad (3.49)$$

Totally differentiating, assuming that initially $E=1$, using equation (3.37) and expressing in matrix form gives:

$$\begin{bmatrix} 1 - A_1 & 0 & -A_2 \\ 0 & 1 - A^*_1 & A^*_2 \\ -I_1 & I^*_1 & I(\eta_I + \eta_x - 1) \end{bmatrix} \begin{bmatrix} dY \\ dY^* \\ dE \end{bmatrix} = \begin{bmatrix} d\delta \\ 0 \\ d\beta \end{bmatrix} \qquad (3.50)$$

The determinant of the left-hand side matrix (D) will be positive if the stability condition of the model is satisfied, since $D > 0$, from equation (3.43). Inverting D and solving for dY, dY^* and dE in terms of $d\delta$ and $d\beta$, gives the following multiplier expressions:

$$dY/d\delta = D^{-1}[(1 - A_1)I(\eta_I + \eta_x - 1) - I^*_1 A^*_2] > 0$$

$$dE/d\delta = D^{-1}[(1 - A^*_1)I_1] > 0$$

$$dY/d\beta = D^{-1}A_2(1 - A^*_1) > 0$$

$$dE/d\beta = D^{-1}[(1 - A_1)(1 - A^*_1)] > 0$$

$$dY^*/d\delta = -D^{-1}A^*_2 I_1 < 0$$

$$dY^*/d\beta = -D^{-1}(1 - A_1)A^*_2 < 0$$

The top four expressions confirm the results of the graphical analysis above. That is, a domestic demand shock raises income and depreciates the exchange rate, if the stability condition is satisfied, while a positive import shock raises domestic income through a depreciation of the exchange rate. The effect of an increase in home demand upon foreign output, however, is negative. The reason for this result is that as the domestic currency depreciates so, by definition, the foreign currency appreciates, which serves to reduce the demand for foreign output. Hence an expansion at home leads to a contraction abroad. If, however,

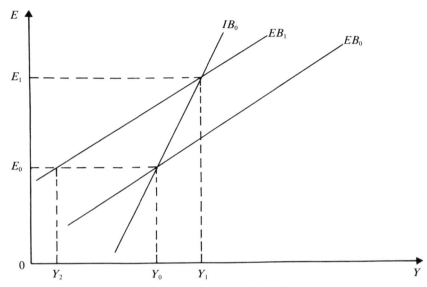

Figure 3.3   A rise in domestic imports in the IEKM

$A_2 = A^*_2 = 0$, then domestic shocks are not transmitted abroad, in which case flexible exchange rates insulate the foreign country from domestic shocks. A positive shock to domestic imports, that is a rise in β, causes a fall in foreign output and a rise in domestic output, since the exchange rate of the home country must depreciate to clear the foreign exchange market, and therefore the foreign currency must appreciate, thereby reducing foreign income. Finally, suppose the increase in domestic demand came entirely from imports, rather than from domestic production, so that $d\delta = d\beta$. In this case the output effects in both countries would be stronger, because the exchange rate depreciation for the home country would need to be larger, thereby inducing larger output effects.

3.4   Empirical evidence on price and income elasticities
So far the theoretical conditions for stability in the foreign exchange market, given constant levels of income and general price levels (Section 3.2) and just constant prices (Section 3.3) have been considered. In this section the empirical literature on the price and income elasticities of demand for exports and imports and the price elasticities of supply of imports and exports is reviewed and the empirical question of stability addressed.

One important problem in assessing this issue in the context of exchange rate dynamics is that most of the studies reviewed here extend over the period of fixed exchange rates as well as over the floating rate period. The problem is that there is not really any reason for believing that the estimates will be the same over the two types of exchange rate regime. A continually changing exchange rate is likely to have rather different implications for prices of traded goods than an exchange rate which is fixed for long periods and changed only discretely by a large amount. This problem is, however, largely ignored here because of the paucity of work purely on the floating exchange rate period.

There are perhaps two main conclusions from the empirical literature on the demand elasticities:

1. The sum of the long-run (defined as greater than or equal to 2 years) price elasticities of demand for imports and exports generally exceed unity for industrial countries. Thus the Marshall–Lerner condition (including infinite supply elasticities) seems to be empirically validated. Goldstein and Khan (1985) estimate that the price elasticity of demand for imports for a typical industrial country lies in the range of -0.5 to -1.0, while the corresponding export elasticity lies in the range of -1.25 to -2.50. Gylfason (1987) reports an average export price elasticity of -1.11 and an average import price elasticity of -0.99 for the 15 largest industrial countries. The sum of these average elasticities is therefore -2.10 and the Marshall–Lerner condition empirically validated in the long run. Gylfason also reports long-run elasticities for nine developing countries, which again show average export and import elasticities of greater than -1.0 and an average sum of -2.6.

2. The short-run (defined as less than 6 months) price elasticities of demand for imports and exports are considerably smaller than the long-run elasticities (with short-run elasticities being about half the size of the long-run elasticities). In this context the low short-run price elasticities may imply instability in the foreign exchange market, although taking mid-point estimates from the range cited above by Goldstein and Khan suggests that this is not necessarily the case.

Empirical work on the price elasticities of supply of exports and imports is rather more sparse than that for demand. The range for a typical industrial country, excluding the USA, seems to be between one and four. These values suggest that even in the presence of low demand elasticities the more general condition for exchange market stability is likely to hold. That is, an exchange rate depreciation will improve the trade balance even if the demand elasticities are less than unity, so long as the supply elasticities are less than infinite. Since the evidence suggests that demand price elasticities are greater than unity in the long run, the lower than infinite export supply price elasticities will diminish the trade balance effects of exchange rate changes. There is also a tendency for the size of the export elasticity to vary positively with the size of the exporting country and negatively with the ratio of exports to real GNP (that is, openness). Thus for the UK the export price elasticity is between 0.8 (Gylfason, 1978) and 1.4 (Goldstein and Khan, 1978), which is rather low considering the size factor.

Income elasticities of demand for a representative industrial country fall in the range of 1 to 2 on both the export and the import sides (Goldstein and Khan, 1985). There are two main implications of this result. First, in the absence of secular increases in the relative price of imports it should be expected that the shares of imports and exports in GNP (in real terms) will be rising over time. A second implication is that, if the income elasticity of demand for a country's imports is much greater than that for its exports, then the country has to face an unpalatable choice: either grow at the same rates as its trading partners and accept a secular decline in its trade balance, or opt for external balance and accept a lower rate of economic growth than its trading partners.

3.5 Conclusions

This chapter has reviewed the Keynesian approach to exchange rate determination in the absence of capital flows. In this case the dynamics of exchange rate adjustment are concerned with stability of the foreign exchange market. This requires that certain elasticity conditions be met so that the exchange rate moves in the right direction in response to exogenous shocks. The exchange rate is assumed to be in continual equilibrium, balancing the export and import values between countries. The policy implications of this approach are that the simple Marshall–Lerner condition is not a sufficient condition for foreign exchange market stability, if the exchange rate change affects the level income. Moreover, in this case floating exchange rates do not insulate the foreign economy from domestic shocks, or vice versa, again because changes in the exchange rate have real effects upon output. This does raise another important paradox since demand expansion abroad causes a recession at home, by appreciation of the home exchange rate, and hence with floating exchange rates domestic governments are unable to argue that domestic recession is caused by foreign recession, since a foreign recession should lead to a domestic boom.

In contrast to the Classical approach discussed in Chapter 2, this approach does not allow floating exchange rates to provide full insulation from foreign disturbances even in the long run. Thus exchange rate changes are real exchange rate changes and are not neutral in their effects on the real economy. This suggests that floating exchange rates are less attractive to policy makers under this approach in comparison with the Classical monetary approach. Niehans (1984) has argued that these approaches are in fact very similar, the main difference being the time horizon of the analysis. The Keynesian models discussed in this chapter are short-term models, which do not require full stock equilibrium, only flow equilibrium, whereas the Classical models of Chapter 2 take a longer-run view of the adjustment process requiring full stock equilibrium. Unfortunately the concepts, short run and long run, do not convert easily into calendar time. To the extent that both of these models ignore international capital movements and exchange rate expectations, neither model is likely to be appropriate in the real world. In the next two chapters it is assumed that the exchange rate is determined exclusively by capital flows and current balance effects are completely ignored.

Notes
1. Equation (3.16) can, of course, also be written in terms of foreign currency, in which case it becomes:

$$T^* = (P_x/E).I^* - P_I^*I = 0.$$

2. Niehans (1984), however, argues that the sign of A_2 could in fact be negative if wealth effect outweighs the income effect. The wealth effect arises as a result of the fact that the rise in import prices will also reduce real wealth. This may lead to individuals reducing their expenditure in order to rebuild their real money balances, and so A_2 would be negative. It is, of course, an empirical question as to whether the income effect or wealth effect dominates.
3. This can be directly obtained from (3.43) by setting $I^*_1 = 0$.

4 The modern monetary approaches

4.1 Introduction

Chapters 2 and 3 have focused on exchange rate models where the only international transactions have been in traded goods and services and the role of money has been solely as a medium of exchange. In this section of the book it is additionally assumed that a domestic and a foreign bond market exist. For simplicity, however, it is also assumed both that domestic and foreign bonds are perfect substitutes and that these asset markets clear instantaneously. Thus the law of one price holds continuously for securities of similar maturity and risk, when denominated in terms of a common currency. In the context of international bond markets this is known as the condition of uncovered interest rate parity. National monies are, however, still assumed to be non-traded and so only domestic residents hold domestic currency and only foreign residents hold foreign currency.

The models in this chapter are in the Classical tradition in that labour markets always clear so that output is supply-determined and there is automatic full employment. The aggregate price level is determined in the money markets, which are also assumed to clear continuously, in contrast to the model postulated in Chapter 2. The real exchange rate is also constant in that purchasing power parity (PPP) is expected to hold continuously. The introduction of domestic and foreign bond markets is the principal innovation and it is the treatment of exchange rate expectations that generates different types of monetary model.

This chapter is divided into four sections. Section 4.2 considers the various kinds of monetary model. The principal difference between these monetary models is in the way that they model exchange rate expectations. Section 4.3 critically examines the empirical evidence for these various models of exchange rate determination. Section 4.4 considers the role of 'news' and of speculative bubbles within the framework of the Rational Expectations Monetary Model (REMM) of the exchange rate. Finally, Section 4.5 concludes with some of the policy implications of this class of exchange rate model.

4.2   The modern monetary models

These models take the Classical monetary model, developed in Chapter 2, as their starting point. They are therefore genuine two-country models which in long-run equilibrium must exhibit full stock equilibrium, in the sense that neither the domestic nor the foreign money stock must be changing. As with their Classical forerunner therefore, the money markets are critical in restoring equilibrium following an exogenous disturbance. This section is divided into two sub-sections. Section 4.2.1 sets out the basic equilibrium model and Section 4.2.2 examines the exchange rate dynamics associated with different expectational hypotheses.

4.2.1   The basic framework

The basic model consists of two behavioural (demand for money) equations and four identities (those for domestic and money market equilibrium, PPP and interest rate parity).

The two behavioural relationships for the domestic and the foreign demand for money are assumed to be identical, with common elasticities. The domestic demand for money is positively related to the level of domestic income and negatively related to the nominal, domestic interest rate. The interest rate term reflects the potential substitutability between domestic money and domestic bonds, with a rise in the rate of interest increasing the opportunity cost of holding money balances and hence reducing the demand for cash. The domestic demand for money function is given by equation (4.1), with the identical foreign demand for money given by (4.2):

$$l_t = p_t + \alpha y_t - \beta r_t \tag{4.1}$$

$$l^*_t = p^*_t + \alpha y^*_t - \beta r^*_t \tag{4.2}$$

where lower-case letters for l, p and y denote the natural logarithms of the nominal money demands, price levels and real incomes respectively, r is the nominal interest rate and asterisks denote foreign country (and foreign currency) variables.

The four identities in the model consist of four market equilibrium conditions. Equilibrium in the home and foreign money markets are given by equations (4.3), where lower case m denotes the logarithm of the nominal money supplies.

$$m_t = l_t \text{ and } m^*_t = l^*_t \tag{4.3}$$

Equilibrium in the international product market is given by absolute purchasing power parity (PPP), exactly as in Chapter 2, which in logarithms is written as:

$$p_t = p^*_t + e_t \qquad (4.4)$$

International bond market equilibrium, which is given by the uncovered interest rate parity condition, is written as:

$$E_t e_{t+1} - e_t = r_t - r^*_t \qquad (4.5)$$

where E_t is the expectations operator. Hence $E_t e_{t+1}$ represents the expected value at time t of the exchange rate in period $t+1$. This condition says that the expected depreciation of the home currency will be equal to the excess of the domestic nominal interest rate over the foreign nominal rate. In other words, the domestic interest rate exceeds the foreign rate to compensate investors for any expected, future depreciation of the currency.

Substituting equations (4.1) and (4.2) into (4.3), solving for p_t and p^*_t and substituting into (4.4), for p_t and p^*_t gives:

$$e_t = (m_t - m^*_t) - \alpha(y_t - y^*_t) + \beta(r_t - r^*_t) \qquad (4.6)$$

This is the basic equation for the modern monetary approach, although it makes no use of the interest rate parity condition, given by equation (4.5). From equation (4.5) the interest rate differential is an endogenous variable, so replacing $r_t - r^*_t$ in (4.6) with its equal from (4.5) gives:

$$e_t = (m_t - m^*_t) - \alpha(y_t - y^*_t) + \beta(E_t e_{t+1} - e_t) \qquad (4.7)$$

To close the model some assumption has to be made about how exchange rate expectations are formed. In the long-run stationary state the exchange rate is assumed not to change, so that $E_t e_{t+1} = e_t$ and therefore $r_t = r^*_t$. The last term of equation (4.7) is therefore zero and equation (4.7) collapses to the Classical Monetary Model (CLMM) of Chapter 2. Interestingly, therefore, the CLMM and the modern monetary approach have the same long-run solution. The short-run dynamics, however, may be very different. These are considered in the next section.

4.2.2 *Expectations and exchange rate dynamics*
The assumption of static expectations used to derive the equilibrium exchange rate is inappropriate when considering exchange rate dynamics. In the literature four methods have been used to model exchange rate expectations: Frenkel's core inflation approach; adaptive expectations;

perfect foresight or rational expectations; and Frankel's real interest rate parity model in conjunction with regressive exchange rate expectations. Each of these alternative hypotheses gives rise to a different type of monetary model, considered below.

Frenkel's core inflation approach   Frenkel (1976) used equation (4.7) to model the German mark exchange rate during the German hyperinflation of the 1920s. To represent the expected change in the exchange rate Frenkel took expectations at time period *t* of the PPP condition, given by equation (4.4) and then subtracted PPP to get:

$$E_t e_{t+1} - e_t = (E_t p_{t+1} - p_t) - (E_t p^*_{t+1} - p^*_t) = \prod_t - \prod^*_t \qquad (4.8)$$

where $\prod_t - \prod^*_t$ is the expected inflation differential between the domestic and the foreign country. Frenkel then replaced the expected change in the exchange rate with the expected inflation differential to give the Core Inflation Monetary Model (CIMM), as in equation (4.9):

$$e_t = m_t - m^*_t - \alpha(y_t - y^*_t) + \beta(\prod_t - \prod^*_t) \qquad (4.9)$$

The assumption used by Frenkel was that the relative expected inflation differential was exogenous and hence independent of the price level.[1] It is important to remember that this model was set up in the context of the German hyperinflation, since in the absence of hyperinflation the assumption of independence between p_t and $\prod_t$ is unlikely to be valid and the model mis-specified. This approach to representing exchange rate expectations is essentially *ad hoc* and not model-consistent. The same criticism applies to the next expectations hypothesis, the adaptive expectations model.

Adaptive expectations   The adaptive expectations hypothesis says that the change in exchange rate expectations depends upon some proportion, $(1 - \theta)$, of the previous period's forecast error, that is

$$E_t e_{t+1} - E_{t-1} e_t = (1 - \theta)(e_t - E_{t-1} e_t) \qquad 0 < \theta < 1 \qquad (4.10)$$

so that if $e_t > E_{t-1} e_t$ then the actual price of foreign currency will be lower than expected and so the expectation of the future level of the exchange rate will be revised downwards according to (4.10). After continuous substitution for the expectations term on the right-hand side of (4.10) the equation becomes

$$E_t e_{t+1} = (1 - \theta)\sum_i \theta^i e_{t-1} \qquad \text{where } i = 1, 2, \ldots, \infty \qquad (4.11)$$

Substituting for the expected value of the exchange rate in (4.7) using (4.11) and rearranging gives

$$(1 + \beta)e_t = [m_t - m^*_t - \alpha(y_t - y^*_t)] + \beta(1-\theta)\sum_i\theta^i.e_{t-1} \qquad (4.12)$$

Employing the Koyck transformation gives the following expression for the exchange rate:

$$e_t = (1+\beta\theta)^{-1}\{(1-\theta L)[m_t - m^*_t - \alpha(y_t - y^*_t)] + \theta(1+\beta)e_{t-1}\} \qquad (4.13)$$

where L is the lag operator such that $(1-\theta L)x = x_t - \theta x_{t-1}$. The spot exchange rate, e_t, therefore depends on current and one-period lagged values of $(m - m^*)$, $(y - y^*)$, and the one-period lagged value of the exchange rate. The merit of this Adaptive Expectations Monetary Approach (AEMM) specification is that it allows temporary, short-run deviations from long-run PPP. This difference equation will be stable if $(1 + \beta\theta) > \theta(1 + \beta)$, which is the case when $\theta < 1$. This is, in fact, nothing more than the standard restriction under adaptive expectations. Moreover, the time path of the exchange rate will be monotonically convergent, since the coefficient on the lagged exchange rate is positive.

There are however, three principal difficulties with adaptive expectations. Firstly, the specification is *ad hoc*, with little theoretical basis. Secondly, the exchange rate will always under-react to shocks, because adaptive expectations are backward-looking. Hence this assumption is more appropriate to slowly moving variables like output than to exchange rates which, like other asset prices, are highly volatile. Thirdly, adaptive expectations imply persistent errors, since any forecast error in the last period is only partially adjusted in the current period. Hence a sharp movement in the exchange rate will give rise to expectations which are persistently incorrect, in that agents could do better using recent information. For these reasons the use of adaptive expectations is rare in the empirical literature.[2]

Rational expectations Expectations are deemed to be rational if they use all the available information to derive an estimate of the future value of the exchange rate. This means that agents do not only use past values of the exchange rate, inflation, budget deficits and so on, but also use information as to what are the expected future out-turns for these variables. This information may be gleaned from newspapers or from formal forecasting models; all that is necessary is that agents use this information to the full. Such expectations will probably turn out to be incorrect, but the important point is that, given the time when the forecast was made, the agents could not have produced a better forecast. This kind of expectations process is modelled by equation (4.14),

$$e_t = E_t e_{t+1} + \Omega_{t+1} \tag{4.14}$$

where Ω_t is a random shock which has a mean value of zero and is serially uncorrelated: that is: $E_t(\Omega_{t+1}) = 0$ and $E_t(\Omega_t\Omega_{t+1}) = 0$. In fact for most of this section it can be assumed that Ω_t is zero, so that equation (4.14) collapses to its non-stochastic form, which is distinguished from its stochastic form by the name 'perfect foresight'. Thus, if there are no random disturbances, the future is perfectly predictable and the forecast made at time t about $t+1$ will be correct.

This information has fundamental implications for equation (4.7). Rearranging (4.7) gives:

$$e_t = [1/(1+\beta)]z_t + [\beta/(1+\beta)]E_t e_{t+1} \tag{4.15}$$

where $z_t = m_t - m^*{}_t - \alpha(y_t - y^*{}_t)$. To solve (4.15) it is necessary to find an expression for $E_t e_{t+1}$. To do this lead equation (4.15) one period and take expectations at time period t. This gives:

$$E_t e_{t+1} = [1/(1+\beta)]E_t z_{t+1} + [\beta/(1+\beta)]E_t e_{t+2} \tag{4.16}$$

The problem now is to find an expression for $E_t e_{t+2}$. The solution, of course, is to advance equation (4.16) one period and take expectations again. This process of successive substitution continues *ad infinitum*. The final solution, however, will be of a form that can be deduced from equation (4.16); that is:

$$e_t = [1/(1+\beta)]\sum_i [\beta/(1+\beta)]^i z_{t+i} \quad \text{where } i = 0,1,\ldots,\infty. \tag{4.17}$$

Thus the current exchange rate depends upon the current values and all expected future values of the exogenous variables. This means that, if the expected future value of the money supply changes, then the current spot exchange rate will also change, without any current variables changing. Thus, if new information becomes available that suggests domestic income will rise next year above the previously expected level, then the current exchange rate will appreciate, in anticipation of this happening. The REMM, first developed by Mussa (1976) and Bilson (1978a, 1978b), therefore explains how the exchange rate can be very volatile despite seemingly stable fundamentals. All that is required is for expectations to change and the exchange rate can move sharply without any change in the fundamentals. The difficulty is that if this model is to be used to predict the exchange rate then forecasts have to be made of the future values of the exogenous variables, z_{t+i}. The statistical processes that are assumed for z_{t+i} will become important determinants of the exchange rate.

The kinds of time series processes for the exogenous variables that have been most commonly employed are: (i) the random walk model, defined as an ARIMA (0, 1, 0) process; (ii) the random walk model with serially correlated errors (Mussa, 1976); (iii) a random walk on the levels and growth of the exogenous variables (Mussa, 1976); and (iv) the random walk model with serially correlated differences, defined as an ARIMA (1, 1, 0) process. Consider each of these statistical processes in turn.

(I) THE RANDOM WALK MODEL: ARIMA (0,1,0) In this simplest case the process for the exogenous variables z_t is specified as:

$$z_t = z_{t-1} + u_t \tag{4.18}$$

where $E(u_t) = 0$, $E(u_t^2) = \sigma_u^2$, $E(u_t u_{t-1}) = 0$

Hence the difference of z_t is a serially uncorrelated, white noise error process. Taking expectations of z_{t+1} at time period t gives: $E_t z_{t+1} = E_t z_t = z_t$. Repeating for period $t+2$ yields: $E_t z_{t+2} = E_t z_{t+1} = z_t$. Therefore expectations of all future values of z_t will be captured by the actual current value of z_t. Although this may seem convenient, it is also rather uninteresting since in this case the model collapses to the ClMM reduced form, with static exchange rate expectations. To see this, substitute for $E_t z_{t+j}$ in equation (4.16), with $E_t z_{t+j} = z_t$ and noting that $\sum_{j=0}[\beta/(1+\beta)]^j = 1 + \beta$, so that

$$e_t = z_t = (m_t - m^*_t) - \alpha(y_t - y^*_t) \tag{4.19}$$

which is identical to a log-linear version of equation (2.4).

(II) THE RANDOM WALK WITH SERIALLY CORRELATED ERRORS This kind of stochastic process is represented as follows:

$$z_t = z_{t-1} + v_t \text{ and } v_t = \rho v_{t-1} + u_t$$

where u_t is white noise as before and $0 < \rho < 1$. Substituting for v_t and taking expectations at t for $t+1$, $t+2 \ldots$, gives:

$$E_t z_{t+j} = z_t + \sum_{j=1} \rho^j v_t \tag{4.20}$$

Substituting in equations (4.16) and (4.17) after some manipulations gives:

$$E_t e_{t+j} = z_t + [\rho/(1+\beta\{1-\rho\})]v_t \tag{4.21}$$

$$e_t = z_t + [1/(1+\beta\{1-\rho\})]v_t \tag{4.22}$$

This result shows that when ρ is small the exchange rate is expected to closely follow the fundamentals, given by z_t, but when ρ is large money holders expect large deviations from the fundamentals. In the extreme case when $\rho = 1$ any disturbance to z_t is expected to last forever, and since v_t and u_t are both random walks in this case, the exchange rate will also follow a random walk.

(III)   RANDOM WALKS ON THE LEVELS AND GROWTH OF Z   Let ξ_t represent the growth of z_t so that:

$$z_t = z_{t-1} + \xi_t + u_t \text{ and } \xi_t = \xi_{t-1} + \delta_t \tag{4.23}$$

where u_t and δ_t are white noise errors with zero means and constant variances σ^2_u and σ^2_δ respectively. If it is assumed that agents have full information, that is they know the processes generating ξ_t, u_t and δ_t, as well as the current value of z_t, then taking expectations of z_{t+j} at time period t gives:

$$E_t z_{t+j} = z_t + \sum_{i=1}\xi_t^i = z_t + j\bar{\xi}_t \text{ where } \bar{\xi}_t = E_t\xi_t \tag{4.24}$$

Substituting back into equations (4.16) and (4.17), but noting that:

$$\sum_{i=1}[\beta/(1+\beta)]^{i-1}i\bar{\xi}_t = (1+\beta)^2\bar{\xi}_t \text{ and } \sum_{i=0}[\beta/(1+\beta)]^i = \beta(1+\beta)$$

gives:

$$E_t e_{t+1} = z_t + (1+\beta)\bar{\xi}_t \text{ and } e_t = z_t + \beta\bar{\xi}_t \tag{4.25}$$

The effect of an unanticipated change in the elements of z_t depends upon whether the source is from u_t or δ_t. If the unanticipated positive shock is to the level of the money supply, for example, the unanticipated increase in the exchange rate also equals u_t, since only m_t, as part of z_t, is affected by such a shock. If, however, the shock is to the rate of growth of the money supply, that is via an unanticipated rise in δ_t, then agents expect, through the first relation in (4.23), a faster rate of growth in m_t in all future periods and the current exchange rate will depreciate by $(1+\beta)\,\xi_t$, since δ_t affects e_t

through ξ_t and through m_t. Bilson (1979) calls this faster depreciation of the domestic currency, due to positive shocks to the rate of growth of the money supply, the 'magnification' effect. The analysis here, however, is perfectly general, in that exogenous disturbances to real income growth, would also have a larger effect on the exchange rate than shocks to the level of real income.

(IV) A RANDOM WALK WITH SERIALLY CORRELATED DIFFERENCES: ARIMA (1,1,0)   This process can be written as:

$$\triangle z_t = \rho \triangle z_{t-1} + u_t \qquad\qquad (4.26)$$

where again u_t is a white noise error process, with a zero mean and constant variance. Taking expectations at time t for period $t+1$ gives: $E_t z_{t+1} = z_t + \rho(\rho \triangle z_{t-1}) = z_t + \rho^2 \triangle z_{t-1}$, which gives the form of the expression for $t+j$ which is:

$$E_t z_{t+j} = z_t + \sum_{i=1} \rho^i \triangle z_t \qquad\qquad (4.27)$$

Substituting into equations (4.16) and (4.17) gives:

$$e_t = z_t + [\beta\rho/(1+\beta-\beta\rho)]\triangle z_t \qquad\qquad (4.28)$$

where the exchange rate is now dependent on a set of observable variables, as in the other cases above.

   The REMM is tested by estimating equation (4.17) simultaneously with one of the statistical processes generating values for the exogenous variables outlined above. This yields a model of the exchange rate with model-consistent expectations.The results of this estimation procedure are discussed in Section 4.3.2.

Frankel's real interest rate parity model and regressive expectations   If exchange rate expectations are assumed to be regressive then the expected change in the exchange rate will be equal to the deviation of the actual exchange rate from its long-run equilibrium multiplied by some speed of adjustment parameter, θ, that is

$$E_t e_{t+1} - e_t = \theta(\overline{e} - e_t) \qquad 0 < \theta < \infty \qquad\qquad (4.29)$$

where θ is the speed of adjustment. Hence if e_t is above $\overline{e}$ the expectation is that the exchange rate will appreciate back towards the long-run equilibrium given by $\overline{e}$. Frankel (1979), used this expectations formation mechanism to derive the Real Interest Parity Model (RIPM) from the basic monetary model. Equating equations (4.29), (4.5) and (4.8) gives:

$$E_t e_{t+1} - e_t = \theta(\bar{e} - e_t) = r_t - r^*_t = (\textstyle\prod_t - \prod^*_t) \qquad (4.30)$$

Frankel replaced $\bar{e}$ with the expression for e_t from (4.9), that is, from Frenkel's CIMM, and rearranged the expression to obtain the quasi-reduced form of the RIPM, given as equation (4.31):

$$e_t = (m_t - m^*_t) - \alpha(y_t - y^*_t) + (\beta + 1/\theta)(\textstyle\prod_t - \prod^*_t) - (1/\theta)(r_t - r^*_t) \qquad (4.31)$$

The interesting feature about this model is that it gives Frenkel's CIMM as a special case, in the long-run equilibrium. The final term is therefore a disequilibrium term, representing deviations from PPP, which in the long run collapses to zero as the nominal interest differential is zero. If, on the other hand, the actual exchange rate adjusts instantaneously to its long-run equilibrium rate, then $\theta \to \infty$, and the model again reduces to the long-run equilibrium exchange rate given by Frenkel's CIMM.

The problem with this approach is that it is neither an equilibrium exchange rate equation nor a properly specified dynamic equation. As noted above, the interest rate differential term represents disequilibrium in the international bond markets and so the equation is not an equilibrium equation. Secondly, it is not a dynamic equation because it only includes contemporaneous variables among the regressors. Furthermore, the inclusion of an endogenous variable on the right-hand side of (4.31) implies that ordinary least squares estimates (OLS) will not be unbiased and that it is not a reduced form equation. To treat equation (4.31) as a directly estimable reduced from equation has, however, been the dominant approach in the empirical literature, as the next section explains.

4.3   The econometric evidence

The monetary models of the exchange rate have been the most widely tested exchange rate models, partly because of their undemanding data requirements. The empirical literature is therefore vast and so rather than attempt to provide a comprehensive review this section focuses on sample results and, wherever possible, on recent contributions.[3] This section is sub-divided into two main sections, the former of which is further sub-divided. Section 4.3.1 examines the empirical problems and results obtained from the estimation of Frenkel's RIPM as represented by the quasi-reduced equation (4.31), of which Frenkel's CIMM, given by equation (4.9), is a special case. The examination of these results is divided into three classes: within-sample tests, out-of-sample tests and cointegration approaches respectively. Section 4.3.2 considers tests of the Rational Expectations Monetary Model (REMM) which employs simultaneous equations estimation procedures.

4.3.1 Tests of the CIMM and RIPM

Within-sample results The early empirical work on the CIMM and RIPM in the late 1970's (Bilson 1978a, 1978b, Hodrick, 1978 and Putnam and Woodbury 1979) seemed to show that the monetary models were reasonably well-supported by the data for the period up to 1978. (See MacDonald, 1988, and Pentecost, 1991 for a detailed discussion of these results.) When the sample period was extended beyond 1978 however, a number of problems arose which cast doubt on the ability of these monetary models to explain the in-sample movements of the exchange rate.

Table 4.1 reproduces some typical results obtained from estimating equations like (4.31). The major problem with these estimates is the consistently wrong sign on the coefficient of the relative money supplies term, which should *a priori*, be positive and equal to unity. From Table 4.1 the coefficient on $(m - m^*)$ is usually negative and not statistically different from zero at the 5 per cent level, the only exception being the results for the Canadian dollar–US dollar exchange rate obtained by Backus (1984). A second related problem is the potential endogeneity of the interest rate differential. With both the money supplies and interest rate differentials on the right-hand side it is certain that an endogenous variable will be included among the regressors since the authorities cannot target both m and r simultaneously. The wrong sign on the money supplies term may therefore reflect the fact that the authorities have set interest rates and allowed the money supply to adjust endogenously. In this case a depreciation of the exchange rate is associated with a rise in the interest rate and a fall in the money supply.

A third problem in this class of results is that of serial correlation. In Table 4.1 all the results exhibit this characteristic. The traditional approach to this problem was to look for forms of mis-specification in the estimated equation, such as: the imposed cross-equation restrictions on the income and interest rate elasticities; the log-linear form as against a non-linear specification; and the likely instability of the demand for money function over time due to the extent of financial innovation in the 1980's. The results of tests for these kinds of mis-specification are reported below, with the results of the alternative approach to the problem of serial correlation, namely cointegration, deferred until the end of this subsection.

The cross-equations restrictions have been tested by Haynes and Stone

Table 4.1   Tests of the CIMM and RIPM quasi-reduced forms

$$e_t = \alpha_0 + \alpha_1(m - m^*)_t + \alpha_2(y^* - y)_t + \alpha_3(\prod - \prod^*)_t + \alpha_4(r - r^*)_t$$

Priors: RIPM: $\alpha_1 = 1, \alpha_2 > 0, \alpha_3 > 0, \alpha_4 < 0$
        CIMM: $\alpha_1 = 1, \alpha_2 > 0, \alpha_3 > 0, \alpha_4 = 0$

	[1]	[2]	[3]	[4]	[5]
α_0	−0.115	0.685	−0.865	0.770	
	(0.25)	(1.68)	(1.90)	(1.84)	
α_1	−0.344	−0.033	−0.865	−0.034	1.097
	(1.31)	(0.50)	(0.94)	(0.52)	(3.54)
α_2	−1.261	−0.356	−0.271	−0.194	−0.463
	(1.53)	(0.55)	(3.43)	(0.29)	(0.82)
α_3	−0.042	−0.000	−0.038	−0.002	−0.106
	(0.34)	(0.00)	(0.35)	(0.05)	(3.00)
α_4			0.041	−0.005	−0.000
			(3.61)	(0.89)	(0.03)
$\bar{R}^2$	0.095	0.359	0.308	0.325	0.43
DW	0.270	1.361	0.564	1.283	0.60
RHO		0.951		0.958	−0.205
		(25.6)		(28.04)	

Notes
Data set: [1] to [4] use DM/$ exchange rate, quarterly from 1974. Q1 to 1984 Q4; [5] uses Can $/US $ exchange rate quarterly, from 1971 Q1 to 1980 Q4.
All equations estimated using OLS, with t-values in parenthesis

Sources: [1] to [4]: Leventakis (1987), Tables 1 and 2, pp. 368–9; [5]: Backus (1984).

(1981), Boothe and Glassman (1987) and by Radaelli (1988). The former studies found the restrictions jointly rejected and the relative money supply restriction individually rejected. Radaelli, on the other hand, found the restrictions not rejected individually on an F-test for the mark–dollar exchange rate in the RIPM. These results suggest that the cross-country restriction is not important in explaining the poor performance of these models.

Meese and Rose (1989) have argued that there may be non-linearities in the demand for money functions, hence the simple log-linear forms are misspecified. Three reasons are offered as to why non-linearities may be important. First, economic time and calendar time may differ – the so-called 'time deformation' problem. This may arise, for example, if the appropriate time scale for foreign exchange markets 'speeds up' in terms of calendar time in periods when there is an unusually large amount of new information to be processed. Second, misspecification of the functional form itself in the empirical model may also lead to manifestations of non-linearities. Third, the data generation process may be intrinsically non-linear. This can arise in rational expectations models where forward-looking agents forecast the future time path of the fundamentals, but expect government reaction functions to be subject to random shocks. This may lead to the agent's appropriate prediction formula, and hence the reduced form exchange rate equation, having a non-linear form. Meese and Rose apply a wide range of parametric and non-parametric tests to different monetary models in an attempt to identify these various types of non-linearity. They find no evidence of time deformation or that inappropriate transformations of fundamentals were responsible for the poor performance of the models. Hence they conclude that 'accounting for non-linearities in current exchange rate models does not appear to be a promising way to improve our ability to explain currency movements' (p. 36).

The third reason cited for likely failure of the monetary model is the instability of the demand for money functions that underlie it. This suggestion by Meese and Rogoff (1983b) has been specifically tested by a number of papers, but especially by Boothe and Poloz (1988), Frankel (1984) and among other things by Smith and Wickens (1986). Frankel's approach is to include a lagged term in relative velocity in a monetary model of the real exchange rate. He finds that not only is this term correctly signed and statistically significant, but that the coefficients on each of the four original variables (relative money supplies, relative real income, relative expected inflation and relative nominal interest rates) are also now significant and of correct sign. In contrast Boothe and Poloz found that allowing for shifts in the demand for money function, due to financial innovation, in a model of the Canadian dollar–US dollar exchange rate, did not help improve the performance of the model. Smith and Wickens, show that, for the sterling–dollar and mark–dollar exchange rates for the period 1973 Q3 to 1982 Q3, both money supply innovations and money demand function errors are important sources of error in the monetary models, although, interestingly, neither of these is as important as those errors stemming from PPP. Moreover, in a recent paper, Baillie and Pecchenino (1991), using a battery of statistical tests, provide strong evidence for a stable, equilibrium demand function for money in both the UK and the USA, noting that the disturbances around the equilibrium are strongly autocorrelated, but stationary and mean-reverting. On balance, therefore, it would seem that instability of the demand for money function is unlikely to be the main reason for the failure of the monetary approach to exchange rate determination.

Out-of-sample forecast tests   There have been two principal techniques used to generate out-of-sample forecasts for the monetary models: the rolling regressions method and the time-varying parameter method. These two methods are considered in turn.

The rolling regressions method in this context was pioneered by Meese and Rogoff (1983a), who estimated the simple monetary models using the instrumental variable (IV) technique, due to Fair (1970), to generate static exchange rate forecasts. The models were estimated over the period March 1973 to November 1976. Forecasts were generated at horizons of one, three, six and twelve months. The data for December 1986 are then added to the sample and the parameters of the model re-estimated using rolling regressions. New forecasts are generated at the same horizons as before. The principal result is that the one-step-ahead random walk model outperforms the reduced form monetary models over all time horizons and exchange rates. It has been suggested, however, by Schinasi and Swamy (1987) that, since Meese and Rogoff's reduced form model does not include a lagged dependent variable, the relevant comparison should be with a multi-step-ahead random walk forecast rather than the one-step-ahead. The use of the one-step-ahead random walk biases the results in favour of the random walk since it is able to utilize information not available to the reduced form model; that is, the lagged value of the nominal exchange rate. Indeed, a rough comparison between the multi-step random walk forecasts reported in Schinasi and Swamy and the average root mean square forecast error (RMSE) of Meese and Rogoff's reduced form predictions shows that the reduced form models actually out perform the random walk for the yen–dollar and mark–dollar exchange rates. This suggests that Meese and Rogoff were too hard in their original conclusions. This is also suggested in a later paper by Meese and Rogoff (1983b) where they demonstrate, using vector autoregressions, that the instruments used to estimate the monetary reduced form in their original paper were not truly exogenous. They overcome this problem by imposing coefficient constraints and re-estimating the RMSE for the same periods as in their initial paper. They discover that, although the coefficient-constrained reduced form still fails to beat the one-step-ahead random walk model for most forecast horizons up to one year, in forecasting beyond one year the monetary model reduced form does outperform the random walk on the RMSE criterion. Although this lends support to the view that the exchange rate may behave in a random way in the short run, it also suggests that in the longer run its path may be more closely related to the fundamentals, which is in contrast to Meese and Rogoff's original results which show a better performance over the one and six month horizons than over the one year horizon.

The time-varying parameters method of obtaining out-of-sample forecasts of the exchange rate is an attempt to overcome the likely instability of the demand for money function noted above. The problem is that the researcher has to specify how the parameters are allowed to vary. Economic theory provides no guidance on this matter and the results are fairly sensitive to the way in which the parameters are allowed to evolve, as the two main papers by Wolff (1985) and Schinasi and Swamy (1987) demonstrate. Wolff assumed the coefficients in the monetary model each follows a random walk process. The results obtained for the mark–dollar, yen–dollar and sterling–dollar exchange rates were relatively unsuccessful in that the monetary model only outperform the random walk in one case (the mark–dollar rate). For all other exchange rates the random walk has a superior out-of-sample forecasting performance. Schinasi and Swamy, on the other hand, impose a first order autoregressive structure on the model parameters. They then estimate the RIPM with and without lagged values of the exchange rate on the right-hand side, to generate out-of-sample forecasts for the sterling, mark and ten exchange rates against the dollar, for 15 periods beyond March 1980. The RMSEs for the monetary approach models are lower than the RMSEs generated by the multi-step random walk model for all exchange rates without lagged dependent variables. The addition of lagged dependent variables sees the RIPM of Frankel (1979) out perform a one-step-ahead random walk model for all the exchange rates.

The interim conclusion from this survey of the reduced-form econometric evidence is that, if static forecasts are compared to a multi-step-ahead random walk model, rather than a one-step-ahead model, then the out-of-sample results are not all that bad, although the stochastic coefficients method seems to have the edge over the fixed parameter method. In the case of dynamic forecasts, the inclusion of lagged dependent variables, or autoregressive time-varying coefficient structures, greatly enhances forecast performance, although of course such specifications are generally *ad hoc*. It is likely, therefore, that the lack of explicit dynamic processes, such as the stock adjustment process or the model-consistent treatment of exchange rate expectations, is an important reason for the flexible price monetary model performing so poorly when confronted with the data. The single most important reason for the failure of the monetary approach, however, seems to be the failure of the PPP assumption (Smith and Wickens, 1986).

Cointegration tests   Several recent papers have attempted to use cointegration techniques to estimate some form of the monetary model. There are three problems that arise in these studies. First, exchange rates and relative prices have been shown not to be cointegrated in Chapter 2 and so it would perhaps be a little surprising if the tests of the quasi-reduced form, which are based on PPP, were to reveal a long-run equilibrium relationship. Secondly, equation (4.31) is not an equilibrium equation, since in full stock equilibrium the interest rate differential will be zero. Hence either the CLMM or the CIMM are usually employed as appropriate models of the equilibrium exchange rate. However, there are cases in the literature (see, *inter alia*, Boothe and Glassman, 1987) where an inappropriate long-run equilibrium exchange rate model has been used. In these cases it is not surprising that cointegration methods have been no more successful than the traditional econometric techniques.

Boothe and Glassman (1987), for example, find that the monthly mark–dollar exchange rate and monthly data on m, y, r and $\prod$ are all individually stationary after first-differencing, that is the series are I(1), but no cointegrating vector is found between the exchange rate and the relative money supplies. The omission of relative income terms from the CLMM and the real income and expected inflation differential terms from the CIMM make this result unsurprising. Baillie and Selover (1987) however, also find that the CIMM does not provide a valid cointegrating regression for the currencies of Canada, France, Germany, Japan and the UK (all against the US dollar), while Sarantis and Stewart (1991), for the period 1973 Q1 to 1990 Q3, find that the US dollar, Deutsche Mark, yen and French franc bilateral exchange rates against sterling are all I(1), together with a number of measures of the money supply, income and interest rates, but no valid cointegrating vector can be found among the monetary model variables. Radaelli (1988), on the other hand, does claim to find a valid cointegrating regression for the yen–dollar exchange rate, although five out of the twelve coefficients have theoretically incorrect signs! In an empirical study of the six principal industrial countries over the period from mid-1972 to mid-1986, McNown and Wallace (1989) report that the variables of the CIMM and CLMM do not cointegrate and hence do not represent an appropriate long-run equilibrium model of the exchange rate. A summary of McNown and Wallace's results are reproduced in Table 4.2.

In contrast to these negative results, MacDonald and Taylor (1992b) have found evidence for the CIMM using the Johansen maximum likelihood procedure (Johansen, 1988; Johansen and Juselius, 1990) and monthly data on the US dollar–sterling exchange rate from January 1976 to December 1988. The results are reproduced in Table 4.3, and show that

Table 4.2   Cointegration tests for the CIMM

$$e_t = \alpha_0 + \alpha_1(m - m^*)_t + \alpha_2(y - y^*)_t + \alpha_3(\prod - \prod^*)_t + u_t$$

Base country is the USA	Restricted model		Unrestricted model	
	DF	ADF	DF	ADF
UK				
1972.M7–1986.M7	− 1.70		− 2.74	
West Germany				
1973.M4–1986.M7	− 2.60*	− 2.39 (12)	− 4.74*	− 3.14 (12)
Japan				
1973.M4–1986.M6	− 1.73		− 1.96	− 2.86 (4)
Canada				
1970.M6–1986.M6	− 3.95*	− 3.00	− 5.27*	− 3.40 (12)
France				
1973.M4–1986.M6	− 4.67		− 4.58	

Notes
The unrestricted model allows different domestic and foreign elasticities and semi-elasticities in the demand for money.
*Denotes serially correlated residuals, based on Q-statistics at 10%.
(.)Denotes number of lags used to calculate the ADF statistics. The critical values for DF and ADF are given in Engle and Yoo (1987).
McNown and Wallace reportedly also test for cointegration with $\alpha_3 = 0$, and obtain very similar results.

signs of the variables in the long-run cointegrating vector are all consistent with the CIMM of Frenkel (1976), although the domestic and foreign parameters are not equal and the income elasticity of the demand for both domestic and foreign money balances is rather large, although not any larger than those reported in some studies of the demand for money: for example, Hendry and Mizon (1978). The error correction form shows excellent diagnostics although it has only moderate explanatory power. Most impressively, the estimated equation outperforms a random walk forecast up to 12 months ahead. Given the other results presented in this section these results are very good and demonstrate the advantages of a longer run of data combined with an appropriate equilibrium model and estimation technique.

The results in this section demonstrate that the CIMM has some support, at least in the case of the US dollar–pound exchange rate, but that in general much of the empirical research in this area has not been well directed.

Table 4.3　Maximum likelihood cointegration and error correction tests of the CIMM

Cointegrating vector

$$e_t - [0.838m_t - 0.641m^*_t - 3.382y_t + 2.643y^*_t + 0.322\prod_t - 0.157\prod^*_t] = RES_t$$

Error correction model

$$\Delta e_t = 0.217\Delta e_{t-2} - 0.691\Delta m^*_t - 0.441\Delta^2 y_{t-2} + 0.013\Delta^2\prod_{t-1} - 0.016\Delta\prod^*_{t-3}$$
$$\quad (2.65) \qquad (1.59) \qquad (1.55) \qquad (2.6) \qquad (2.00)$$
$$+ 0.010\Delta r_t - 0.017\Delta r_{t-1} + 0.009\Delta^2 r^*_t - 0.024RES_{t-1} - 0.126$$
$$\quad (2.5) \qquad (3.4) \qquad (2.25) \qquad (2.18) \qquad (2.14)$$
$$R^2 = 0.26; \ \eta_2(6, 134) = 0.60; \ \eta_3(6, 128) = 1.14; \ \eta_4(2, 138) = 0.46;$$

where t-values are in parentheses and the η_i's are distributed as F, where:
η_2 is the Lagrange multiplier test for serial correlation (critical value at 5% = 2.41),
η_3 is the ARCH statistic (critical value at 5% = 2.52),
η_4 is a RESET misspecification test (critical value at 5% = 3.69).

Source: MacDonald and Taylor, (1992b), pp. 13 and 15.

4.3.2　Test results of the REMM

The REMM has the advantage over the CIMM and RIPM of treating exchange rate expectations in a model-consistent, that is, rational way. The problem, as noted above, is that expectations have to be generated of the future values of the exogenous variables prior to estimation of the model. How these expectations are generated is largely an *ad hoc* matter. Empirically ARIMA (1,1,0) and ARIMA (3,1,0) processes have been employed by Hoffman and Schlagenhauf (1983) and Finn (1986) respectively. It is primarily these results that are reported in this section.

Hoffman and Schlagenhauf (1983) use an ARIMA (1,1,0) process for the forcing variables and so their estimating equation is similar in form to that of (4.28) above; that is:

$$e_t = c + (m_t - m^*_t) - \alpha(y_t - y^*_t) + [\beta\rho_m/(1+\beta-\beta\rho_m)]\triangle m_t$$
$$- [\beta\rho_m^*/(1+\beta-\beta\rho_m^*)]\triangle m^*_t - [\alpha\beta\rho_y/(1+\beta+\beta\rho_y)]\triangle y_t$$
$$+ [\alpha\beta\rho_y^*/(1+\beta-\beta\rho_y^*)]\triangle y^*_t \qquad (4.32)$$

This equation can be re-parameterized to give:

$$e_t = k + (m_t - m^*_t) - \alpha(y_t - y^*_t) + \theta_1\triangle m_t + \theta_2\triangle m^*_t + \theta_3\triangle y_t, \theta_4\triangle y^*_t \qquad (4.33)$$

and

$$e_t = k + \theta_5 m_t - \theta_6 m^*{}_t - \theta_7 y_t - \theta_8 y^*{}_t + \theta_1 \triangle m_t + \theta_2 \triangle m^*{}_t + \theta_3 \triangle y_t$$
$$\quad + \theta_4 \triangle y^*{}_t \tag{4.34}$$

where

$$\theta_1 = [\beta\rho_m/(1+\beta-\beta\rho_m)]$$
$$\theta_2 = [\beta\rho_m{}^*/(1+\beta-\beta\rho_m{}^*)]$$
$$\theta_3 = [\alpha\beta\rho_y/(1+\beta+\beta\rho_y)]$$
$$\theta_4 = [\alpha\beta\rho_y{}^*/(1+\beta-\beta\rho_y{}^*)]$$

Equations (4.32) and (4.33) impose the usual monetary model restrictions of unit elasticity of money supplies and equal income elasticities for home and foreign countries. From equation (4.34), only β is not identified elsewhere in the system. This suggests three restrictions, given by equation (4.35):

$$\theta_1(\rho_m{}^*\theta_2 - \theta_2 - \rho_m{}^*) = \theta_2(\rho_m\theta_1 - \theta_1 + \rho_m)$$
$$\theta_1(\rho_y\theta_3 - \theta_3 - \alpha\rho_y) = \theta_3(\rho_m\theta_1 - \theta_1 + \rho_m) \tag{4.35}$$
$$\theta_1(\rho_y{}^*\theta_4 - \theta_4 - \alpha\rho_y{}^*) = \theta_4(\rho_m\theta_1 - \theta_1 + \rho_m)$$

If these restrictions are valid then both the original structure (4.17) and the forecasting equations (4.26) are consistent with rational expectations. Hence a test of these restrictions should be regarded as a test of the internal consistency of the REMM.

Hoffman and Schlagenhauf estimate equations like (4.26) for m, m^*, y and y^* jointly with (4.32) using full information maximum likelihood (FIML) to give constrained estimates, and (4.26) with (4.34) for unconstrained estimates, for three exchange rates, dollar–mark, dollar–franc and dollar–pound, using monthly data for the period 1974 (June) to 1979 (December). A sample of their results is given in Table 4.4. The tests for rational expectations and for rational expectations and the monetary model restrictions are not rejected by the data. The estimates of the structural parameters obtained all have the correct signs and are significant at the 5 per cent level.

Finn (1986) provides similar simultaneous equations evidence for the REMM. Estimated over the period May 1974 to December 1982 for the US dollar–pound exchange rate, with real income terms generated by an ARIMA (1,1,0) model and the money supply terms generated by an ARIMA (3,1,0) model, Finn finds that FIML estimation of the REMM, together with the time series processes, outperforms a naive version of the modern monetary approach. Out-of-sample forecasting tests show that the 'model performs as well as the RW [random walk] model' (p. 190), particularly over the three-month and six-month forecast horizons. Woo (1985) also tests the REMM, with a partial adjustment mechanism on the demand for real money balances, using FIML for the US dollar–Deutschmark exchange rate between March 1974 and October 1981. Woo finds that all the parameters have the expected signs, plausible magnitudes and that the cross equation restrictions implied by the REMM cannot be rejected. Moreover in out-of-sample forecast tests the REMM out performs the random walk at various forecast horizons up to one year.

These studies of the REMM to the exchange rate seem to find evidence to support the model where a large number of other studies have failed. It is tempting to conclude that the combination of model-consistent expectations and superior econometrics shows that, if tested properly, the monetary approach is supported by the data. These studies, however, are not without weaknesses. Firstly, these results seem inconsistent with the results for PPP, reported in Chapter 2, where even long-run PPP is a somewhat doubtful empirical proposition. These studies, in contrast, seem to say that PPP holds on a month-to-month basis. Secondly, as noted by Baillie and McMahon (1989), the ARIMA (1,1,0) and ARIMA (3,1,0) models are really models of extrapolative, rather than rational, expectations because of the autoregressive element in these processes. Moreover, single equation models with an autoregressive structure perform much better than those models without such a parameter, because the exchange rate time path is very similar to a random walk. Hence for all this econometric sophistication it may be that both of these studies are simply mimicking a random walk process. Thirdly, as tested in this subsection, the model does not allow for unanticipated shocks to the fundamentals although this question will be taken up in the next section. Ultimately, then, although these studies represent an advance on previous work, the jury is still out as to the consistency of the monetary models with the data.

4.4   News and speculative bubbles

The monetary models discussed in this chapter have tied the exchange rate to the so-called fundamentals: domestic and foreign money supplies and income. In this section two extensions of the Rational Expectations Monetary Model (REMM) are considered, which permit deviations from these fundamentals. One such extension is to test the importance of 'news', as suggested by Frenkel (1981b). 'News' is any information which surprises agents and which may cause a revision of their expected value of the spot exchange rate. In other words, to what extent is the exchange rate

Table 4.4 Tests of the REMM

| | West Germany | | UK | |
	Restricted	*Unrestricted*	*Restricted*	*Unrestricted*
θ_1	1.869	1.186	3.330	3.020
	(0.78)	(0.84)	(0.75)	(0.83)
θ_2	−0.429	−0.148	−0.157	0.211
	(0.16)	(0.20)	(0.26)	(0.33)
θ_3	−0.496	0.245	−0.190	0.185
	(0.47)	(0.47)	(0.42)	(0.42)
θ_4	−0.025	0.055	−0.364	−0.371
	(0.23)	(0.29)	(0.14)	(0.17)
θ_5	1.000	0.788	1.000	0.664
		(0.55)		(0.66)
θ_6	−1.000	−0.307	−1.000	−0.475
		(0.36)		(0.40)
θ_7		−0.873		−0.349
		(0.35)		(0.31)
θ_8		1.365		0.525
		(0.43)		(0.25)
α	1.177		0.493	
	(0.32)		(0.22)	

Likelihood ratio tests of the restrictions

RE: $\chi^2(3) = 0.64$ RE: $\chi^2(3) = 6.38$

RE + MA: $\chi^2(6) = 1.05$ RE + MA: $\chi^2(6) = 6.59$

Test of structural parameters

$\alpha = 1.507 \ (0.24)$ $\alpha = 0.508 \ (0.14)$

$\beta = 1.784 \ (0.82)$ $\beta = 1.782 \ (1.06)$

Standard errors in parentheses

Critical values for χ^2 at 5%: $\chi^2(3) = 7.815$, $\chi^2(6) = 12.592$.

Source: Hoffman and Schlagenhauf (1983).

susceptible to unanticipated shocks? This issue will be examined in Section 4.4.1. A second extension of the REMM concerns the existance of speculative bubbles (Blanchard, 1979). Speculative bubbles emerge because, although the exchange rate may be already overvalued, speculators are still demanding the currency because they expect a further short-run appreciation before the currency falls back to its equilibrium level given by the fundamentals. Agents therefore expect to be able to sell the currency again before the crash happens. This literature will be briefly considered in Section 4.4.2.

4.4.1   *The news*

The REMM of the equilibrium exchange rate shows that the exchange rate depends upon all current and expected future values of the fundamentals. Therefore, providing agents' forecasts are correct, the exchange rate is tied to the fundamentals. 'News' allows the exchange rate to deviate from its fundamentals by postulating unforeseen and unforeseeable events which alter agents' forecasts of the fundamentals. News in this context is taken to mean any new information which is of relevance to the determination of the exchange rate and which was unanticipated in the previous period.

Using the notation developed in the discussion of the REMM, rational agents' forecast of the spot exchange rate at period t for period $t + 1$ will be $E_t e_{t+1} = b E_t z_{t+1}$, where z_t represents the fundamentals and b is a constant parameter. Then the forecast error will be equal to:

$$e_t - E_t e_{t+1} = b[z_t - E_t z_{t+1}] + u_t \qquad (4.36)$$

where the term in brackets is the 'news', the unanticipated change in the fundamentals, and u_t is a random error term. Rational expectations are crucial in two respects. First, because agents are assumed to know the true structure of the model linking e_t to z_t it also implies that the expectations of those two variables will also be linked. Second, it follows that the news will be that part of the fundamentals which are not only unforeseen, but also unforseeable, using the information set available at time t. Hence news terms are random terms. Assuming that agents are risk-neutral $E_t e_{t+1} = f_t$, where f_t is the logarithm of the forward exchange rate, equation (4.36) can be written as:

$$e_t = f_t - \beta[z_t - E_t z_{t+1}] + u_t \qquad (4.37)$$

To give this 'news' equation empirical content, a model of the fundamentals must be specified and, also, how expectations $E_{t-1} z_t$ are to be formed. The fundamentals are usually represented by the monetary model and expectations generated by time series or regression methods.

The first study of 'news' by Frenkel (1981b) used interest rates as the fundamentals for the US dollar–pound and pound–Deutsche Mark exchange rates. Autoregressions were used to generate the expected series for the interest rates. Frenkel found that for only one case, that of the

Table 4.5   Tests of the news

$$e_t = \beta_0 + \beta_1 f_t + \gamma_1[(m - m^*)_t - E_{t-1}(m - m^*)_t] + \gamma_2[(y - y^*)_t$$
$$- E_{t-1}(y - y^*)_t] + \gamma_3[(r - r^*)_t - E_{t-1}(r - r^*)_t] + u_t$$

Author	[1]	[1]	[1]	[1]	[2]
News	AR(3)	AR(3)	AR(3)	AR(3)	ARIMA
Estimation	SURE	SURE	SURE	SURE	2SLS
Country compared to the USA	France	West Germany	Italy	UK	UK
Coefficients					
β_0	−0.155	0.032	0.248	−0.024	−0.056
	(0.113)	(0.018)	(0.119)	(0.01)	(0.016)
β_1	0.951	0.957	0.962	0.970	0.927
	(0.037)	(0.02)	(0.02)	(0.02)	(0.02)
γ_1	0.359*	0.372*	0.084	0.103	0.096
	(0.142)	(0.18)	(0.19)	(0.15)	(0.28)
γ_2	0.182	0.243*	−0.046	0.006*	0.159*
	0.123)	(0.109)	(0.102)	(0.002)	(0.087)
γ_3	−0.005	0.011	−0.022*	0.007	−0.008*
	(0.02)	(0.02)	(0.01)	(0.02)	(0.003)

Notes
Standard errors in parentheses.
*Significant news coefficient at 5%.

[1] Edwards (1982), monthly data sampled from June 1973 to September 1979.
[2] Copeland (1984), monthly data sampled from January 1973 to May 1983.

dollar–pound rate, was the news coefficient statistically significant, when it took a positive sign. Although these results are deemed to be supportive of the REMM, the fundamentals should also include money supplies and real income terms. Edwards (1982) relates unanticipated exchange rate changes to unanticipated money supplies, income and interest rates for the period June 1973 to September 1979, for the same exchange rates as Frenkel. Table 4.5 shows that these results are only weakly supportive of the news model, with only five of the 12 news coefficients significant at the 5 per cent level. Copeland (1984) also estimates this model of the news for the sterling–dollar exchange rate over the period January 1973 to May 1983, using two-stage least squares (2SLS), where more positive results in favour of news are discovered.

Finally, MacDonald (1983) uses Barro's technique (Barro, 1977) of recovering unanticipated components from the residuals of a regression of the variable concerned on a vector of explanatory variables. The z_t variables are home and foreign money supplies and news about these variables is generated by regressing them upon price inflation, real income, interest rates, the current balance and the budget deficit. For six currencies against the US dollar (Canadian dollar, Australian dollar, pound sterling, French franc, German mark, Swiss franc) for the period 1972 Q1 to 1979 Q4, using the Seemingly Unrelated Regressions Estimator (SURE) due to Zellner (1962), MacDonald finds poor results in that only in the Deutsche Mark–US dollar equation are the news terms significant and even then they generally have the wrong sign!

4.4.2   Bubbles

In the case of 'news', agents were assumed to be surprised by unexpected changes in the fundamentals, which caused them to revise their expectations of the future path of the fundamentals and hence of the exchange rate. Bubbles, on the other hand, are exchange rate movements which are inconsistent with the fundamentals and are driven by non-economic variables such as 'fads' or 'whims' of the speculators independently of the fundamentals.[4]

A rational bubble occurs when market participants continue to buy a currency which is already overvalued in terms of its fundamentals, in the expectation of making a short-run gain as the currency appreciates further, before finally falling back to the long-run equilibrium level determined by the fundamentals. Hence the speculators have to judge the probability of the bubble bursting before the end of the next period. Suppose the expected rise in the exchange rate is $E_t e_{t+1} - e_t$ and that the rate of increase per time period is given by x_t. Speculators anticipate this rate of increase to continue for the next period with a probability of π, and hence expect to earn profits equal to πx_t per unit of foreign currency held. On the other hand, the probability of a collapse in the bubble is $(1-\pi)$ with losses equal to $(1-\pi)(\bar{e} - e_{t+1})$ per unit of foreign currency held, where $\bar{e}$ is the equilibrium exchange rate given by fundamentals. Using the uncovered interest rate parity condition, given by equation (4.5), gives

$$(E_{t+1}e_t - e_t) = r_t - r^*_t = (1-\pi)(\bar{e} - e_{t+1}) + \pi x_t \tag{4.38}$$

This equation shows that, even if $r^*_t > r_t$, so that a future depreciation of the foreign currency is expected, speculators will continue to purchase foreign currency if x_t is positive. Moreover, this simple relationship shows that, if a currency is overvalued and still appreciating, then the rate of appreciation must be rising over time because the loss on each unit of currency will be greater the further the spot rate is from the underlying equilibrium exchange rate. Rearranging (4.38) gives

$$x_t = (r_t - r^*_t)/\pi + (e_{t+1} - \bar{e})/[(1 - \pi)/\pi] \tag{4.39}$$

which says that x_t rises, that is, the rate of increase in e_t rises, for given values of π, $r_t - r^*_t$ and e_t.

To test the bubbles hypothesis three alternative approaches have been used: runs tests, excess volatility tests and specification tests. Evans (1986) tests for a speculative bubble in the US dollar–sterling exchange rate over the period 1981–84, by testing for a non-zero median in excess returns, using a non-parametric test, similar to a runs test. These kinds of test attempt to identify a significant deviation in the number of positive excess returns from the number that would be expected if the distribution of excess returns had a zero median. Evans rejects the zero median hypothesis for excess returns in the US dollar–sterling exchange rate which he interprets as consistent with a speculative bubbles. One problem with this result is that it does not seem plausible to assume that the dollar was driven by a speculative bubble over a four-year period when, by definition, a speculative bubble can only account for short-run exchange rate movements over a period of a few months. An alternative explanation, consistent with Evans's results, is that agents in the foreign exchange market had irrational expectations.

The excess volatility tests are based upon the difference between the fundamental solution for the exchange rate with and without bubbles. The fundamentals solution is:

$$e_{t+1} = bE_t e_{t+1} + z_{t+1} \text{ or } e^F_t = \sum_i b^i E_t z_{t+1} \tag{4.40}$$

With perfect foresight, $E_{t-1} e_t = e_t$, so that $e^F_t = \sum_i b^i z_{t+i}$. The actual solution for the exchange rate, e^A_t, will differ from e^F_t, by any error in forecasting z_t, that is:

$$e^A_t = e^F_t + u_t \tag{4.41}$$

where $u_t = \sum b^i (z_{t+i} - E_t z_{t+1})$. Since u_t is independent of e^F_t, then:

$$V(e^A_t) = V(e^F_t) + V(u_t) \text{ and} \tag{4.42}$$

$$V(e^A_t) > V(e^F_t) \tag{4.43}$$

Equation (4.43) says that the observed variance will exceed the variance due to fundamentals. If there are bubbles, B_t, present in the actual exchange rate, then, with perfect foresight, $e_t = e^F_t + B_t$. Substituting for e^F_t, from equation (4.41), gives:

$$e^A_t = e_t - B_t + u_t \qquad (4.44)$$

so that $V(e^A_t) = V(e_t) + V(B_t) + V(u_t) - 2CV(e_t, B_t)$. Since the covariance between e_t and B_t cannot be assumed *a priori* to be zero or negative, then it follows that violation of inequality (4.43) would be *a priori* evidence of excess volatility and the presence of bubbles. Huang (1981) uses this approach to test for bubbles in the REMM for the US dollar–Deutsche Mark, US dollar–sterling and UK pound–Deutsche Mark exchange rates over the period March 1973 to March 1979. His results are supportive of excess volatility and hence of speculative bubbles. Flood and Hodrick (1990), however, show that this kind of test is not well suited to testing for bubbles since it is conditional on the assumed model, and there are other explanations for the violation of the inequality apart from bubbles.

The third approach used to test for bubbles is the specification test method used by Meese (1986). This method involves comparing two estimates of b derived from different versions of the Rational Expectations Monetary Model. Equation (4.45) gives the basic REMM model, where μ_t is a white noise error term:

$$e_t = bE_t e_{t+1} + \mu_t \qquad (4.45)$$

b can be estimated directly, replacing $E_t e_{t+1}$ with e_{t+1}, and using McCallum's Instrumental Variable estimator (McCallum, 1976) to give a consistent estimate of b, say $\tilde{b}$. This estimate is valid whether or not bubbles exist. The alternative estimate of b, call it $\hat{b}$, is derived from the market fundamentals model given by equation (4.40), which, written to include an error term and lagging one period, is given as:

$$e^F_t = \sum b^i E_t z_{t+1} + u_t \qquad (4.40')$$

where it is assumed that z_t follows an AR(1) process of the form

$$z_t = \phi z_{t-1} + w_t \qquad (4.46)$$

where w_t is a white noise error term. Taking expectations at time t, gives $E_t z_{t-1} = \phi^i z_t$, and the closed model for (4.40') is:

$$e^F_t = (1 - b\phi)^{-1} z_t + u_t = v z_t + u_t \qquad (4.47)$$

Under the assumption of no bubbles, equations (4.45) and (4.47) give an alternative estimate of b, which is only consistent in the absence of bubbles.[5] Thus Hausman's specification test (Hausman, 1978) can be used to discriminate between the two estimates of b. Meese's use of this test indicates very strong evidence for bubbles during the period October 1973 to November 1982, for the US dollar–Deutsche Mark and US dollar–sterling exchange rates, in the context of the REMM. West (1987) conducts some additional bubble tests on the US dollar–Deutsche Mark exchange rate between June 1974 and May 1984, using a variance bounds-type test (LeRoy and Porter, 1981). West concludes that exchange rate variability, in the absence of bubbles, is consistent with the standard monetary model used by Meese, augmented to include money demand errors and deviations from PPP as additional fundamentals.

Flood and Garber (1980) note that an omitted variable problem can bias bubble tests towards rejection of the no bubbles hypothesis. Since the standard monetary models in general predict poorly (see Section 4.3.1), it is likely that, when bubble tests are conducted, bubbles will be found. If the models are false, rejection of the null hypothesis of no bubbles cannot be attributed to bubbles alone since it could also be due to misspecification of the model.

4.5 Conclusions

The modern monetary approach, especially the rational expectations version, makes a considerable technical advance on the Classical model, discussed in Chapter 2. Unfortunately, the model is based on the rather dubious foundation of continuous PPP, which makes any forecast of the long-run equilibrium exchange rate somewhat difficult. Moreover, the dynamic path for the exchange rate is constrained to follow the path of the fundamentals with deviations explained by either news, which causes revision to the future path of the fundamentals and hence the exchange rate, or to short-run speculative bubbles, which are a genuine disequilibrium phenomenon, independent of the fundamentals. The notion of short-run overshooting of the exchange rate that was present in the Classical model is only compatible with the flexible price approach considered in this chapter to the extent that speculative bubbles push the rate away from PPP. This is not the same, however, as having exchange rate overshooting as an integral part of the adjustment process.

Empirically the monetary models have only rarely been tested properly. The REMM and the CIMM are the only models with a genuine equilibrium exchange rate specification, while estimates of the REMM have in general been more successful than those for the CIMM. The development of cointegration techniques shows that in many cases it is in the representation of the long-run equilibrium exchange rate that the CIMM is most vulnerable. An alternative approach to the equilibrium exchange rate is considered in Chapter 5.

Notes
1. Frenkel (1976) also argued that the real income terms could be omitted since they contributed very little to the determination of the exchange rate in this period of hyperinflation. The fact that $\prod - \prod^* = r - r^*$, using (4.8) and (4.5), led Frenkel to proxy inflation expectations by the long bond yield, thus making the empirical model observationally equivalent to (4.6).
2. For an exception see Somanath (1986).
3. MacDonald (1988) reviews much of the earlier literature.
4. Miller and Weller (1990) show the implications of a bubble affecting the fundamentals, rather than being independent of the fundamentals, as are all the models in this section. They also use a sticky-price, rather than a flexible-price, model.
5. To see that the estimate of b is only consistent in the absence of bubbles, consider a model with bubbles as: $e_t = e_t + B_t$. Then the estimate of b is given as:

$$\hat{v} = [\sum(e^F_t + B_t)z_t]/\sum z^2_t$$

$$\text{plim } \hat{v} = \text{plim}[\sum(e^F_t z_t)/\sum z^2_t] + \text{plim}[\sum(B_t z_t)/\sum z^2_t]$$
$$= v + \text{plim}(1/N)[\sum(B_t z_t)/\sum z^2_t]$$

where N is the sample size. Therefore $\hat{v}$ is an inconsistent estimator of v.

5 The Mundell–Fleming approaches

5.1 Introduction

The model developed by Fleming (1962) and Mundell (1963) of the open economy with unemployed resources has had a tremendous impact on international monetary economics. In essence these authors extended the early Keynesian income-expenditure approach, developed in Chapter 3, to include international capital movements in the model. The model retained a fixed price assumption so that exchange rate changes are changes in the real exchange rate, rather than in the nominal rate, as in Chapter 4. This model therefore accords more with recent empirical evidence which has shown large movements in real exchange rates. The version developed in this chapter will follow Mundell (1963) in that perfect capital mobility is assumed so that uncovered interest rate parity holds whereby domestic and foreign bonds are perfect substitutes. This implies that the model is fully consistent with the stock view of capital movements, developed by Tobin (1958) and in an open economy context by Branson (1968), McKinnon and Oates (1966) and McKinnon (1969) and that used by the modern monetary approach of Chapter 4. This is in contrast to the original model of Fleming (1962), although it can be developed as a special case of that model. This class of models is typically small-country models, in that the foreign economy is not explicitly modelled with foreign variables assumed exogenous in the domestic behavioural equations.

The outline of this chapter is as follows. Section 5.2 reviews the Mundell–Fleming fixed-price model of the exchange rate and its insulation properties under various assumptions about exchange rate expectations. This extends the original models of Mundell and Fleming, both of which focused solely upon static expectations. Section 5.3 considers three recent models in the Mundell–Fleming tradition, but which allow for some flexibility of the general price level in the long run by introducing a price adjustment equation into the standard Mundell–Fleming model. These are the sticky-price model of Dornbusch (1976a, 1976b), the core inflation model of Buiter and Miller (1981) and the model of Devereux and Purvis (1990) which additionally incorporates an aggregate supply equation in which a real exchange rate appreciation increases the supply of domestic output. Section 5.4 examines the econometric evidence for some of these models with particular emphasis on the notion of exchange rate overshooting. Section 5.5 summarizes the principal conclusions of the chapter.

5.2   The fixed-price Mundell–Fleming model

This section is divided into two parts. Section 5.2.1 sets out the basic model for a small open economy and examines the responsiveness of the model to autonomous domestic and foreign shocks. Section 5.2.2 then explores the dynamics of the model by considering alternative assumptions about expectations formation, while retaining the assumption of fixed prices. Models with flexible prices in the long run will be considered in Section 5.3.

5.2.1   The basic model with static expectations

The Mundell–Fleming model consists of three main markets (a domestic goods market, a domestic money market and a foreign exchange market), with the domestic bond markets omitted from explicit treatment following Walras' Law. The model consists of four assets: domestic money, foreign money, a domestic bond and a foreign bond. In the version of the model developed in this chapter, domestic and foreign money are held only by local residents and domestic and foreign bonds are assumed to be perfect substitutes, thus enabling the domestic financial sector to be represented by a single equation for money market equilibrium (the LM schedule). The goods market equilibrium is essentially that used in Chapter 3, where unemployed resources, constant returns to scale and fixed money wages result in a perfectly elastic 'extreme' Keynesian aggregate supply schedule. Hence domestic output is demand-determined and represented by the IS schedule. The foreign exchange market is dominated by capital movements, due to the assumption of perfect substitutability between domestic and foreign assets, and so is represented by a perfectly elastic BP line.

In this chapter the behavioural relations are assumed to be log-linear functions to facilitate comparison with the monetary models of capital flows, rather than to be consistent with the flow models of Chapter 3. Domestic demand, a, is assumed to be directly related to the level of output, y, the level of government spending on goods and services, g, and the real exchange rate, $e-p$, and negatively related to the domestic rate of interest, r. Therefore domestic aggregate demand is given by:

$$a = \alpha y + g - \beta r + \gamma(e-p) - i \tag{5.1}$$

where i is an exogenous import shock and Greek letters denote the constant parameters of the system. Since output is demand-determined in this model, the goods market supply curve is simply:

$$y = a \tag{5.2}$$

and goods market equilibrium (the IS curve) is given by:

$$y = \alpha y + g - \beta r + \gamma(e-p) - i \tag{5.3}$$

Domestic and foreign monies are only held by domestic and foreign residents, respectively, and therefore the demand for money in each country is independent of the demand in the other country. Hence domestic money market equilibrium (the LM curve) is given by

$$m - p = l = \phi y - \eta r \tag{5.4}$$

where m is the logarithm of the nominal money supply, p is the logarithm of the aggregate price level, l is the logarithm of the real demand for money, which is assumed to depend positively upon the logarithm of domestic income and inversely on the domestic rate of interest.

The equilibrium in the foreign exchange market (the BP curve) is given by the current and capital accounts of the balance of payments. The current account is assumed to depend inversely upon the level of domestic demand and directly upon the real exchange rate. Capital flows are assumed to depend directly upon the interest rate differential, adjusted for the expected depreciation of the exchange rate over the period of holding the foreign asset. Equation (5.5) represents balance of payments equilibrium where the sum of the current and capital accounts always equal zero, because of the floating exchange rate assumption. That is,

$$b = \xi y + \upsilon(e-p+p^*) - i + \theta(r-r^*-E\dot{e}) = 0 \tag{5.5}$$

where θ represents the degree of capital mobility and $E\dot{e}$ is the expected depreciation of the domestic currency. Because domestic and foreign bonds are assumed to be perfect substitutes, arbitrage ensures that the bond yields are continually equalized in domestic currency, which implies that $\theta \to \infty$, and equation (5.5) collapses to equation (5.6); that is:

$$r = r^* + E\dot{e} \tag{5.6}$$

The static model can be represented in a two-quadrant diagram, as in

Figure 5.1. The *IS* curve slopes down in (r,y) space since a fall in the rate of interest stimulates domestic absorption, via the implicit investment function, thereby raising aggregate demand which is matched by an equal rise in aggregate supply. The *LM* curve slopes up because, as income rises the demand for money increases; therefore, for a given real money supply, the rate of interest must rise to reduce the demand for money in order to maintain money market equilibrium. The *BP* line represents equilibrium in the foreign exchange market on the assumption of perfect capital mobility. Formally these relationships are obtained by differentiating equations (5.3), (5.4) and (5.6) respectively to give:

$$[\partial r/\partial y]_{IS} = -(1-\alpha)/\beta < 0$$

$$[\partial r/\partial y]_{LM} = \phi/\eta > 0$$

$$[\partial r/\partial y]_{BP} = \xi/\theta = 0 \text{ (since } \theta \to \infty)$$

The lower quadrant of Figure 5.1 depicts schedules for external balance (*EB*) and internal balance (*IB*) in (e,y) space. The *EB* line has a positive slope (remember the figure is inverted) since a depreciation of the exchange rate (a rise in *e*) will stimulate export demand and hence raise domestic income, which in turn raises import demand, so restoring current account balance. The *EB* line is drawn on the assumption of a given capital account, therefore a rise in the domestic rate of interest, which leads to a capital inflow, will shift the *EB* line up to the right, since *e* will need to fall (appreciate) at every level of income. The *IB* line will also have a positive slope, since a rise in *e* will stimulate demand and raise domestic output. The slope of the *IB* line is, however, assumed to be less responsive to exchange rate changes than the *EB* schedule, because it embodies a proportion of non-traded goods which are unresponsive to exchange rate changes. The *IB* line therefore has a steeper slope than the *EB* line.[1] Mathematically:

$$[\partial e/\partial y]_{IB} = (1-\alpha)/\gamma > 0$$

$$[\partial e/\partial y]_{EB} = \xi/\nu > 0$$

To complete the specification of the model a hypothesis is required for the expected depreciation of the exchange rate in equations (5.5) and (5.6). Following Fleming (1962) and Mundell (1963) the assumption of static expectations can be employed which implies that the exchange rate is not expected to change, so $Ee = 0$. This simple model can be used to

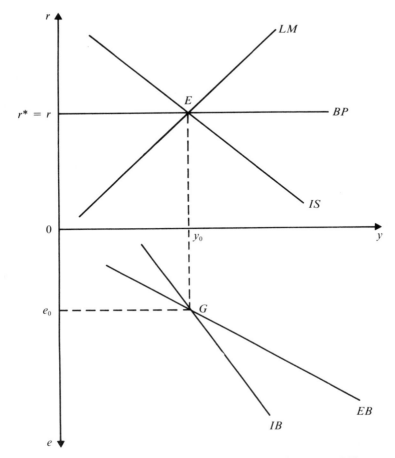

Figure 5.1   Equilibrium in the Mundell–Fleming Model (MFKM)

generate some very powerful policy advice. To examine these policy implications, consider two kinds of domestic policy shock – a monetary shock and a fiscal policy shock – and two kinds of foreign shock – an exogenous increase in imports (through a rise in i) and an increase in the foreign rate of interest (captured by a rise in r^*).

Domestic shocks   Consider the effects of an increase in the money supply. In terms of Figure 5.2, from the initial equilibrium at E, the LM_0 schedule will shift to the right to LM_1, so that domestic equilibrium implies a potential balance of payments deficit and a depreciation of the exchange rate. The rise in e (a depreciation) improves the current account balance, on the assumption that the augmented Marshall–Lerner condition is satisfied,[2] because the lower exchange rate encourages a switch towards domestic output by foreign residents and the IS_0 schedule moves to the right, to IS_1, giving simultaneous internal and external balance at F. At F the level of income has increased from y_0 to y_1. In the lower quadrant of Figure 5.2, the EB schedule shifts down to intersect IB_0 at H, since the depreciation of the exchange rate leads to a current balance surplus at G, thereby necessitating a larger capital outflow, which shifts EB_0 down to EB_1.

An expansionary fiscal policy, on the other hand, will give rise to an

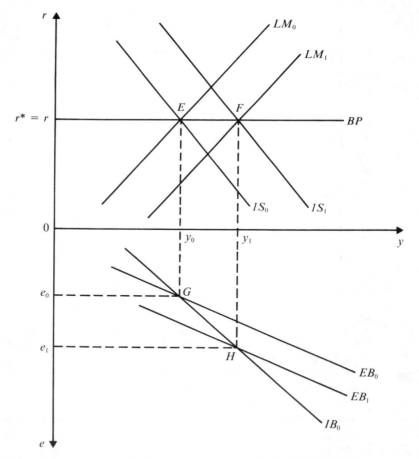

Figure 5.2   A rise in the domestic money supply in the MFKM

appreciation of the exchange rate which will completely crowd out the increase in government expenditure. An exogenous increase in government expenditure will shift the IS_0 curve to the right, to IS_1, in Figure 5.3. This leads to a potential rise in the rate of interest above the world rate, and hence a larger foreign inflow of capital which will appreciate the exchange rate. The appreciation of the exchange rate implies that domestic exports become more expensive abroad, while foreign imports become cheaper in the home economy, thereby reducing the net exports of the home country, shifting the IS_1 curve back to the left, to IS_0. In the lower quadrant of the diagram the fiscal expansion shifts the IB line up

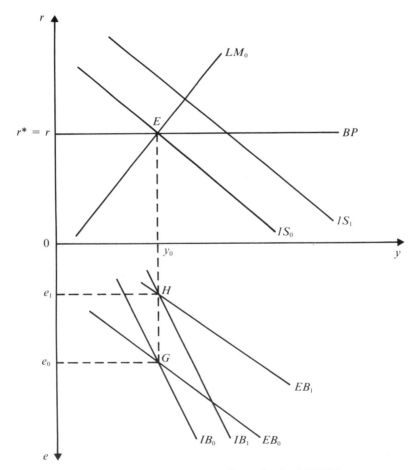

Figure 5.3   A rise in government expenditure in the MFKM

to IB_1, since a higher exchange rate is now required to give internal balance for every level of y. The larger capital inflow into the domestic economy, however, implies that external balance requires a higher level of the exchange rate for every current account position and so the EB_0 schedule shifts up to the right, to intersect IB_1 at H. Hence in the case of a fiscal expansion the exchange rate is higher and income is unchanged at the initial equilibrium level.

These results can be derived more formally by totally differentiating equations (5.3), (5.4) and (5.6), setting $E\dot{e} = dp = dp^* = 0$ to give solutions for dy and de in terms of the exogenous variables. That is:

$$\begin{bmatrix} (1-\alpha) & -\gamma \\ -\phi & 0 \end{bmatrix} \begin{bmatrix} dy \\ de \end{bmatrix} = \begin{bmatrix} -\beta dr^* + dg - di \\ -\eta dr^* - dm \end{bmatrix} \tag{5.7}$$

which yield

$$[dy/dm] = 1/\phi > 0 \qquad [de/dm] = (1-\alpha)/\gamma\phi > 0$$

$$[dy/dg] = 0 \qquad [de/dg] = -1/\gamma < 0$$

Foreign shocks   Floating exchange rates completely insulate domestic output from trade balance shocks when there is perfect capital mobility. To see this, consider the effect of an exogenous fall in domestic net exports. In Figure 5.4, the fall in exports shifts the EB_0, IB_0 and IS_0 schedules down to the left to EB_1, IB_1 and IS_1, respectively. At the points F and J, for a given capital inflow, there is an external deficit which causes the exchange rate to depreciate, thereby shifting IS_1 back to IS_0 and moving the model along the IB line in the lower quadrant until the new equilibrium position is established at H, where the level of domestic real income is unchanged at y_0 and the exchange rate has depreciated to e_1. Domestic output is, therefore, completely insulated from trade balance shocks.

An increase in the foreign rate of interest is illustrated in Figure 5.5, with the foreign rate of interest rising from r^*_0 to r^*_1. At the initial equilibrium at E, there is now a potential balance of payments deficit as more capital flows abroad, causing the EB line to shift down to EB_1. A depreciation of the exchange rate follows, which shifts the IS_0 curve up to the right, to IS_1, as the trade balance improves. The final equilibrium is at F where output is higher, at y_1, and the exchange rate lower. In this case domestic output is not insulated from foreign monetary shocks.

Once again the comparative static effects of these shocks can be examined by looking at equation (5.7). The relevant derivatives are:

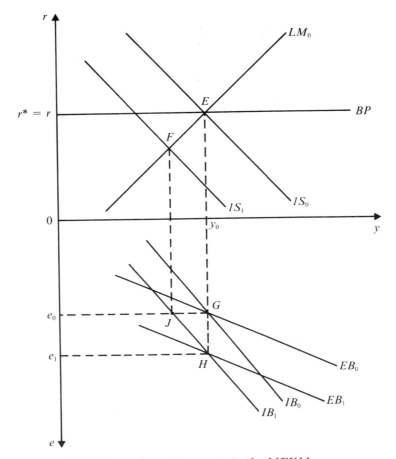

Figure 5.4   A fall in net domestic exports in the MFKM

$$[dy/di] = 0 \qquad [de/di] = 1/\gamma > 0$$

$$[dy/dr^*] = \eta/\phi > 0 \qquad [de/dr^*] = \beta/\gamma + (1-\alpha)\eta/\gamma\phi > 0$$

The conclusion to this section is that, under static expectations real shocks, either domestic or foreign, are unable to influence the level of domestic real income, but nominal shocks are able to raise domestic output through their impact on the exchange rate. The exchange rate is therefore critical in the transmission of nominal disturbances to the real sector of the economy.

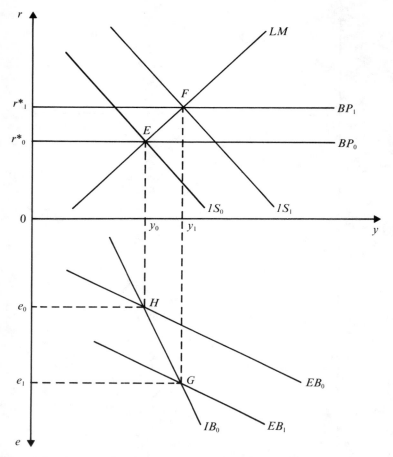

Figure 5.5   A rise in foreign interest rates in the MFKM

5.2.2   *Expectations and exchange rate dynamics*
In this sub-section the assumption of static expectations will be relaxed
in favour of two alternative hypotheses about the generation of expectations concerning the future path of the exchange rate: the regressive
and perfect foresight expectations hypotheses.

Regressive expectations   Regressive expectations are able to reverse
some of the conclusions noted in the previous section; in particular the
effectiveness of fiscal policy maybe restored. Regressive expectations can
be represented by:

$$E(\dot{e}) = \mu(\bar{e} - e) \qquad 0 < \mu < \infty \tag{5.8}$$

This equation says that the expected change in the exchange rate depends upon the difference between the current exchange rate and the equilibrium exchange rate, $\bar{e}$. If e exceeds the equilibrium value then there is an expectation that e will appreciate (fall) back to the equilibrium level. Similarly, if the current value is below the equilibrium value then it is expected that the rate will depreciate (e will rise) back to the equilibrium. Substituting (5.8) into the uncovered interest rate parity condition (5.6) gives

$$r = r^* + \mu(\bar{e} - e) \tag{5.9}$$

which shows that r can now deviate from r^* if e is not at its equilibrium level. Hence r will be above r^* if the exchange rate is expected to depreciate, and below r^* if the exchange rate is expected to appreciate. Substituting for r in equations (5.3) and (5.4) using (5.9), and setting $dp = dp^* = 0$, gives the following system for y and e:

$$\begin{bmatrix} 1-\alpha & -(\beta\mu+\gamma) \\ -\phi & -\eta\mu \end{bmatrix} \begin{bmatrix} dy \\ de \end{bmatrix} = \begin{bmatrix} dg - di - \beta dr^* - \beta\mu de \\ -dm - \eta dr^* - \eta\mu de \end{bmatrix} \tag{5.10}$$

where the determinant of the left-hand side matrix is $A = -[(1-\alpha)\eta\mu + \phi(\beta\mu+\gamma)] < 0$. Solving for y and e gives the following domestic policy multipliers:

$$[dy/dg] = -\eta\mu/A > 0 \qquad\qquad [de/dg] = \phi/A < 0$$

$$[dy/dm] = -(\beta\mu+\gamma)/A > 0 \qquad [de/dm] = -(1-\alpha)/A > 0$$

Fiscal policy is now seen to have some effect upon output and monetary policy is less potent than under static exchange rate expectations, since $[(1 - \alpha)\eta\mu/(\beta\mu+\gamma)] > 0$.

In Figure 5.6, a monetary expansion will shift LM_0 to LM_1. At point D there is a potential balance of payments deficit, since r has fallen below r^*. This will cause a higher capital outflow from the domestic economy, shifting EB_0 to EB_1, and depreciating the exchange rate. As the exchange rate falls, the IS curve will begin to shift to the right, as the trade balance improves. Simultaneously, however, the BP line will shift down to BP_1, since the rise in e, from e_0 to e_1, enables the domestic interest rate to fall below the world rate. The new equilibrium, F, is reached when output is

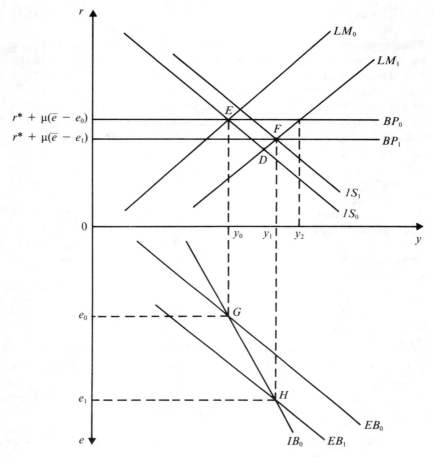

*Figure 5.6   An increase in the money supply in the MFKM with regressive
expectations*

at y_1. Monetary policy is therefore less effective in raising output if
exchange rate expectations are regressive, rather than static, since under
static expectations output would rise to y_2 rather than to y_1, as the
exchange rate depreciation is smaller. On the other hand, as the qualitative fiscal policy multiplier above shows, the effectiveness of fiscal policy
is enhanced. The reason is that the initial exchange rate appreciation
generates expectations of a future depreciation and therefore the capital
inflow is moderated compared to the static expectations case. In Figure
5.7, the rise in government expenditure shifts both the IS_0 and IB_0 lines

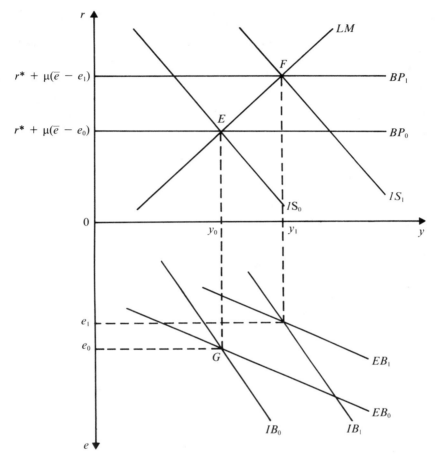

Figure 5.7   An increase in government spending in the MFKM with regressive expectations

to the right, to IS_1 and IB_1, respectively. Since the domestic interest rate is now above the foreign rate there is a larger capital inflow, which shifts EB_0 to EB_1, and the exchange rate appreciates from e_0 to e_1, shifting the BP line up to BP_1. The final equilibrium will be at F, with domestic income higher at y_1 and the domestic price of foreign currency lower at e_1. In this case, therefore, fiscal policy will be effective in raising domestic output, despite the existence of perfect capital mobility.

The adoption of regressive expectations also modifies the insulation properties of the flexible exchange rate system with respect to exogenous trade and foreign interest rate shocks. In the case of a decline in net exports the exchange rate will depreciate, giving rise to expectations of a future appreciation of the exchange rate, thus allowing the domestic interest rate to fall below the foreign rate. For a given money stock the fall in the interest rate raises the demand for money, leading to an excess demand for money which is eliminated by a fall in the level of income. Hence the decline in net exports results in a fall in real domestic income, unlike the static expectations case where income was fully insulated from the fall in net exports. In terms of the equation system above, the net export multipliers are formally:

$$[dy/di] = \eta\mu/A < 0 \qquad [de/di] = -\phi/A > 0$$

compared with zero and $1/\gamma$ with static expectations. So the effect on output is larger, while that on the exchange rate is smaller. On the other hand, for a foreign interest rate shock the insulation properties of a floating exchange rate are improved if exchange rate expectations are regressive. A fall in the foreign rate of interest will cause an appreciation of the domestic currency, but this will generate expectations of a future depreciation, and so the fall in income will be moderated as exports increase in the future to partially offset the higher capital outflow. In terms of the formal comparative statics:

$$[dy/dr^*] = -\eta\gamma/A > 0 \qquad [de/dr^*] = [-\phi\beta - \eta(1-\alpha)]/A > 0$$

which compare to η/ϕ and $[(1-\alpha)\eta + \beta/\gamma]/\gamma\phi$ under static expectations.

Perfect foresight expectations   Perfect foresight expectations imply that the expected change in the exchange rate next period based on information available in this period is exactly the change which occurs. That is:

$$E(\dot{e}) = \dot{e} \tag{5.11}$$

so that the uncovered interest rate parity condition is:

$$r = r^* + \dot{e} \tag{5.11'}$$

In this version of the model, however, this assumption gives rise to an unstable (non-convergent) time path. To see this, solve equation (5.3) for y, substitute for y in (5.4) and then replace r with its equivalent from (5.11'). The resulting first-order differential equation for the exchange rate is:

$$\dot{e} = [\phi\gamma/\{\eta(1-\alpha)+\phi\beta\}]e + \text{constants} \qquad (5.12)$$

Stability requires that the term in brackets be negative, but it is unambiguously positive, so the model is monotonically divergent. This is a typical problem with perfect foresight models, in that they usually exhibit saddle path stability. In this version of the model with only one-dimensional dynamics this kind of stability is ruled out and instability must result. A saddle path equilibrium, however, can be established in this model in a number of ways.[3] To be consistent with the assumption of fixed prices maintained throughout this section, equation (5.2) is modified to allow output to adjust only slowly to aggregate demand. Equation (5.2) is therefore replaced with:

$$\dot{y} = \omega(a-y) \qquad 0 < \omega < \infty \qquad (5.13)$$

where ω is the coefficient of partial adjustment. Solving equations (5.1) and (5.3) for a and r respectively and then using (5.11′) substituting into (5.5) and (5.13) yields a simultaneous first-order dynamic system of the form:

$$\begin{bmatrix} \dot{e} \\ \dot{y} \end{bmatrix} = \begin{bmatrix} 0 & \phi/\eta \\ \omega\gamma & \omega(\alpha-1-\gamma\phi/\eta) \end{bmatrix} \begin{bmatrix} e \\ y \end{bmatrix} \qquad (5.14)$$

The necessary and sufficient condition for stability is that the determinant of the 2x2 matrix B, be negative, which gives a saddle path. Since $B = -\omega\gamma\phi/\eta < 0$ a saddle path equilibrium exists.

Figure 5.8 gives a diagrammatic treatment. The $\dot{y} = 0$ schedule slopes up in (e,y) space because a higher value of output requires a lower exchange rate, for all the additional output to be demanded. Formally, with $\dot{y} = 0$, $de/dy = (1-\gamma\phi/\eta)/\gamma > 0$. The $\dot{e} = 0$ schedule is vertical because the coefficient b_{11} in the B-matrix in (5.14) is zero. This means that the rate of change in the exchange rate is independent of the level of the exchange rate. The direction arrows in Figure 5.8 show, because $b_{22} < 0$, that the arrows point towards the $\dot{y} = 0$ line for each given level of e. On the other hand, the direction arrows point away from the $\dot{e} = 0$ line for each value of y. Hence the saddle path will have a negative slope equal to: $\phi\eta/\lambda_2 < 0$, where $\lambda_2 < 0$ is the stable root (see Appendix to this chapter).

Now consider an unanticipated rise in the money supply. In Figure 5.9, the unanticipated rise in m causes the $\dot{e} = 0$ schedule to shift to the right since a rise in m raises the level of output for each value of the exchange rate. The $\dot{y} = 0$ line also shifts to the right because the higher

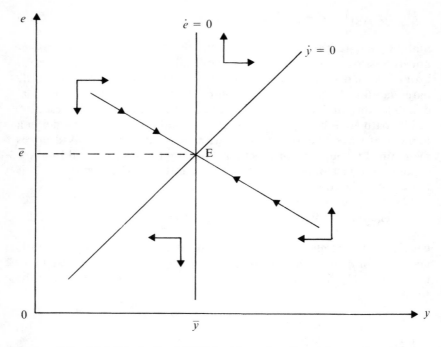

Figure 5.8   Stability in the MFKM with perfect foresight expectations

money supply induces a lower rate of interest which stimulates demand and output. The new equilibrium is at G, with a higher level of output. Whether the exchange rate is higher or lower in the final equilibrium seems to be an empirical question, depending upon the extent of the shifts in the two schedules, but in fact it can be shown that e will always depreciate, since the $\dot{e} = 0$ line will always shift further to the right than the $\dot{y} = 0$ line at any level of e.[4] The model assumes that the money market adjusts instantaneously, whereas the goods market only clears slowly, according to the size of ω, and therefore in the short run the exchange rate will overshoot its final equilibrium position, to reach e'_0 in Figure 5.9, as it jumps to clear the money market, before output has time to rise. Only when output begins to increase, thereby raising the demand for money, will the exchange rate begin appreciating back towards its long-run equilibrium position at e_1. This short-run overshooting of the exchange rate is caused by the different speeds of adjustment between the goods market, which clears only slowly, and the money market which

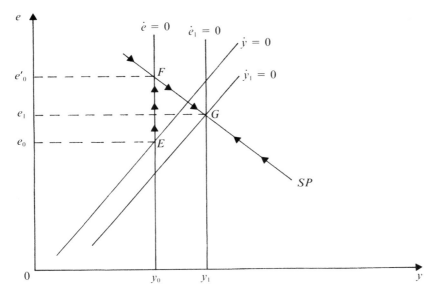

Figure 5.9   An unanticipated rise in the money supply in the MFKM with perfect foresight expectations

clears instantaneously. Thus an unanticipated monetary expansion gives rise to short-run exchange rate overshooting.

A fiscal policy expansion that is also unanticipated is shown in Figure 5.10. The crucial point here is that only the $\dot{y} = 0$ schedule shifts to the right, and therefore there is no exchange rate overshooting (or in this case, undershooting) in the short run. The reason for this is that the increase in government expenditure raises demand and output, but the higher output raises the demand for money. With a fixed money supply the exchange rate has to appreciate immediately to generate expectations of a future depreciation, to enable the rate of interest to rise above the world interest rate, while maintaining uncovered interest parity. Therefore the exchange rate jumps on to the new stable saddle path SP, in Figure 5.10, along the $\dot{e} = 0$ line, to give a final equilibrium at F.

This somewhat technical analysis has shown that fiscal policy is impotent at raising output in an open economy with a floating exchange rate, perfect foresight expectations and perfect asset substitutability, while, on the other hand, an unanticipated monetary policy change is able to bring about a permanent rise in output. In other words the Mundell–Fleming results discussed in Section 5.2.1 above are robust when perfect foresight

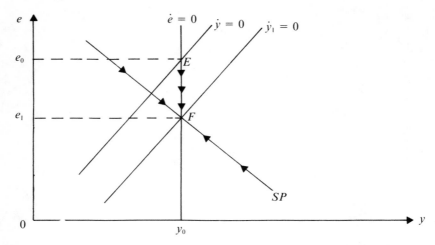

*Figure 5.10   An unanticipated rise in government spending in the MFKM
with perfect foresight expectations*

exchange rate expectations are allowed into the model, providing that
there is also a 'slowly moving' variable, such as output, to ensure the
possibility of saddle path stability. An alternative approach has been to
permit the price level to rise in response to excess demand; this is the
approach adopted in the next section.

5.3   Sticky-price models

In this section three alternative supply-side hypotheses are considered to
that used in the standard Mundell–Fleming model given by equation
(5.2). The first alternative hypothesis is that employed by Dornbusch
(1976a) whereby, although the price level is sticky in the short run, in the
long run it rises, albeit sluggishly, in response to excess demand in the
goods market. The second hypothesis, due to Devereux and Purvis
(1990), additionally allows for the real exchange rate to affect both the
supply of domestic output and the level of real money balances. This
model allows for domestic output to be crowded out by an appreciation
of the exchange rate. The third hypothesis, due to Buiter and Miller
(1981), includes a core rate of inflation in the model, thereby leading to a
modification of the demand-side to allow for real interest rate effects on
domestic expenditure. These three alternative hypotheses are considered
in the following three sections.

5.3.1 The Dornbusch model

In what has become a classic paper Dornbusch (1976a) proposed that, rather than output adjusting to equate demand and supply in the goods market, the supply of output could be assumed fixed, as in the Classical approach, and that the general level of prices could rise (fall) in response to excess demand (supply). In addition to this Dornbusch used regressive, rather than rational, expectations although the results obtained regarding the efficiency of monetary and fiscal policy are identical. Formally Dornbusch combines equations (5.1) (5.4) (5.5) and (5.8) with the price level adjustment equation (5.15) replacing equation (5.2):

$$\dot{p} = \pi(a - y) \qquad \pi > 0 \tag{5.15}$$

The solution for this model is not the same as that in Section 5.2.2 above, because without perfect foresight expectations the solution will not involve a saddle path, although the overshooting of the exchange rate in the short run is still an important feature of the solution. Substituting equation (5.1) into (5.15), inverting (5.4) to give an expression in terms of the rate of interest, and substituting this into the equation for $\dot{p}$ gives goods market equilibrium as:

$$\dot{p} = \pi[\gamma e - (\gamma + \beta/\eta)p + g + (\beta/\eta)m - (1 - \alpha + \beta\phi/\eta)y] \tag{5.16}$$

In Figure 5.11 the locus $\dot{p} = 0$ shows the equilibrium values of e and p which clear the goods market. The schedule has a positive slope because a depreciation of the exchange rate will be associated with higher levels of demand and hence higher prices to maintain goods market equilibrium. Formally:

$$\partial e/\partial p = [1 + \beta/\eta\gamma] > 1 \tag{5.17}$$

This expression shows that the slope of the $\dot{p} = 0$ line is greater than unity. This is because an exogenous increase in the price level lowers demand, both by a relative price effect and a higher interest rate, which is necessary to maintain money market equilibrium, necessitating a more than proportionate increase in the exchange rate to restore equilibrium. Points to the right of the $\dot{p} = 0$ locus are points of excess demand for goods and are associated with rising price levels. Asset market equilibrium is obtained by writing (5.4) in terms of p and substituting for r from (5.9). Since in equilibrium $e = \bar{e}$, the equilibrium price level is given by: $\bar{p} = \eta r^* + m - \phi y$. Subtracting $\bar{p}$ from p and rearranging gives:

$$(e - \bar{e}) = -(1/\eta\mu)(p - \bar{p}) \tag{5.18}$$

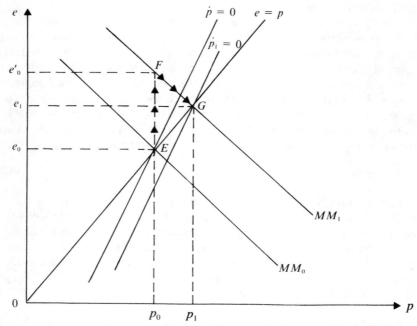

Figure 5.11   An increase in the money supply in a sticky-price model (SPKM)

which is the schedule for money market equilibrium. The slope of this line, as shown in Figure 5.11, is negative. Thus for money market equilibrium a rise in p above $\bar{p}$ implies that real money balances have fallen, requiring an increase in the interest rate to maintain money market equilibrium, which in turn requires an expectation of exchange rate depreciation, so e must appreciate relative to $\bar{e}$. This will worsen the trade balance but be offset by a large capital inflow.

A crucial feature of the adjustment process is, as before in the flexible output case, that the asset market clears instantaneously while the goods market adjusts only slowly. In Figure 5.11, starting from the equilibrium at E an increase in the money supply will shift the MM line to the right since a higher value of p is required to clear the market, given that y is fixed. Since the money market equilibrium schedule implies that both m and p are homogeneous then the price level must rise in proportion to the money supply in the long run, so the final equilibrium at G will have higher levels of both e and p. If prices are sticky in the short run, while asset markets always clear, the exchange rate will depreciate instantly to

F to clear the money market, thereby allowing expectations of a future appreciation to allow *r* to fall below its initial value. As goods market prices rise so the exchange rate can appreciate back towards its long-run equilibrium value at *G*. The extent of this short-run overshooting is given by totally differentiating the price level equation, noting that $de = dm = dp$ and that *y* and r^* are constant, gives $de/dm = (1 + 1/\mu\beta)$, where $0 < \mu\beta < 1$. That is, a 1 per cent rise in the money supply has a larger than 1 per cent effect on the exchange rate. Moreover, the extent of overshooting depends upon the interest elasticity of the demand for money, β, and the regressive expectations coefficient μ. Thus, if the interest elasticity of money demand is low, any change in the money supply will result in a relatively large change in the interest rate and will be mirrored by a large overshoot of the exchange rate. In the long run the fall in the interest rate leads to an excess demand for goods, which in this model raises prices and reduces the real money supply. The lower supply of real balances allows the interest rate to rise, which produces an incipient capital inflow which appreciates the exchange rate simultaneously, permitting interest rate parity to be maintained continuously.

An increase in government expenditure in this context, as before, does not lead to exchange rate overshooting. This is shown in Figure 5.12. From the initial equilibrium at *E* the fiscal expansion shifts the $\dot{p} = 0$ schedule to the right. For a given level of the money supply the rate of interest must rise, to persuade non-bank private sector investors to buy bonds, to finance the higher level of spending. This stimulates a capital inflow which causes the exchange rate to appreciate until a future depreciation is expected. The appreciation of the exchange rate lowers the demand for domestic money balances, hence generating an excess supply. To maintain money market equilibrium, given that *m*, *y* and *p* are all fixed, requires that the long-run equilibrium exchange rate, $\bar{e}$, falls (appreciates), to offset the effect of the appreciation of the exchange rate on the money market. The fall in *e* causes the money market equilibrium locus to shift to the left, to MM_1 in Figure 5.12. It also requires a long-run appreciation in the real exchange rate and so the $e - p$ locus also swivels round to the right. The new short-run equilibrium is reached at *F*, where the fiscal expansion is completely crowded out by the appreciation of the exchange rate. Point *F* also happens to be the new long-run equilibrium position, with both money and goods markets in equilibrium. In this case the exchange rate does not overshoot in the short run, but adjusts instantaneously and monotonically. The model in the next sub-section shows how fiscal policy shocks may also give rise to real exchange rate volatility and overshooting.

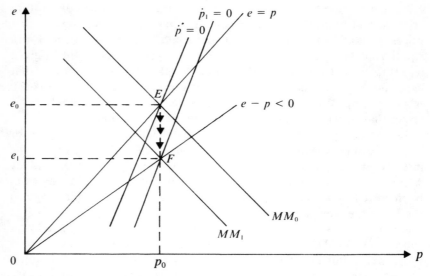

Figure 5.12   An increase in government spending in a SPKM

5.3.2   The Devereux and Purvis model

The model in this sub-section is a generalization of the models of the previous sections. The basic structure is similar, with identical relationships for demand, inflation and with perfect foresight exchange rate expectations. The generalization comes from the explicit specification of a linkage from the real exchange rate $(p - e)$ to the level of domestic output, y. This also has implications for the money market equilibrium schedule and the stability of the model. From the point of view of economic policy it demonstrates that real, fiscal shocks may also generate volatile exchange rate movements.

The supply curve is assumed to have the form:

$$\dot{y} = \sigma(p - e) \tag{5.19}$$

where $\sigma > 0$, so that a real exchange rate appreciation raises domestic output. Underlying this specification is the labour market, in which the demand depends negatively on the real product wage $(w - p)$ and the supply depends positively on the consumption-based real wage, $(w - p_c)$, where the consumer price index, p_c, is defined as: $p_c = \beta_1 e + \beta_2 p$. Hence a real appreciation, that is a rise in $(p - e)$, allows for a simultaneous rise in the consumption-based real wage and a fall in the product-based real wage, so that the levels of employment and output are increasing functions of the real exchange rate, as in (5.19). The supply side of the model is completed with the partial adjustment of prices to excess demand, exactly as given by equation (5.15) above.

The demand side of the model consists of the uncovered interest rate parity condition, equation (5.6), assuming perfect foresight exchange rate expectations, the demand for output function, as given by equation (5.1), and money market equilibrium as given by equation (5.20):

$$m - p_c = \phi(y + p - \beta_1 e - \beta_2 p) - \eta r \qquad (5.20)$$

where $\beta_1 + \beta_2 = 1$ and the right-hand side term in parentheses allows for the effect of real depreciation on real income. Equation (5.20) can be simplified to give:

$$m - \delta_1 e - \delta_2 p = \phi y - \eta r \qquad (5.20')$$

where $\delta_1 + \delta_2 = 1$, $\delta_1 = \beta_1(1 - \phi)$ and $\delta_2 = \beta_2 + \phi(1 - \beta_2)$. The steady-state solutions show that a permanent rise in government expenditure, g, causes a steady-state appreciation in the nominal and real exchange rates, and therefore a rise in domestic output, although the price of domestic goods may rise or fall, depending on the sign of $\delta_1 - \sigma\phi$. Formally:

$$
\begin{aligned}
e - p &= -[(g - \alpha r^*)/C] \\
p &= m - [(\delta_1 - \phi\sigma)/C]g + [\eta + \beta(\delta_1 - \sigma\phi)/C]r^* \\
e &= m + [(\delta_2 + \phi\sigma)/C]g - [\beta(\delta_2 - \sigma\phi)/C - \eta]r^*
\end{aligned}
\qquad (5.21)
$$

where $C = -\sigma[(1 - \alpha) + \gamma] < 0$

The dynamics are captured by two differential equations in e and p. It is assumed that output is demand-determined in the short run, so replacing demand with output in the equation for goods market equilibrium, and then using this equation together with (5.20) and the interest rate parity condition, gives the equation for e. Substituting for y in equation (5.15) gives the dynamic reduced form for p. The system is therefore:

$$
\begin{bmatrix} \dot{e} \\ \dot{p} \end{bmatrix} = D^{-1} \begin{bmatrix} [\delta_1(1 - \alpha) + \phi\gamma] & [\delta_2(1 - \alpha) - \phi\gamma] \\ p[(\gamma\eta - \beta\delta_1) + \sigma D] & -\pi[(\eta\gamma + \beta\delta_2) + \sigma D] \end{bmatrix} \begin{bmatrix} e \\ p \end{bmatrix} + \begin{bmatrix} D^{-1}[\phi g + (\alpha - 1)m - Dr^*] \\ D^{-1}[\pi\eta g + \pi\beta m] \end{bmatrix}
$$

where $D = (1 - \alpha)\eta + \beta\phi > 0$

The determinant from this system is $-\pi(1-\alpha)[\eta\gamma + \sigma D + \phi\gamma\beta(1-\alpha)^{-1}]$ < 0, so the system gives a saddle path equilibrium. Interestingly, however, in this case the exchange rate equilibrium schedule and stable arm can have either negative or positive slopes, depending upon the sign of the term $\delta_2(1-\alpha) - \phi\gamma$. These two cases are illustrated in Figure 5.13. The constant inflation locus is always positively sloped in this model, since a rise in p requires a lower exchange rate to hold the real exchange rate constant in the long-run equilibrium.

Consider an unanticipated rise in government expenditure, g. From the long-run equilibrium equations the nominal and the real exchange rates must appreciate, leaving e and $(e - p)$ lower in the final equilibrium. The price level may rise or fall, however, depending upon the sign of $(\delta_1 - \sigma\phi)/\beta$. Here it is assumed that the price level falls in the long run, which implies that the direct effect of the exchange rate change on the price level is greater than the indirect effect via higher aggregate supply; or more technically, σ is small compared with δ_1 and ϕ is strictly less than unity. In this case the short-run dynamics of the model are given in Figure 5.13A. The rise in g shifts the $\dot{e} = 0$ line in to the left and the $\dot{p} = 0$ schedule out to the right, although the shift in the $\dot{e} = 0$ line will always be greater than that in the $\dot{p} = 0$ line, given the assumptions above. The long-run equilibrium moves from A to C in Figure 5.13A although in the short run, if prices are sticky downwards, there will be exchange rate overshooting. This occurs since the exchange rate has to appreciate to maintain uncovered interest parity, because the higher demand for goods raises money demand, so for a given supply of money the interest rate must rise to clear the money market. Hence the exchange rate appreciates immediately generating expectations of a future depreciation. When prices start to fall, the demand for money starts to decline and the exchange rate will depreciate back towards its final equilibrium as interest rates fall. From Figure 5.13A it can be seen that if the price level does not fall in the long-run equilibrium then the exchange rate does not overshoot in the short run.

Figure 5.13B shows another case where the exchange rate does not overshoot in the short run, that is, when the $\dot{e} = 0$ line has a positive slope. An unanticipated rise in government expenditure in this case shifts the $\dot{e} = 0$ line up to the left (and the $\dot{p} = 0$ line out to the right as before) so that the new long-run equilibrium is at point C. With sticky prices in the short run, the exchange rate immediately depreciates to e_0, but then continues to depreciate further to e_1, to reach the long-run equilibrium without overshooting. This case is consistent with a rapid adjustment of the goods market to excess demand and a high income elasticity of demand for money.

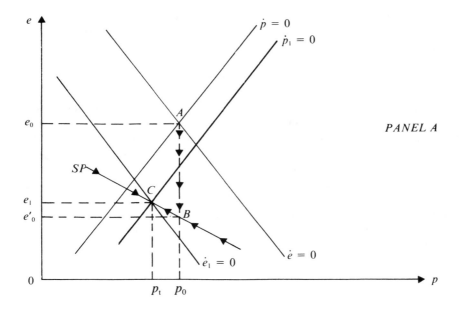

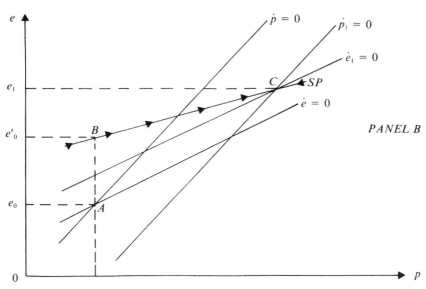

Figure 5.13   An unanticipated increase in government spending in a SPKM with exchange rate effects on aggregate supply

A monetary expansion in this model which is unanticipated does not have such ambiguous effects in the long run. The price level rises and the exchange rate depreciates in direct proportion to the change in the money supply, so that the real exchange rate is unaffected in the long run and so the final equilibrium will be along a 45-degree line from the origin in Figure 5.13. Short-run overshooting, however, is only a feature of the model when the stable saddle path is negatively sloped. As with the fiscal policy case, if the arm has a positive slope the exchange rate converges monotonically. This model can therefore be regarded as a generalization of the Dornbusch model with two principal conclusions. Firstly, with rapidly clearing goods markets the likelihood of exchange rate over-shooting is reduced, even for unanticipated monetary disturbances. Secondly, a fiscal expansion may give rise to short-run overshooting if the money markets adjust more quickly than goods markets, if the income elasticity of the demand for money is low and the price level falls in the long run.

5.3.3   The Buiter–Miller model

This model attempts to mimic the position in the late 1970s when inflation was a persistent condition in many Western economies. The model shares the money market equilibrium condition of the traditional Mundell–Fleming model and the assumption of perfect foresight expectations. The inflation equation is essentially the same as that used by Dornbusch (1976a) and Devereux and Purvis (1990), although it includes an additional term in trend inflation, x, as in equation (5.15′) below, which in turn is equal to the trend growth in the money supply, $\dot{m}$.

$$\dot{p} = \pi(a-y) + x \qquad\qquad (5.15')$$

$$x = \dot{m} \qquad\qquad (5.22)$$

This extension of the model necessitates a modification to the aggregate demand equation since, with a positive rate of inflation, the relevant rate of interest will be the real rate, $r - \dot{p}$, assuming that expected inflation equals actual inflation, and not the nominal rate, r. The modified aggregate demand equation is:

$$a = \alpha y + g - \beta(r-\dot{p}) + \gamma(e-p) \qquad\qquad (5.1')$$

The long-run equilibrium solutions for p and e are obtained as follows. Inverting (5.4), using (5.6) and noting that in the long-run solution $\dot{e} = x$, the equilibrium price level is simply:

$$\bar{p} = m - \phi y + \eta(r^* + x) \tag{5.23}$$

For the long-run level of e, set $\dot{p} = 0$, $a = y$ and substitute for p into (5.1') from (5.23) to get:

$$\bar{e} = [(1 - \alpha - \gamma\phi)/\gamma]y - (1/\gamma)g + m + [(\beta + \gamma\eta)/\gamma]r^* + \eta x \tag{5.24}$$

The equations for the real exchange rate, c, and real money balances, l, are as follows:

$$\bar{c} = \bar{e} - \bar{p} = [(1 - \alpha)/\gamma]y - (1/\gamma)g + (\beta/\gamma)r^* \tag{5.25}$$

$$\bar{l} = \bar{m} - \bar{p} = \phi y - \eta(r^* + x) \tag{5.26}$$

Therefore a rise in government expenditure leads to an appreciation in the real exchange rate while a rise in the foreign interest rate and the level of domestic output will give rise to a real depreciation of the equilibrium exchange rate.

The dynamics of the model are given by equations (5.6) and (5.15') which can be written in terms of real money balances and the real exchange rate:

$$\dot{p} = \pi(a - y) + \dot{m} \tag{5.27}$$

$$\dot{c} = \dot{e} - \dot{p} = r - r^* - \pi(a - y) - x \tag{5.28}$$

Assuming output is demand-determined in the short-run these equations reduce to:

$$\dot{m} - \dot{p} = \dot{l} = -\pi a \tag{5.27'}$$

$$\dot{e} - \dot{p} = \dot{c} = -\pi a + r - r^* - x \tag{5.28'}$$

To solve for $\dot{l}$ and $\dot{c}$ substitute into (5.27') and (5.28') for a and r from the aggregate demand and money market equations (5.1') and (5.4) respectively, to obtain:

$$\begin{bmatrix} \dot{c} \\ \dot{l} \end{bmatrix} = F^{-1} \begin{bmatrix} \gamma(\phi - \pi\eta) & -1 \\ -\eta\gamma\pi & -\pi\beta \end{bmatrix} \begin{bmatrix} c \\ l \end{bmatrix} + F^{-1} \begin{bmatrix} \eta & -F \\ 0 & \pi\eta\beta \end{bmatrix} \begin{bmatrix} r^* \\ x \end{bmatrix} \tag{5.29}$$

where

$$F = [\eta(1 - \beta\pi) + \beta\phi] > 0$$

Stability requires that the determinant be negative to give a saddle path equilibrium. This determinant is: $F^{-1}[-\pi\gamma\{\beta(\phi - \eta\pi) + \eta\}]$, which is negative if $\phi > \pi\eta$. In Figure 5.14 the $l = 0$ line is the locus of l and c that give a stationary level of real money balances. It has a negative slope because $dc/dl = -\beta/\gamma\eta < 0$ from (5.29). The $\dot{c} = 0$ line denotes the combinations of l and c which give the long-run equilibrium solution for c. This schedule is of ambiguous slope with $dc/dl = [\gamma(\phi - \pi\eta)]^{-1}$ which is positive if $\phi > \pi\eta$. This is likely to be the case if price adjustment is slow (so that π is small). This is also the necessary and sufficient condition for stability as the direction arrows in Figure 5.14 show. For any level of c, a position to the right of the $l = 0$ line implies an excess supply of real money balances which depresses the rate of interest, causing excess demand for goods, which in turn pushes up the price level thereby reducing the level of real money balances back towards equilibrium, as shown by the horizontal arrows. For any level of l, a point directly below the $\dot{c} = 0$ locus implies an excess demand for domestic currency, which for given interest rates and income leads to a further appreciation of the exchange rate which worsens competitiveness, as shown by the vertical arrows in Figure 5.14.

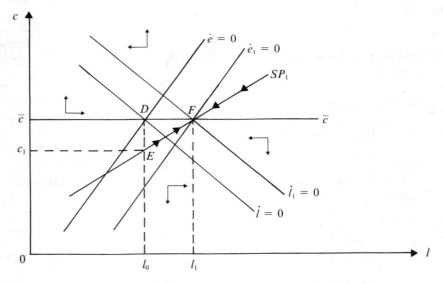

Figure 5.14   An unanticipated cut in monetary growth in the CIKM

Consider an unanticipated reduction in the rate of monetary growth which is announced and implemented simultaneously. The monetary contraction shifts the $\dot{l}=0$ and $\dot{c}=0$ lines out to the right, although it does not affect the level of competitiveness in the long run. Therefore the long-run level of competitiveness must be along the horizontal line $\bar{c}$ in Figure 5.14. From the long-run equilibrium equations it is also clear that the level of real money balances depends negatively on the core rate of monetary growth, so that the demand for real money balances must have increased. The new long-run equilibrium position is given by point F in Figure 5.14 and the new saddle path by the line SP_1. As with the other models in this class, the assumption of differential speeds of adjustment in the goods and assets markets means that in the short run the exchange rate will overshoot its final equilibrium. The reduction in the rate of monetary growth, with a constant stock of money balances, will raise the demand for real money balances, and the lower rate of interest must be offset by the expectation of an exchange rate appreciation. Thus the exchange rate and hence competitiveness both jump onto the new saddle path at E. The money market is cleared at E by a fall in output which in turn is induced by the real exchange rate appreciation and an increase in the real rate of interest. Once prices begin to fall, the nominal interest rate falls and the exchange rate will be depreciating as the new equilibrium is approached. The increased demand for real balances is satisfied in the new equilibrium because the inflation-adjusted interest rate has fallen, making interest-bearing assets less attractive. In the new equilibrium all real variables are unchanged and the model exhibits the Neoclassical properties also possessed by the models in Chapter 4.

Finally, consider an unanticipated increase in the level of the money stock. Since the price level and the exchange rate are homogeneous of degree one with respect to the money supply the final equilibrium must be one in which l and c are unchanged, that is at E in Figure 5.15. The increase in the money supply increases liquidity so the real exchange rate must jump to c_2 and, since the exchange rate will be expected to appreciate to equilibrium, the nominal interest rate will fall on impact and output will expand. Over time this increases the price level, reduces real money balances, raises the interest rate and appreciates the exchange rate, so eventually the system returns to E. Thus, if a cut in the rate of growth of the money supply is combined with an increase in the level of the money supply then the interest rate will be prevented from rising, and the exchange rate from appreciating. Therefore the reduction of domestic output may be curtailed if cutting money supply growth is combined with a policy of raising the stock of money in the system.[5]

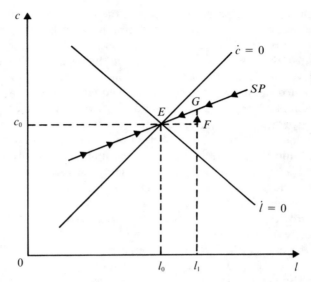

Figure 5.15 An unanticipated rise in the money supply in the CIKM

5.4 The econometric evidence

The empirical evidence can be divided into two classes: tests of the Dornbusch overshooting model and tests of the Buiter–Miller core inflation model. In each case there are both single equation and simultaneous equation tests which will be discussed in Sections 5.4.1 and 5.4.2 respectively.

5.4.1 The Dornbusch overshooting model

The Dornbusch model has not been extensively tested.[6] In this section two tests of the model are considered: those by Driskill (1981) and Demery (1984) for the Swiss–US dollar exchange rate using three-monthly data[7] and those tests in a series of similar papers by Papell (1984, 1985, 1988) for the other major currencies using quarterly data. The approach in both cases has been to convert the continuous time, small-country theoretical model into a discrete time, two-country empirical model. In the papers by Driskill and Demery the model is reduced to two dynamic equations, one for the price level and the other for the exchange rate, while Papell uses systems estimators to also generate predictions for the exogenous variables in the model, consistent with the rational expectations approach.

To convert Dornbusch's model into a two-country model for prices and the exchange rate, Driskill defines all variables in relative terms. The equation for relative prices, for example, is the logarithm of the domestic price level minus the logarithm of the foreign price level, and denoted in discrete time as:

$$\tilde{p}_{t+1} = \tilde{p}_t + \pi(\tilde{a}_t - \tilde{y}_t) \tag{5.15'}$$

where the tildes denote a domestic value relative to a foreign value, that is, $\tilde{z} = z - z^*$. Substituting into (5.15′) for a and r, using relative versions of equations (5.1) and (5.4) and lagging one period gives:

$$\tilde{p} = a_0\tilde{y}_{t-1} + a_1\tilde{p}_{t-1} + a_2\tilde{m}_{t-1} + a_3e_{t-1} + a_4\tilde{g}_{t-1} + w_t \tag{5.30}$$

where

$$\begin{aligned}
a_0 &= \pi\{\alpha - 1 - (\beta\phi/\eta)\} & a_1 &= \{1 - \pi\gamma - \pi\beta/\eta\} \\
a_2 &= \{\pi\beta/\eta\} & a_3 &= \pi\gamma \\
a_4 &= \pi
\end{aligned}$$

and w_t is the error term. Equation (5.30) is a first-order difference equation in relative prices. The empirical equation for the exchange rate is attained by using the uncovered interest rate parity equation combined with regressive exchange rate expectations, where the long-run equilibrium exchange rate, $\bar{e}$, is replaced by the relative money supply, $\tilde{m}_t$. Substituting for r_t from the money market equilibrium equation and for $\tilde{p}_t$ from (5.30) above gives:

$$e_t = b_0 + b_1e_{t-1} + b_2\tilde{m}_t + b_3\tilde{m}_{t-1} + b_4\tilde{p}_{t-1} + b_5\tilde{y}_t + b_6\tilde{y}_{t-1} + b_7\tilde{g}_{t-1} + v_t \tag{5.31}$$

where v_t is the error term and the overidentified reduced form coefficients are as follows:

$$\begin{aligned}
b_1 &= -\pi\gamma/\mu\eta = -a_3/\mu\eta < 0 & b_4 &= (1 - \pi\beta/\mu\eta^2 - \pi\gamma/\mu\eta) = -a_1/\mu\eta < 0 \\
b_2 &= (1 + 1/\mu\eta) > 1 & b_5 &= -\phi/\mu\eta < 0 \\
b_3 &= \pi\beta/\mu\eta^2 = a_2/\mu\eta > 0 & b_6 &= \pi(\alpha - 1 - \beta\phi/\eta)/\mu\eta < 0 \\
b_7 &= -a_4/\mu\eta < 0
\end{aligned}$$

The Dornbusch model implies that the following four restrictions are valid:

$$b_1 < 0$$
$$b_2 > 1$$

$$b_4 < 0$$
$$b_1 + b_2 + b_3 + b_4 = 1$$

The sign and size of b_2 indicates short-run overshooting and the constraint that the sum of the first four b's sum to unity is equivalent to long-run PPP. Furthermore, since the price level rises only after the exchange rate has overshot its long-run equilibrium, prices rise as the exchange rate appreciates back towards equilibrium and so b_4 must be negative.

Driskill (1981) uses single equation estimation procedures to estimate the quasi-reduced form for the Swiss franc–US dollar exchange rate for the period 1973–7, using three-monthly data. The terms in government expenditure are not strictly part of the Dornbusch model and so are not included in the estimated version of the model. The income terms also had to be omitted because the proxies used for Swiss income data were insignificant. Secondly, two dummy variables were added to the exchange rate equation: OIL, to capture the effects of the oil embargo and cuts in Arab oil production in December to February 1973–74, and SEAS, which captures the pronounced year-end demand for Swiss francs by Swiss firms for end-of-year 'window dressing' of their financial statements. Prior to estimation of the exchange rate equation the relative money supply term was tested to see if it followed a random walk. Since this hypothesis could not be rejected, the assumption that all changes in the relative money supply were unanticipated seemed justified, although, as noted by Demery (1984), this means that the error terms in equations (5.30) and (5.31) are of a moving average type and not autoregressive, as assumed by Driskill.

Table 5.1 reports the tests of the Dornbusch overshooting model by Driskill and Demery. Driskill's results do not offer much support for the model with incorrect signs on a_2, b_1 and b_4 in both restricted and unrestricted versions of the model. There is, however, strong evidence of exchange rate overshooting with $b_2 > 2$ and strongly significant. Both of Driskill's equations have an R^2 greater than 0.96 and the restricted and unrestricted coefficients are very similar in magnitude and size. Demery (1984) re-estimates the model, using the same data set, by maximum likelihood methods to obtain efficient estimates of the parameters and to test the implied cross-equation restrictions, not tested by Driskill. Demery's estimates are rather different from Driskill's, for two reasons. First, Demery uses a moving average error process as implied by the theoretical model, and not an autoregressive error as used by Driskill. Second, the oil dummy is not included in Demery's tests for technical reasons. Demery's coefficients differ considerably in magnitude and sign from those of Driskill; in particular, in the unrestricted form the coefficient on b_2 is less than unity, suggesting exchange rate undershooting. Demery explicitly tests two restrictions using the likelihood ratio procedure. LR_1 tests the complete set of restrictions implied by the Dornbusch model on the reduced form. These restrictions are rejected at the 5 per cent level, since the estimated value exceeds the tabulated critical

Table 5.1   Tests of the Dornbusch model

| | Driskill (1981) | | | Demery (1984) | |
	Unrestricted	Restricted*		Unrestricted	Restricted*
Coefficients					
a_0	0.06	0.57		0.891	0.751
	(1.90)	(1.84)			
a_1	0.76	0.71		0.622	0.563
	(4.58)	(4.47)			
a_2	0.37	0.29		0.546	0.491
	(1.96)	(1.86)			
a_3	−0.03			−0.045	−0.054
	(0.74)				
b_0	−2.22	−2.38		−1.659	−1.301
	(2.82)	(2.89)			
b_1	0.43	0.55		0.530	0.016
	(3.65)	(4.48)			
b_2	2.37	2.30		0.522	1.301
	(5.73)	(4.92)			
b_3	−2.45	−2.69		−0.505	−0.148
	(5.60)	(5.79)			
b_4	0.93	0.84		0.830	−0.170
	(2.23)	(1.91)			
Seas	−0.06	−0.06		−0.039	−0.028
	(5.47)	(5.11)			
Oil	0.15	0.16			
	(7.61)	(7.25)			
ρ	0.35	0.21	q	0.315	0.541
				LR_1 = 15.12 [9.49]	
				LR_2 = 11.09 [7.81]	

Notes
*Restrictions are: $a_1 + a_2 + a_3 = 1$ and $\sum_i b_i = 1$, where $i = 1, \ldots, 4$. LR statistics are likelihood ratio tests of Dornbusch model restrictions, including and excluding the PPP restriction respectively. ρ is the first-order serial correlation coefficient and q the first-order moving average coefficient. The t-ratios are in parentheses.

value in brackets in Table 5.1. This test includes the PPP restriction which is unlikely to hold. Demery therefore tests the validity of the other restrictions, excluding PPP. The LR_2 statistic, however, again exceeds its critical value, leading to a rejection of the restrictions. Therefore, somewhat contrary to Driskill's results, it seems that overshooting is not an important feature in the case of the Swiss–US dollar exchange rate.

Papell (1988) tests the Dornbusch model using constrained maximum likelihood techniques which incorporate cross-equations restrictions and the assumption of rational expectations for the effective exchange rate indices of Germany, Japan, the UK and the USA using quarterly data from 1973 Q2 to 1984 Q4. In this model most of the structural parameters have plausible values, but the critical parameter for overshooting is δ_2, the coefficient on the price level in the exchange rate equation. If δ_2 is positive then there is exchange rate overshooting but if it is negative then undershooting prevails. The results obtained are reported below in Table 5.2. This table shows that half the coefficients are positive and half negative. The only country where overshooting seems a credible hypothesis is West Germany, while Japan seems to display the characteristics of undershooting. For the UK and the USA the results are weak, with δ_2 insignificantly different from zero.

Table 5.2. Papell's estimates of exchange rate overshooting

		Germany	Japan	UK	US
Constrained Model	δ_2	0.62	−0.16	−0.02	0.09
Semi-constrained	δ_2	0.39	−0.51	0.09	−0.18
Model		(1.83)	(2.17)	(0.75)	(0.17)

Note
Asymptotic *t*-values in parentheses

Source: Papell (1988), extracted from Tables 1 and 3.

Papell (1984) estimates a two-country version of the Dornbusch overshooting model, assuming rational expectations and postulating endogenous money supplies. Monetary policy in both countries is assumed to be responsive to exchange rate and price level changes. The estimated model consists of six equations which are estimated structurally using constrained maximum likelihood techniques and quarterly data for the USA and West Germany for the period 1973 Q3 to 1981 Q4. The

strongest result is that, while US monetary policy is strongly accommodating of prices, German policy is sufficiently offsetting for the combined
monetary policies not to be able to induce exchange rate undershooting.
Thus exchange rate overshooting is a strong result to emerge from this
extended Dornbusch model. Papell (1985) extends the model further by
incorporating imperfect capital mobility and a real uncovered interest
rate differential to test the Deutsche Mark and yen effective exchange
rates over the same period as the German–US study. The results are
consistent with those obtained by Papell (1988); that is, with overshooting of the mark and undershooting of the yen. Attempts to estimate the
model for the USA and UK effective exchange rates failed to yield any
sensible significant results, which Papell attributes to the change in the
money supply rule during the period, as both monetary authorities
became less accommodating.

5.4.2   Tests of the core inflation model

Barr (1989) tests the Buiter–Miller model for the UK effective exchange
rate index for the period 1973–82, using quarterly data (giving 37 observations). To make the theoretical model presented in Section 5.3 above
suitable for estimation, Barr adds a vector of additional exogenous
variables to the equation for domestic demand. This vector includes
variables such as the oil price, denoted p^{oil}, which reflects the UK's oil-
producing capacity, domestic capacity output, which is proxied by the
domestic capital stock, denoted, k, and two variables to capture changes
in the world economy: the world real interest rate, i^* and the level of
world output, y^*. The estimated quasi-reduced form of the Buiter–Miller
model is therefore of the form:

$$l_t = b_1 l_{t-1} + b_2 c_{t-1} + b_3 i^*_{t-1} + b_4 \mu_{t-1} + b_5 x_{t-1} + b_6 p^{oil}_{t-1} + b_7 y^*_{t-1} \\ + b_8 k_{t-1} + v_{1t}$$

$$c_t = h_1 l_t + h_2 c_{t+1} + h_3 i^*_t + h_4 \mu_t + h_5 x_t + h_6 p^{oil}_t + h_7 y^*_t + h_8 k_{t-1} + v_{2t}$$

where the v_{1t} and v_{2t} are error terms, x_t is the expected core rate of
inflation and μ_t is the expected rate of growth of the money supply,
which is zero in the equation for competitiveness. The *a priori* signs are:

$$b_1 < 1, b_2 \gtrless 0, b_3 > 0, b_4 = 1, b_5 < 0, b_6 < 0, b_7 < 0, b_8 > \quad 0$$

$$h_1 > 0, h_2 > 0, h_3 \gtrless 0, h_4 = 0, h_5 > 0, h_6 < 0, h_7 > 0, h_8 < 0$$

The single equation estimates for each of these equations are given in
Table 5.3.

The real balances equation is estimated by OLS and shows no sign of first-order serial correlation, according to Durbin's H test. The very high R^2 is mainly due to the fact that l_t is highly dependent on l_{t-1}. All the coefficients are correctly signed with the coefficient on future monetary growth, b_4, not significantly different from unity. Note that higher core inflation, x, reduces the stock of real money balances in the long run. The competitiveness equation is estimated by instrumental variables (IV), to instrument out the explanatory variable, c_{t+1}, using McCallum's errors in variables method (McCallum, 1976). Barr reports several sets of results for the competitiveness equation, depending in part on the set of instruments chosen for c_{t+1}. The version reported in Table 5.3 passes Sargan's IV test (Sargan, 1958) given by $z(3)$ and the results show no signs of serial correlation, given by $z(1)$, which is distributed as chi-squared. The coefficients are well-defined and consistent with the theore-

Table 5.3   Tests of the core inflation model

Single equation estimates

$$l_t = 0.76l_{t-1} + 0.05c_{t-2} + 2.50i^*_{t-3} - 2.90x_{t-2} - 1.65x_{t-4} - 0.46y^*_{t-2}$$
$$\quad (15.2) \qquad (5.00) \qquad (5.95) \quad (-4.83) \quad (-2.75) \quad (-5.11)$$
$$\quad - 0.05p^{oil}_{t-2} + 0.64k_{t-4} + 1.12\mu_{t-1} + \text{const} + \text{seasonals}$$
$$\quad (-7.14) \qquad (5.33) \qquad (14.0)$$

$R^2 = 0.995$; Durbin's $H = 0.59$; $F = 588.4$.

$$c_t = 0.75l_t + 0.75c_{t+1} - 5.08i^*_t + 13.51x_{t-1} + 10.22x_{t-3} + 1.85y^*_t$$
$$\quad (2.78) \quad (7.5) \quad (-2.95) \qquad (3.72) \qquad 1.56 \qquad (2.31)$$
$$\quad - 1.65k_{t-3} + \text{const} + \text{seasonals}$$
$$\quad (-1.81)$$

$R^2 = 0.874$; $z(1) = 1.13$; $z(2) = 3.88$; $z(3) = 1.77$

Instruments: $\mu_{\tau-1}$, $\mu_{\tau-2}$, $\mu_{\tau-3}$, $\mu_{\tau-4}$, c_{t-1}

Simultaneous equations estimates

$$l_t = 0.80l_{t-1} + 0.06c_{t-2} + 2.77i^*_{t-3} - 3.60x_{t-2} - 0.051x_{t-4} - 0.42y^*_{t-2}$$
$$\quad (20.0) \qquad (3.0) \qquad (6.60) \quad (-6.43) \quad (-1.46) \qquad (-5.25)$$
$$\quad - 0.04p^{oil}_{t-2} + 0.56k_{t-4}$$
$$\quad (-4.0) \qquad (5.6)$$

$$c_t = 0.47l_t + 0.84c_{t+1} - 4.52i^*_t - 4.89x_t + 8.72x_{t-1} + 1.05x_{t-3}$$
$$\quad (3.92) \quad (28.0) \qquad (-3.48) \quad (-1.76) \quad (2.71) \qquad (0.53)$$
$$\quad + 0.81y^*_t + 0.08p^{oil}_t - 0.90k_{t-3}$$
$$\quad (40.5) \qquad (4.00) \quad (-4.29)$$

Source: Barr (1989), from Tables 2.1, 2.3 and 2.4.

tical model, although the interest rate effect is not very strong and the oil price is dropped because of its insignificance.

The simultaneous equations results from non-linear estimation are not very much different from the single-equation results reported. Most of the differences lie in the competitiveness equation, in particular the coefficients on real money balances and current core inflation, which changes sign, but remains insignificant. Overall, Barr regards the results as encouraging, while noting that the money market equilibrium part of the model does not do particularly well.

5.5 Conclusions

This chapter has reviewed some of the developments in modelling exchange rate behaviour in the context of the Mundell–Fleming tradition of fixed or sticky prices. This model extends the income-expenditure approach developed in Chapter 3 to include international capital flows, where domestic and foreign assets are assumed to be perfect substitutes. Within this framework goods markets are assumed to be slowly clearing while asset markets are in continuous equilibrium. This may give rise to exchange rate overshooting, as in the Classical Monetary Model of Chapter 2, although for a different reason. In this case it is the differential adjustment speeds of the goods and asset markets whereas in the CLMM it was the stickiness in non-traded goods prices which gave rise to exchange rate overshooting. The Mundell–Fleming approach therefore has an advantage over the modern monetary approaches of Chapter 4 in that overshooting can occur and hence real exchange rate changes can take place, at least in the short run. Given the very large movements in real exchange rates over the recent floating rate period, the Mundell–Fleming approach seems, intuitively, more plausible.

The empirical evidence, however, suggests that exchange rate overshooting is not a widely supported important empirical phenomenon. Evidence has been found for overshooting of the Deutsche Mark in the 1970s, although for other currencies, as with the Swiss–US dollar rate, the dollar and sterling effective exchange rates, little evidence is found for overshooting. Indeed, there is evidence to support undershooting of the exchange rate for the yen effective exchange rate, the Swiss Franc–US dollar rate and the sterling and US dollar effective exchange rate indices.

The principal limitation of this class of exchange rate model is the assumption of perfect capital mobility (and hence perfect substitutability of domestic and foreign assets) which does not permit the trade balance to influence the path of the exchange rate or make the exchange rate susceptible to switches in asset preferences. Given that the results of

Demery (1984), Driskill (1981) and Papell (1985) are constant with an exchange rate model which exhibits imperfect capital mobility, so that the trade balance can have a direct influence upon the exchange rate, exchange rate models which allow for stock–flow interaction are the subject of the next two chapters.

Notes
1. This condition is also important for the stability of the model. This assumption was also employed by both Mundell and Fleming in the 1960s.
2. See Chapter 3 for the appropriate conditions.
3. See for example, Pentecost (1984) and Devereux and Purvis (1990).
4. Because $1/\beta\phi > 1/\eta[(\alpha-1)-\beta\phi]$.
5. Buiter and Miller (1981) claim that the UK authorities' decision not to 'claw back' the sterling M3 overshoot in the second half of 1980 amounted to this kind of joint policy action.
6. It has usually been nested in the quasi-reduced form of Frankel's RIPM (Frankel, 1979). Not only have these tests been unsuccessful but there are doubts about the methodology. See Chapter 4.
7. The quarterly data were generated by averaging three-monthly end of period figures. This gives a sample of only 19 observations, beginning in March 1973 and ending in November 1977.

Appendix: Mathematics of saddle path equilibria

Let us postulate a general second-order dynamical system:

$$\begin{bmatrix} \dot{X} \\ \dot{Z} \end{bmatrix} = \begin{bmatrix} a_{11} & a_{12} \\ a_{21} & a_{22} \end{bmatrix} \begin{bmatrix} X \\ Z \end{bmatrix} \tag{A5.1}$$

where X is a potential jump, or free variable, and Z is a slow-moving variable. For this system to exhibit saddle path stability a necessary and sufficient condition is that $Det(A) < 0$. This requires the elements on the main diagonal to have opposite signs and those on the other diagonal to have like signs. If X is the jump variable then $a_{11} > 0$ and $a_{22} < 0$. This second-order system will have two roots, λ_1 and λ_2, one of which is stable ($\lambda_2 < 0$) and one of which is unstable ($\lambda_1 > 0$). The stable arm is the saddle path equilibrium.

The solution has the following form:

$$\dot{X} = a_{11}X + a_{12}Z \tag{A5.2}$$

re-arranging to give:

$$Z = (\dot{X} - a_{11}X)/a_{12} \tag{A5.3}$$

Differentiating (A5.3) with respect to time gives

$$\dot{Z} = (\ddot{X} - a_{11}\dot{X})/a_{12} \tag{A5.4}$$

Substituting this into the equation for $\dot{Z}$ gives:

$$\ddot{X} - (a_{11} + a_{22})\dot{X} + (a_{11}a_{22} - a_{21}a_{12})X = 0 \tag{A5.5}$$

This solution has the general form given by (A5.6):

$$X(t) = A_1 exp(\lambda_1, t) + A_2 exp(\lambda_2, t) \tag{A5.6}$$

From (A5.3) and using (A5.6) the expression for Z becomes:

$$Z(t) = [\{\lambda_1 A_1 exp(\lambda_1, t) + \lambda_2 A_2 exp(\lambda_2, t)\} \\ - a_{11}\{A_1 exp(\lambda_1.t) + A_2 exp(\lambda_2, t)\}]/a_{12} \tag{A5.7}$$

$$Z(t) = -(A_1/a_{12})(a_{11} - \lambda_1)exp(\lambda_1, t) - (A_2/a_{12})(a_{11} - \lambda_2)exp(\lambda_2, t) \tag{A5.8}$$

Setting $A_1 = 0$ in (A5.6) and (A5.8) gives:

$$X(t) = A_2 exp(\lambda_2, t) \qquad\qquad (A5.9)$$

$$Z(t) = -(A_2/a_{12})(a_{11} - \lambda_2)exp(\lambda_2, t) \qquad\qquad (A5.10)$$

Writing (A5.9) in terms of A_2 and substituting for A_2 in equation (A5.10) gives:

$$Z(t) = -X(t)(a_{11} - \lambda_2)a_{12} \qquad\qquad (A5.11)$$

from which it can be seen that the slope of the stable arm is:

$$dZ/dX = -(a_{11} - \lambda_2)/a_{12} \qquad\qquad (A5.12)$$

where the expression in parentheses is unambiguously positive, since λ_2 is the stable root ($\lambda_2 < 0$). The sign of the overall expression depends crucially upon the sign of a_{12}: if $a_{12} > 0$ then the saddle path has a negative slope and if $a_{12} < 0$ the saddle path has a positive slope.

6 The currency substitution approach

6.1 Introduction

Currency substitution models are a specific kind of monetary model, in which domestic and foreign residents hold both home and foreign currencies. In these models bond markets are not explicitly represented and so there are no rates of interest. The interesting new feature of this class of small, open-economy models is that they attempt to integrate the current and capital accounts of the balance of payments through wealth effects. Domestic wealth can only be increased by the accumulation of foreign currency arising from a current balance surplus. Only when there is current account balance will domestic wealth be unchanging and the model be in equilibrium. In this chapter and the next these so-called stock–flow interaction models are the focus of attention. It is also important to recognize the distinction between exchange rate models concerned with currency substitution and currency substitution *per se*. Most of the attempts to model currency substitution have not been in the context of small, open-economy exchange rate models which emphasize stock–flow interaction, but rather of domestic demand for money equations with an additional explanatory variable for foreign interest rates consistent with currency substitution in the context of integrated world capital markets (Bilson, 1979). Some of this empirical work is briefly reviewed in Section 6.4 below, but it does not represent a direct test of the empirical validity of this class of exchange rate models.

It is also important to stress at the outset that it is difficult to distinguish between currency substitution and the more usual concept of capital mobility. Indeed, it is likely that currency substitution is part of a wider process of portfolio diversification (see Chapter 7). McKinnon (1982) for example, distinguishes between direct and indirect currency substitution. Direct currency substitution occurs when economic agents have an incentive to hold a portfolio of non-interest bearing currencies and substitute between such currencies on a risk-return criterion. Indirect currency substitution, on the other hand, arises because of the substitutability of non-money assets, which, McKinnon argues, is empirically more important. To understand this hypothesis, assume that economic agents revise upwards their expectations of the return on foreign bonds, because they expect the domestic currency to depreciate. They will therefore wish to sell domestic bonds and buy foreign bonds, which causes upward pressure on the domestic interest rate and perhaps some downward pressure on the foreign interest rate. With a given domestic demand for money function and a fixed money supply the domestic interest rate cannot rise, and so the increased demand for foreign bonds gives rise to an appreciation of the exchange rate. The exchange rate continues to appreciate until the expected depreciation of the exchange rate is exactly equal to the interest rate differential between the home and foreign countries.

In this chapter two models are considered where foreign money is held by domestic residents and in which there is interaction between the current and capital accounts of the balance of payments. These models have monetary approach characteristics in that they assume uncovered interest rate parity, purchasing power parity and full employment of factor inputs. In Section 6.2, we consider the models of Kouri (1976) and the extension by Calvo and Rodriguez (1977), to include a distinction between traded and non-traded goods, and hence relative prices and the elasticities condition (see Chapter 3). This class of models focuses not upon the money supply, as other monetary models, but rather on its rate of growth. Section 6.3 considers the model of Niehans (1977), where there is assumed not to be instantaneous asset market clearing and which therefore presents a large variety of dynamic paths for the exchange rate. Section 6.4 briefly considers the limited evidence on currency substitution, in the context of capital market integration, which suggests that this class of models may not be consistent with the observed pattern of asset substitutability.

6.2   The instantaneous asset market adjustment models

The models of this section are based on that of Kouri (1976). This model makes Classical assumptions with regards to the goods market, in that prices are perfectly flexible and all goods are traded, so that absolute purchasing power parity (PPP) holds and there is automatic full employment. For simplicity, the foreign price level, P^*, is set equal to unity so that $P = E$. The model has only two assets, domestic money, M, and foreign money, M^*, neither of which bears interest, exactly like the Classical model of Chapter 2, although the important difference here is that domestic residents may hold foreign money. Because of the small country assumption, foreign residents do not hold domestic money. This model is examined in Section 6.2.1 below, with the extension by Calvo and Rodriguez (1977) to allow for non-traded goods developed in sub-Section 6.2.2.

6.2.1   The basic model

Asset market equilibrium in this class of model is made up of the wealth identity and equilibrium conditions in both home and foreign money markets. Domestic residents real wealth, w, in terms of foreign currency is defined as:

$$w = M/E + M^* \tag{6.1}$$

where E is the nominal exchange rate (which is equal to P). Domestic residents' real demand functions for the home and foreign asset are given as:

$$L = L(\prod, w) \text{ and } L^* = L^*(\prod, w) \tag{6.2}$$

where

$$L_1 < 0, \ L_2 > 0 \text{ and } L^*_1 > 0, \ L^*_2 > 0$$

with subscripts denoting the partial derivatives of the appropriate variables and where $\prod$ is the expected rate of depreciation of the exchange rate which, through PPP, is identical to the expected rate of inflation and money supply growth. In equilibrium the demands and supplies are equal, so that:

$$M/E = L(\prod, w) \text{ and } M^* = L^*(\prod, w) \tag{6.3}$$

but through the wealth constraint only one of these equations is independent. Therefore substituting for w, from equation (6.1), into the domestic currency equilibrium condition in (6.3) gives:

$$M/E = l\,(\prod, M^*) \tag{6.4}$$

where

$$l_1 = L_1/(1 - L_2) < 0 \text{ and } l_2 = L_2/(1 - L_2) > 0$$

Equation (6.4) is the asset market equilibrium relationship since, if the domestic money market is in equilibrium and wealth is constant, then, via Walras' Law, the domestic market for foreign currency must also be in equilibrium. This relation is shown in Figure 6.1 as the AA schedule, which is drawn for a given expected rate of depreciation and has a positive slope of l_2.

Because foreign residents do not hold domestic currency assets, the only way that domestic residents can acquire foreign currency is by running a current account surplus. This will in turn add to domestic real wealth and appreciate the exchange rate. The current account balance (CAB) is defined as the difference between domestic (consumption) expenditure, C, and output, Y, which is, by definition, equivalent to the change in the domestic holdings of foreign money:

$$\dot{M}^* = \text{CAB} = Y - C(w,Y) \qquad C_1 > 0, C_2 > 0 \qquad (6.5)$$

where a dot above a variable denotes a time derivative and consumption is assumed to be a positive function of domestic real wealth and income. Since Y is fixed at full employment by perfectly flexible prices, it can be dropped from the equation. Then substituting for w, from (6.1) gives:

$$\dot{M}^* = F(w) = F([M/E] + M^*) \qquad F_1 < 0 \qquad (6.6)$$

Substituting for w in the foreign money equilibrium equation (6.3) gives

$$\dot{M}^* = l^*(\textstyle\prod, M/E) \qquad (6.7)$$

where

$$l^*_1 = L^*_1/(1 - L^*_2) > 0 \text{ and } l^*_2 = L^*_2/(1 - L^*_2) > 0$$

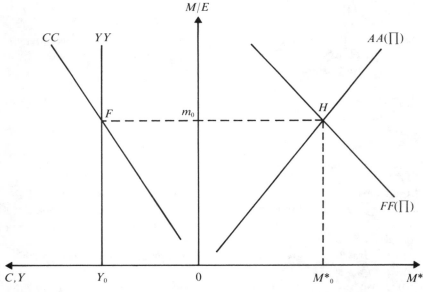

Figure 6.1   Equilibrium in the small-country Currency Substitution Monetary Model (CSMM)

Replacing M/E and $M*$ in (6.6) with their equivalents from (6.4) and (6.7) gives the equation for the balance of payments:

$$\dot{M}* = B(\textstyle\prod, M*, M/E) \tag{6.8}$$

where

$$B_1 = F_1(l_1 + l^*_1) \gtrless 0 \qquad B_2 = F_1 l_2 < 0 \qquad B_3 = F_1 l^*_2 < 0$$

This equation is depicted on Figure 6.1 by the FF schedule, which is drawn for a given level of $\prod$ and along which $\dot{M}* = 0$. It has a slope of $-(l_2/l^*_2) < 0$. To the right of FF, $M*$ is falling and so there is a current account deficit, whereas points to the left of the FF line are points of current account surplus, with $M*$ rising.

The model is in equilibrium where the AA and the FF lines intersect at H, with real domestic money balances of m_0 and foreign money balances of M^*_0. At point H the balance of payments is in equilibrium and so there is no accumulation of foreign money by domestic residents and so the current account must also be in balance. This flow equilibrium is demonstrated in the left-hand quadrant of Figure 6.1. The YY line represents the level of domestic output, which is assumed to be fixed, and the CC line is the level of domestic consumption (absorption), which has a positive slope of $(1/C_1) > 0$, since domestic consumption rises as wealth rises (that is, as E falls for a given level M). Where the CC and YY lines intersect the balance of payments on current account is in equilibrium, with domestic absorption equal to domestic output.

This model can now be used to examine the effects of two types of shock: a flow shock, captured by central bank intervention in the foreign exchange market and a stock disturbance, represented by an increase in the rate of growth of the domestic money supply, which is reflected in a rise in $\prod$.

Central bank purchase of domestic currency   In Figure 6.2 this is illustrated as a fall in foreign money balances from M^*_0 to M^*_1. The wealth constraint of equation (6.1) must be satisfied and so the new temporary equilibrium is at B on the AA line, with lower real home money balances (m_1). In fact, because the domestic money supply, M, is fixed, the exchange rate must have depreciated from E_0 to E_1, thereby raising the value of the foreign money balances held by the non-bank private sector, in order to satisfy the wealth constraint. The point B is not a full equilibrium position, however, because it is below the FF line, and therefore domestic residents are accumulating foreign assets, as is reflected in the current account,

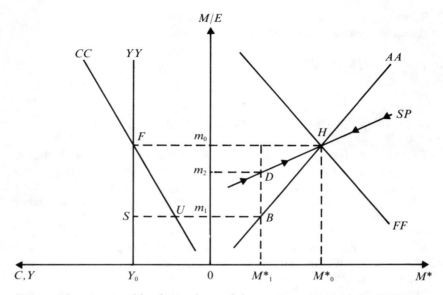

Figure 6.2   A central bank purchase of domestic currency in the CSMM

which is in surplus, shown by the distance SU, in the left-hand quadrant. This surplus has arisen because the depreciation of the exchange rate has made home goods more competitive in foreign markets. This surplus at B is gradually eliminated as the exchange rate starts to appreciate and domestic residents acquire the optimal amount of foreign money. Thus there is a movement up the AA and CC lines, back towards the initial equilibria and at F. Once at F the current account surplus is completely eliminated and stock equilibrium restored. Notice that in this story a flow disturbance has only a transitory effect on the exchange rate and the balance of payments, exactly as in the traditional monetary approach.

The analysis of the previous paragraph is based on the assumption of static exchange rate expectations. Kouri (1976) shows that the analysis is almost identical under perfect foresight expectations, the only difference being the extent of the exchange rate depreciation. Under perfect foresight, $\prod = \dot{E}/E$, hence re-arrangement of equation (6.4) gives:

$$\dot{E}/E = \varepsilon(M/E, M^*) \qquad \varepsilon_1 < 0, \quad \varepsilon_2 > 0 \tag{6.4'}$$

and substituting this into the balance of payments accumulation equation (6.8) and re-arranging gives:

$$\dot{M}^* = b(M/E, M^*) \tag{6.8'}$$

where

$$b_1 = (B_1\varepsilon_1 + B_3) \gtrless 0 \qquad b_2 = (B_1\varepsilon_2 + B_2) \gtrless 0$$

Hence the second order dynamic system is:

$$\begin{bmatrix} \dot{E} \\ \dot{M}^* \end{bmatrix} = \begin{bmatrix} a_1 & a_3 \\ b_1 & b_3 \end{bmatrix} \begin{bmatrix} E \\ M^* \end{bmatrix} \qquad\qquad (6.9)$$

The determinant of the 2×2 matrix is unambiguously negative, indicating a saddle path solution. Moreover, since both coefficients in the top row are positive, the saddle path will have a negative slope in (E, M^*) space and therefore, a positive slope in $(M/E, M^*)$ space. Hence in Figure 6.2, the stable arm of the saddle path will slope up, passing through point H, as indicated by the SP locus. In this case it is now easy to see that an unanticipated purchase of foreign currency by the central bank will again cause an immediate depreciation of the home currency, but this depreciation will not be as great as under static expectations, where E rose to reduce real balances to m_1, because agents will foresee an expected future appreciation of the exchange rate. In this case speculators with long-run perfect foresight cushion the exchange rate against discrete, once-and-for-all changes in the money stock.

An increase in the rate of growth of the money supply   Consider now a stock-shift effect, arising from an increase in the rate of growth of the money supply. Because there is full employment and no interest rates, an increase in the rate of growth of the money supply is equivalent to an increase in the expected rate of depreciation of the exchange rate. In this case, therefore, it makes little sense to assume static expectations, where the exchange is not expected to change, because, if the rate of growth of the money supply is increased, the exchange rate will depreciate faster. Therefore in this case only perfect foresight expectations are considered.

    In terms of Figure 6.3 an actual and expected increase in the rate of growth of the domestic money supply will shift both the AA and the FF schedules. The AA line will move out to the right, to A_1A_1, since home residents will be substituting foreign money for domestic money as the value of domestic money declines and lower domestic real balances will be held in the new long-run equilibrium. The FF line, however, may shift either to the right or the left, depending upon the strength of the substitution effect and therefore the real value of foreign balances held in the new equilibrium may be larger or smaller. Following Kouri, Figure 6.3 assumes that the FF line shifts to the right, which implies that $l_1 > l^*_1$.

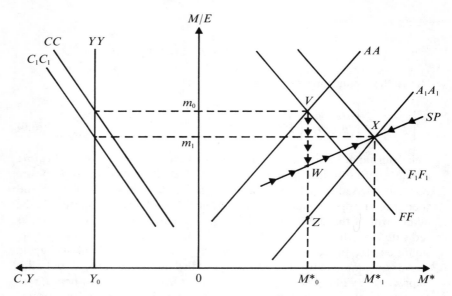

Figure 6.3   An increase in the rate of growth of the money supply in the CSMM

Starting from point V in Figure 6.3, an increase in the rate of growth of the domestic money supply shifts the AA and FF loci to the right, to A_1A_1 and F_1F_1, respectively. The exchange rate will immediately depreciate to W on the stable arm of the saddle path (labelled SP). At this point the current balance is in surplus, despite an increase in consumption, caused by the higher level of real wealth. At W the exchange rate partly reverses its initial depreciation and appreciates up the saddle path towards the new long-run equilibrium at X, where the current account surplus has been completely eliminated and full stock equilibrium is attained.

The assumption that $l_1 > l^*_1$ is important in determining the dynamic path of the exchange rate. It specifically lessens the extent of the depreciation of the home currency and ensures exchange rate overshooting in the short run. If the FF schedule shifted to the left, however, and foreign money balances were the same or lower in the final equilibrium than in the initial position, then there would be no exchange rate overshooting. From Figure 6.3 it can be seen that, if the foreign balances are the same in the final equilibrium, the exchange rate jumps instantaneously to its final equilibrium position at Z without over- or undershooting, whereas if foreign balances are lower in the final equilibrium position the exchange rate will initially undershoot its long-run equilibrium position.

Hence the extent of the exchange rate change and its dynamic adjustment path depend crucially upon the magnitudes of the shifts of the two schedules and on the direction of the movement in the *FF* locus.

In this model expectations about the exchange rate are important for the actual dynamic path that results, but the direction of movement is the same. There is no role for relative prices in this model, the necessary condition for stability being simply that foreign asset accumulation reduces the current account surplus. In the next section the model is extended to include non-traded goods and hence relative price effects.

6.2.2 The model with non-traded goods

This section extends the model of the previous section to include non-traded goods. This follows papers by Calvo and Rodriguez (1977) and Frenkel and Rodriguez (1982) and overcomes one of the criticisms of Kouri's model in that relative price effects are now permitted to influence trade flows.

The structure of the asset markets is identical to Kouri's, hence only the foreign money is traded and equations (6.1) for real wealth and (6.2) and (6.3) for asset demands and supplies are the same. The asset market equilibrium condition is expressed as the ratio of home money to foreign money, so dividing the equation for M/E by M^* in (6.3) gives:

$$[M/(EM^*)] = L/L^* = N(\dot{E}/E) \qquad N_1 < 0 \qquad (6.10)$$

where perfect foresight is assumed and arguments in w are suppressed. Equation (6.10) shows that the desired ratio of home to foreign money declines as the rate of depreciation of the home currency increases.

The main novelty in this model concerns the specification of the goods markets. The home country now produces a traded good and a non-traded good. For the traded good the home country is a price-taker, being only a small supplier in the world market, so the law of price holds, that is: $P^T = EP^{T*}$. For ease of exposition the foreign country price is set equal to one so that $P^T = E$. The relative price of the traded to the non-traded good is given as $q = P^T/P^N$ which can be written as E/P^N and which is equal to the real exchange rate. The production of traded and non-traded goods depends therefore upon their relative price, thus:

$$Y^T = Y^T(q) \qquad \text{where} \qquad Y^T_1 > 0 \qquad (6.11)$$

$$Y^N = Y^N(q) \qquad \text{where} \qquad Y^N_1 < 0 \qquad (6.12)$$

Hence an increase in the relative price of the traded good (q) leads to an increase in the production of the traded good and to a decline in the production of the non-traded good. The demands for the traded good, C^T, and for the non-traded good, C^N, are written as:

$$C^T = C^T(q,w) \qquad \text{where} \qquad C^T_1 < 0, \quad C^T_2 > 0 \qquad (6.13)$$

$$C^N = C^N(q,w) \qquad \text{where} \qquad C^N_1 > 0, \quad C^N_2 > 0 \qquad (6.14)$$

where a rise in the price of the traded good lowers consumption of that good and raises the consumption of the non-traded good and a rise in real wealth raises the demand for both goods.

The market for domestically produced non-traded goods is assumed to clear continuously since prices are perfectly flexible, so that:

$$Y^N(q) = C^N(q,w) \qquad (6.15)$$

Moreover, since $Y^N_1 < 0$, $C^N_1 > 0$ and $C^N_2 > 0$, equation (6.15) defines a unique relationship between q and w, as follows:

$$dq/dw = C^N_2/(Y^N_1 - C^N_1) < 0$$

so that

$$q = q(w) \qquad q_1 < 0 \qquad (6.16)$$

The line $q(w)$ in the left-hand quadrant of Figure 6.4 depicts this equilibrium relationship between the real exchange rate and the level of real wealth. Since the non-traded goods market must clear continuously the model must always be on $q(w)$.

The traded goods market does not have to clear within the country because any excess demand can always be met from imports. Hence any excess of domestic demand for the traded good over domestic production gives rise to a trade balance deficit and a loss of foreign currency, that is:

$$\dot{M}^* = CAB = Y^T(q) - C^T(q,w) \qquad (6.17)$$

Therefore the current account balance will be an upward-sloping locus in (w,q) space, since, as real wealth rises, consumption rises, causing a deterioration in the current account. To offset the effect of a rise in wealth on the current balance a rising real exchange rate is needed. More formally, totally differentiating (6.17) with $CAB = 0$ gives: $dw/dq = [Y^T_1 - C^T_1)/C^T_2] > 0$, which is the slope of the TT locus in Figure 6.4. Note that above

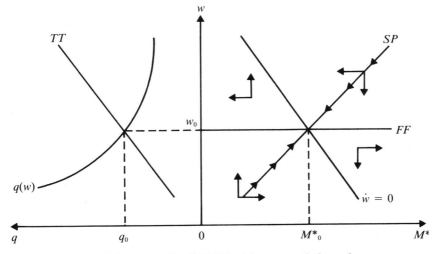

Figure 6.4   Equilibrium in the CSMM with non-traded goods

the *TT* locus are points of trade deficits and below the *TT* line points of surplus. To be on the *TT* line is only a long-run equilibrium requirement.

Using equation (6.16) the accumulation of foreign money balances can be written in terms of the stock of real wealth:

$$\dot{M}^* = m(w) \qquad m_1 > 0 \tag{6.18}$$

The rate of change in the stock of real wealth is given by equation (6.19), where the term $\dot{M}^*$ is given by equation (6.18) and the term in brackets is the time derivative of domestic real money balances, that is the rate of growth of the money supply, $x = \dot{M}/M$ less the percentage change in the exchange rate, $\dot{e} = \dot{E}/E$

$$\dot{w} = (M/E)[x - \dot{e}] + m(w) \tag{6.19}$$

From equation (6.10), for asset market equilibrium, using equation (6.1), $\dot{e}$ can be written as:

$$\dot{e} = (1/N_1)[w - M^*]/M^* \tag{6.20}$$

Substituting into (6.19) gives:

$$\dot{w} = (w - M^*)[x - \{1/N_1\}\{(w/M^*) - 1\}] + m(w) \tag{6.21}$$

Equations (6.18) and (6.21) are the key dynamic equations of the model which are represented diagrammatically in Figure 6.4. From (6.18), if $\dot{M}^* = 0$, then the slope of the foreign asset accumulation schedule will be zero in (w, M^*) space, as shown in Figure 6.4 by the *FF* locus. On the other hand, equation (6.21) may be assumed to have a negative slope, since as M^* rises a depreciation of the exchange rate is necessary to keep real wealth constant, for a given level of the domestic, nominal money supply. The qualitative dynamics of the system are given by the direction arrows on Figure 6.4. These arrows indicate that a saddle path equilibrium must exist for the system to be stable, one such path being denoted by the *SP* line.

Consider now a monetary policy change. In the context of this model, consider the effect of an unexpected increase in the rate of growth of the money supply, μ. From equation (6.21) it can be seen that a rise in μ will shift the $\dot{w} = 0$ line out to the right, from $\dot{w} = 0$ to $\dot{w}_1 = 0$ in Figure 6.5. At the initial equilibrium point A, the exchange rate will depreciate to B, overshooting its long-run level. At B, however, real wealth has fallen, but because the non-traded goods market must clear the real exchange rate, q, must rise to maintain the model on $q(w)$. The higher real exchange rate reduces consumption of traded goods and encourages the consumption of non-traded goods, while simultaneously encouraging the production of traded goods relative to non-traded goods. Hence at B a trade surplus emerges which gives rise to a gradual appreciation of the exchange rate and an accumulation of foreign money. Stock equilibrium is re-estab-

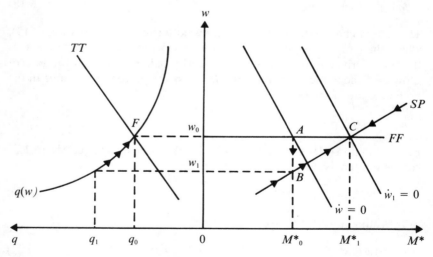

Figure 6.5   *An unanticipated rise in monetary growth in the CSMM with non-traded goods*

lished at point C in Figure 6.5, where the foreign money holdings are higher, reflecting the higher level of real wealth.

In the Currency Substitution Monetary Models (CSMM) considered up to now, instantaneous stock adjustment has been a specific feature, as has the need to consider changes in the rates of growth of the money supply, rather than the stock of money as in Classical monetary model. In the final model of this chapter, an alternative, arguably more general, model is developed to address these issues.

6.3   A model with slow asset market adjustment

The models of Kouri and Calvo and Rodriguez have addressed the question of stock–flow interaction in models with instantaneous stock adjustment and perfect foresight expectations. Exchange rate dynamics depended upon an increase in the rate of growth of the money supply, rather than a change in the level of the money supply. The model in this section, due to Niehans (1977), does not assume perfect foresight or instantaneous stock adjustment, although it still permits full stock–flow interaction. This model shows that exchange rate dynamics are extremely complicated and that many dynamic adjustment paths are plausible.

The economy is assumed to be small with flexible prices maintaining goods and labour market equilibrium enabling the analysis to focus on the asset markets. Domestic residents hold two assets, domestic money and foreign money, which are imperfect substitutes in that positive balances of both monies are held in equilibrium. Under full employment the domestic demand for each asset is a constant-elasticity function of the expected depreciation of the domestic currency. In logarithms these asset demand functions are written as:

$$l - p = \alpha + \lambda(e - \bar{e}) \tag{6.22}$$

$$l^* - p^* = \alpha^* - \lambda^*(e - \bar{e}) \tag{6.23}$$

where $l - p$ is the desired demand for real domestic money balances, λ denotes the constant elasticity of the demand for real balances with respect to the expected change in the exchange rate, with all parameters defined to be greater than zero, and asterisks denote foreign-money de-nominated variables. The problem of exchange rate expectations is by-passed by Niehans who assumes that the expected rate and the equilibrium rate, $\bar{e}$, are the same for given levels of the exogenous variables and that the speed with which the actual exchange rate adjusts to the expected equilibrium rate does not matter. The adjustment of actual asset stocks to desired demands is not instantaneous, the real money balances being adjusted by a constant proportion of the difference between desired and actual balances:

$$\dot{m} - \dot{p} = \mu(l-m) \tag{6.24}$$

$$\dot{m}^* - \dot{p}^* = \mu^*(l^*-m^*) \tag{6.25}$$

where μ, $\mu^* > 0$ and dots above a variable denote time derivatives. The domestic money supply is assumed to be an exogenously given constant as is the foreign price level, so that the equations for l and l^* can be substituted into (6.24) and (6.25) to obtain dynamic equations for p and m^*, respectively, to give:

$$\dot{p} = -\mu[\alpha + \lambda(e-\bar{e}) + p-m] \tag{6.26}$$

$$\dot{m}^* = \mu^*[\alpha^* - \lambda^*(e-\bar{e}) + p^* - m^*] \tag{6.27}$$

Equation (6.26) shows that domestic prices are determined by the excess demand for domestic cash balances and equation (6.27) shows that capital exports depend upon the excess demand for foreign cash balances. In Figure 6.6, the domestic zero inflation locus is denoted by $\dot{p} = 0$. This has a slope of $-(1/\lambda)$ from equation (6.26), and is drawn in (e, p) space for given values of the domestic money supply and the equilibrium exchange rate.

Under floating exchange rates the change in private foreign cash balances is equal to the current account balance. Therefore, if the current balance depends only upon the real exchange rate, with the foreign price level normalized to unity, balance of payments equilibrium can be expressed as:

$$\dot{m}^* = \delta - \beta(p-e) \qquad \beta > 0 \tag{6.28}$$

where β represents the sum of the demand elasticities of home exports and imports which will be less than unity, if the Marshall–Lerner condition is to be satisfied.[1] A rise in e (a depreciation) will therefore improve the trade balance of the home country, thereby leading to a larger current account surplus and greater export of capital. When the current account of the balance of payments is in balance there will be no foreign capital accumulation or decumulation. In Figure 6.6, therefore, current account balance is given by the $\dot{m}^* = 0$ locus. This has a slope of unity, from (6.28), since a depreciation of the exchange rate must be exactly matched by a rise in the domestic price level to maintain a constant real exchange rate and current account balance.

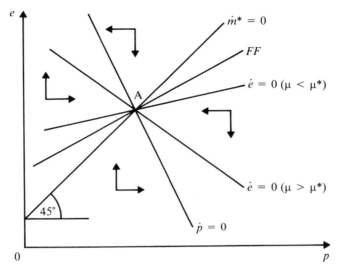

Figure 6.6   Equilibrium in Niehans' currency substitution model (CSMM)

Equating equations (6.27) and (6.28) for the capital flow and the current account balance respectively enables an expression to be derived for the exchange rate consistent with balance of payments equilibrium; that is:

$$e = (\beta + \mu^*\lambda^*)^{-1}[\beta p - \mu^* m^* + c_1] \tag{6.29}$$

where $c_1 = [\mu^*(\alpha^* + \lambda^* e + p^*) - \delta]$. In Figure 6.6, this balance of payments equilibrium condition is denoted by the *FF* line. It has a positive slope because a rise in the domestic price level must be offset by a depreciation of the exchange rate if equilibrium is to be maintained. Formally, the slope is given by $[\beta/(\beta + \mu^*\lambda^*)] > 0$ from (6.29), which shows that the slope depends not only upon the responsiveness of the trade account to changes in the real exchange rate, but also on the speed of adjustment of foreign money balances and the elasticity of foreign money balances with respect to the exchange rate. In Figure 6.6, points to the right of the *FF* locus are points of balance of payments deficit, since the price level is too high for a given value of the exchange rate, while all points to the left of *FF* are points of balance of payments surplus.

The exchange rate dynamics are given by differentiating equation (6.29) with respect to time and substituting for p and m^* from (6.26) and (6.28). This gives:

$$\dot{e} = (\beta + \mu^*\lambda^*)^{-1}\beta[(\mu^* - \mu)p - (\mu^* + \mu\lambda)e + \mu(\lambda e + m)] + c_2 \tag{6.30}$$

where the constant

$$c_2 = (\beta + \mu^*\lambda^*)^{-1}[c_1 - \beta\mu\alpha - \mu^*\delta]$$

The exchange rate equilibrium line, defined by $\dot{e} = 0$, may have a positive or negative slope, depending upon the relative speeds of adjustment of the domestic and foreign money demands. If the domestic money market clears faster than the foreign market, so that $\mu > \mu^*$, then the $\dot{e} = 0$ schedule has a negative slope, and if $\mu < \mu^*$ the schedule has a positive slope. These alternative schedules are shown in Figure 6.6. For given values of e and m (6.26) and (6.30) are a system of linear differential equations in p and e. The system is stable with a positive determinant and a negative trace, given by:

$$Det = [\mu(\mu^* + \mu\lambda) + \mu^* - \mu] > 0 \qquad (6.31)$$

$$Tr = -\mu - \beta(\beta + \mu^*\lambda^*)^{-1}(\mu^* + \mu\lambda) < 0 \qquad (6.32)$$

The direction arrows in Figure 6.6 confirm the stability of the system. A perverse reaction of the trade balance, however, if strong enough, could result in some instability, although this possibility is ignored here.

The following set of Figures 6.7 to 6.9 show three kinds of dynamic adjustment and time paths for the exchange rate. Figure 6.7 assumes that foreign real money balances adjust more slowly than domestic balances so that $\mu^* < \mu$ and the $\dot{e} = 0$ line has a negative slope. Starting from point A an increase in the domestic money supply will raise the equilibrium price level and nominal exchange rate to p_1 and e_1 respectively. To maintain balance of payments equilibrium the exchange rate must initially depreciate to be on the FF line at point B. The direction arrows from point B indicate that the exchange rate will not overshoot the long-run equilibrium, and therefore adjustment is monotonic to the stable equilibrium at C. The flow lines in the diagram show that the price level may or may not overshoot during the adjustment process. Note, however, that this overshooting is not an inherent feature of the model dynamics, but a possible feature of the adjustment process itself.

Figure 6.8 illustrates the alternative case with domestic money balances assumed to adjust more slowly than foreign money balances, so that $\dot{e} = 0$ is upward-sloping. After an initial exchange rate depreciation from A to B, prices and the exchange rate rise towards the new equilibrium at C. In the early part of the adjustment process prices and the exchange rate move in the same direction, although the exchange rate may oscillate as it approaches the new equilibrium, when prices and the exchange rate may

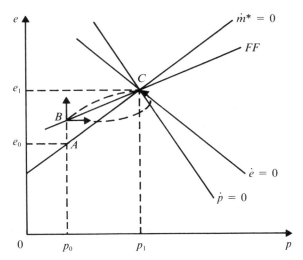

Figure 6.7   An increase in domestic money supply in Niehans' CSMM with
$\mu^* < \mu$

move in opposite directions. As drawn in the figure, the balance of payments is in surplus in the early stages of the adjustment process (that is above $\dot{m}^* = 0$ schedule) although it moves into deficit in the second part of the adjustment process.

Figure 6.9 illustrates a third case. Again domestic money balances are assumed to adjust more slowly than foreign balances, although in this case the $\dot{e} = 0$ line is assumed to be steeper than the *FF* line. In this case there is an immediate depreciation of the exchange rate, followed by an appreciation (and a fall in the domestic price level) which reduces the trade balance surplus and pushes it into deficit. The exchange rate resumes its depreciation which may lead to both the exchange rate and the price level overshooting the final equilibrium at *C* in the course of the adjustment process.

This model demonstrates that overshooting is a temporary phenomenon which depends on the relative speeds of adjustment of home and foreign asset markets. The model postulates a regressive exchange rate expectations hypothesis, although the speed of adjustment is assumed to be equal to unity for simplicity. Values of greater or less than unity do not change the dynamics. In the case of static expectations, where $e = \bar{e}$, the adjustment path is along the *FF* line, which in this case is identical to the $\dot{m}^* = 0$ line. Prices and the exchange rate therefore rise and fall together in equal proportion, since the slope of the *FF* line is unity. With perfect

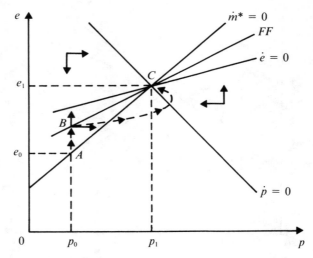

Figure 6.8   An increase in domestic money supply in Niehans' CSMM with
$\mu^* > \mu$

foresight expectations the model can be shown to be unstable, although this mathematical result makes no economic sense, since with slowly adjusting asset markets there are no economic forces to make the exchange rate jump onto a stable saddle path.

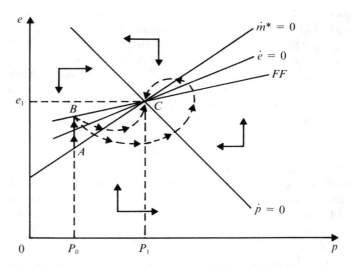

Figure 6.9   Exchange rate overshooting in Niehans' CSMM

This chapter has discussed two principal models of exchange rate dynamics featuring currency substitution which integrate both capital account flows and trade balance flows as joint determinants of the exchange rate. The principal limitation of these models is the restricted asset choice to only foreign and domestic money excluding all interest-bearing assets.[2] Such assets will be included in the next chapter on portfolio balance models of the exchange rate. Before this extension is considered a brief review of the empirical evidence on currency substitution is provided.

6.4   Empirical evidence for currency substitution

The evidence for currency substitution is not strong, although this may reflect the difficulty of distinguishing between capital mobility and currency substitution. Capital mobility consists of two hypotheses: that of asset substitutability and speed of asset market adjustment. If the speed of adjustment is assumed to be instantaneous, as in the models of Kouri and Calvo and Rodriguez, then currency substitution can be regarded as a sub-set of asset substitution. Moreover, the reasons for domestic residents holding foreign currency, which, typically carries low or zero rates of interest, are perhaps more likely to be related to transactions balances held as a consequence of trade flows, which in turn, are likely to be a small proportion of total money holdings with a low interest rate elasticity.

The currency substitution models of the exchange rate discussed in this chapter have not been explicitly tested like the other models of the exchange rate in Chapters 4 and 5. The reason for this is that this class of exchange rate models only really capture the notion of direct currency substitution. By excluding interest rates from the demand for money functions, they also exclude bond markets from the analysis and hence the possibility of indirect currency substitution between domestic and foreign currencies. McKinnon (1982), as noted in the introduction to this chapter, has argued that this kind of indirect substitution is likely to be more important than that of direct substitution. For this reason this class of exchange rate models may be regarded as of limited empirical validity.

Tests of the currency substitution exchange rate models have been based upon a version of the monetary approach without full stock–flow interaction. In these models the coefficient on the interest rate, or interest rate differential, is interpreted as the coefficient of currency substitution, although this could equally be interpreted as the degree of substitution between money and bonds. This problem of how to interpret the interest rate coefficient plagues all empirical studies of currency substitution.

Miles (1978, 1981) provided one of the first tests of currency substitution. The non-bank private sector is assumed to hold M_0/P cash balances out of the total wealth real wealth, w. Miles assumes that domestic and foreign real money balances are inputs into a constant elasticity of substitution production function for money services. This production function is maximized subject to an asset constraint of the form:

$$M_0/P = (1+r)(M/P) + (1+r^*)(M^*/P^*) \tag{6.33}$$

which reflects the assumption that there is an opportunity cost to holding real cash balances, r, and that this opportunity cost may differ between domestic and foreign balances. Maximizing the money services production function, subject to the asset constraint and assuming purchasing power parity (PPP) is maintained, Miles obtains:

$$ln(M/M^*E) = \alpha + \sigma ln[(1+r)/(1+r^*)] \tag{6.34}$$

where σ is the elasticity of substitution between domestic and foreign money. This equation was used by Miles to test for currency substitution between the Canadian residents' Canadian dollar and the US dollar holdings, US residents' US dollar and foreign currency holdings and West German residents' German Deutsche Mark and foreign currency holdings. A summary of the results is presented in Table 6.1. For each of the countries the elasticity of substitution is significant in the floating exchange rate period. A general weakness of these results is that when foreign interest rates rise domestic residents may switch from both domestic and foreign money into foreign bonds. In other words, the size and significance of σ may reflect, at least in part, the elasticity of substitution between foreign bonds and foreign money, rather than simply currency substitution. Moreover, the estimates do not appear to be particularly robust, with the Durbin–Watson statistics in equations [1] and [3], suggesting a dynamic misspecification of the model.

In a recent paper, Bergstrand and Bundt (1990) employ the cointegration methodology to test for currency substitution on private sector non-bank foreign dollar holdings, using a similar theoretical framework to Miles. Evidence is reported in favour of long-run currency substitution, which is strongest for Italy (rationalized by Italy's high and variable rates of inflation), although the evidence does not support short-run currency substitution. There are, however, a number of limitations in this work. The long-run cointegrating vectors are not reported, which means that the impact effects of the individual variables cannot be ascertained. This omission is rather surprising since the long-run results are claimed to be the strongest. Secondly, a coefficient of unity is imposed on the price level, but recent work by Pentecost and Mizen (1992) suggests that this restriction is unlikely to be supported by the data.

Table 6.1 Miles' estimates of currency substitution

	[1]	[2]	[3]
α	2.79	5.61	3.71
	(16.1)	(39.3)	(5.70)
σ	5.78	5.08	2.78
	(1.83)	(3.38)	(2.23)
R^2	0.79	0.72	0.89
DW	1.27	1.96	2.28
rho	0.80	0.81	0.97

where *t*-values are in parentheses and *DW* is the Durbin-Watson statistic.

Notes
[1] Canadian $–US $ for the period 1970 Q3–1975 Q4.
[2] US $–foreign currency holdings, for the period 1971 Q3–1978 Q3.
[3] German DMark–foreign currency holdings, for the period 1971 Q3–1978 Q3.

Source: Miles (1978, 1981).

Cuddington (1983) estimates a domestic demand for real money balances function of log-linear form:

$$m - p = \beta_0 + \beta_1 y - \beta_2 r - \beta_3(r^* + x) - \beta_4 x + \beta_5(m - p)_{t-1} \qquad (6.35)$$

where y is the log-level of real income, r is the nominal rate of interest, x is the expected depreciation of the home currency (proxied by the forward premium) and where the coefficient β_4 is interpreted as measuring the extent of currency substitution. Cuddington finds that, using data from the 1960s and 1970s for the UK, Canada, the USA and West Germany, both for narrow and broad measures of money, the hypothesis of currency substitution is only evident from the West German data. Moreover, the extent of capital mobility, measured by β_3, is only significant for the USA. Cuddington's results are also subject to a number of econometric problems. In particular, the presence of serial correlation suggests that the model is misspecified, and if interest rates are endogenous variables, then the estimates will also be subject to simultaneous equations bias.

Pentecost and Mizen (1992) test for currency substitution between sterling balances held by non-residents and the principal local foreign currencies within the European Monetary System, between March 1976 and December 1989 using a SURE framework (Zellner, 1962). They find that UK sterling balances held by non-residents are not close substitutes for local foreign currency balances in either the short or the long run, using both the money services production function framework of Miles and the portfolio balance model of Cuddington. These results are therefore very much in line with the earlier evidence summarized by Spinelli (1983), who concluded that currency substitution is never found to be high, not even for two highly integrated economies, such as the USA and Canada, and that statistically significant cross-elasticities are not easy to detect with estimated values so low that they tend to fall between one-quarter and one-tenth of those for the own interest rate elasticities.

6.5 Conclusions

The currency substitution models presented in this chapter represent a theoretical advance on the models of earlier chapters by integrating both capital and trade account influences on the exchange rate. The exchange rate is therefore determined jointly by financial markets and goods markets, through the interaction of stock and flow variables. The principal limitation of these models is that the asset choice is very restricted, consisting only of domestic currency and foreign currency and hence the models only allow for direct currency substitution, which, as noted at the outset, is likely to be rather less significant than indirect substitution.

The econometric evidence for the existence of currency substitution is very weak. Although the evidence presented in this chapter is not entirely consistent with the theoretical models presented here, since interest rates (and implicitly bond markets) are present, it provides little encouragement for this class of exchange rate models. Exchange rate models in which domestic money, domestic bond and foreign bond markets all interact are the subject of the portfolio balance models in the next chapter.

Notes

1. See Chapter 3
2. Note, however, a recent paper by Zervoyianni (1988) which introduces the domestic and foreign bond markets into a model of currency substitution. This is very similar to the portfolio balance approach, which is discussed in Chapter 7, and summarized, complete with currency substitution extensions, by Branson and Henderson (1985).

7 The portfolio balance approach

7.1 Introduction

The portfolio balance models of exchange rate determination stem from the work on portfolio theory and the demand for money by Markowitz (1952) and Tobin (1958). The central feature of the portfolio balance approach to exchange rate determination is that domestic and foreign non-money assets are assumed to be imperfect substitutes, rather than perfect substitutes as in the monetary and Mundell–Fleming approaches (see Chapters 4 and 5, respectively). In these models money is usually assumed to be non-traded so that only domestic residents hold domestic money, although Branson and Henderson (1985) and Zervoyianni (1988) also allow for currency substitution. Because domestic and foreign assets are only imperfect substitutes, uncovered interest rate parity does not hold in this class of model. Thus international investors will hold a diversified portfolio of non-money assets, the proportion of each asset in the portfolio depending upon its particular risk-return characteristics. These particular risk characteristics may include such factors as default risk, exchange rate risk, political risk and differential tax liabilities, all of which serve to drive a wedge between the yields on similar securities.

Stock–flow interaction is introduced into the portfolio balance model by making the demand for domestic money and assets depend upon the level of non-bank private wealth. Private-sector wealth is accumulated and decumulated through current account surpluses and deficits, as in the currency substitution models of Chapter 6, which in turn affects the exchange rate and the level of private-sector wealth, which in turn feed back into private expenditures and the demand for money. It is important to note that the inclusion of wealth effects is distinct from imperfect asset substitutability. Wealth effects have been added to the Mundell–Fleming model with perfect capital mobility by Branson and Buiter (1983), Pentecost (1984) and Driskill and McCafferty (1985) to give results for the exchange rate that are in many respects identical to those developed in this chapter.

The portfolio balance model has its origins in the Keynesian tradition of fixed prices (McKinnon and Oates, 1966; Branson, 1968), although it has recently been used in a Classical framework by Dornbusch and Fischer (1980). In this chapter the former approach is employed, although this is not important for the conclusions reached. Indeed, the model developed here largely assumes away the real side of the economy. The goods market can be introduced, as demonstrated by Allen and Kenen (1978) and Branson and Buiter (1983), but at the cost of much greater complexity, without adding much to the understanding of the exchange rate dynamics.

This chapter is divided into five sections, as follows. In Section 7.2 the short-run asset market-clearing relations are set out with imperfect capital mobility, and the exchange rate dynamics examined under both static and perfect foresight expectations. In Section 7.3 the empirical evidence for the portfolio balance approach is considered. This is not as well developed as that for the monetary models of the exchange rate since the reduced form typically includes the levels of foreign and domestic bond stocks outstanding held by both domestic and foreign residents, on which data are generally not available. The lack of data on the ownership of foreign currency assets has led to indirect tests of the portfolio balance model through the interest rate parity condition. These tests are considered in Section 7.4 where evidence of non-zero risk premia can be regarded as evidence of imperfect asset substitutability and hence supportive of the Portfolio Balance Model (PBKM). Section 7.5 summarizes the main results from this chapter.

7.2   A portfolio balance model

This section is divided into two parts. In sub-section 7.2.1 the short-run, static portfolio balance model of the non-bank private sector with imperfect asset substitutability is set out, without reference to the real sector of the economy. In sub-section 7.2.2 the dynamics of the exchange rate are considered under different assumptions about exchange rate expectations.

7.2.1   Short-run asset market equilibrium

Total domestic nominal wealth, W, is made up of domestic residents' holding of domestic money, M, domestic residents' holdings of domestic bonds, B, and domestic residents' holdings of foreign currency assets, F^*. Domestic residents are assumed not to hold foreign currency, M^*. Therefore domestic non-bank private sector wealth, measured in domestic currency, is defined as:

$$W = M + B + EF^* \tag{7.1}$$

where E is the exchange rate defined in terms of the domestic price of foreign currency. The asset market equilibrium conditions for each of these three assets are given as:

$$M = m(r, r^* + \varepsilon\dot{e})W \qquad m_1 < 0, m_2 < 0 \tag{7.2}$$

$$B = b(r, r^* + \varepsilon\dot{e})W \qquad b_1 > 0, b_2 < 0 \tag{7.3}$$

$$EF^* = f(r, r^* + \varepsilon\dot{e})W \qquad f_1 < 0, f_2 > 0 \tag{7.4}$$

where $\varepsilon\dot{e}$ is the expected change in the exchange rate. The principal characteristic of the demand equations (7.2) to (7.4) is that the scale variable is the level of wealth and that the demand functions are all homogeneous in wealth, which allows them to be written in nominal terms (assuming homogeneity in prices and real wealth, prices cancel out) as in Tobin (1969). The asset supplies are exogenous and fixed. Equation (7.2) shows that money demand is inversely related to the yields on both domestic and foreign securities. Equations (7.3) and (7.4) indicate that domestic and foreign bond demands depend positively upon the own rate of interest and inversely on the rate of interest on the other asset. The assets are assumed to be gross substitutes, so that $|b_1| > |f_1|$ and $|f_2| > |b_2|$. The case where the assets are perfect substitutes is given by, $f_1 = b_2 \to \infty$, in which case equations (7.3) and (7.4) collapse to the uncovered interest rate parity condition:

$$r = r^* + \varepsilon\dot{e} \tag{7.5}$$

and the financial sector of the model collapses to the money market equilibrium condition, given by (7.2) and the interest rate parity condition given by (7.5), as in the Mundell–Fleming model[1] of Chapter 5.

The three asset market equilibrium equations can be depicted in (E,r) space, for given levels of $r^* + \varepsilon\dot{e}$ and asset stocks, as in Figure 7.1, where the MM locus gives money market equilibrium. It has a positive slope, given by:

$$[dE/dr]_{MM} = -(Wm_1/mF^*) > 0$$

A rise in E will require a rise in the home rate of interest to maintain money market equilibrium. This comes about because a rise in E raises the domestic currency value of foreign bonds, thereby increasing wealth. The higher level of wealth raises the demand for domestic money and, with the supply of domestic money fixed, the domestic rate of interest must rise to eliminate the excess demand and restore equilibrium. The BB locus has a negative slope given by:

$$[dE/dr]_{BB} = -(Wb_1/bF^*) < 0.$$

In this case, the rise in domestic wealth caused by a rise in E, creates an

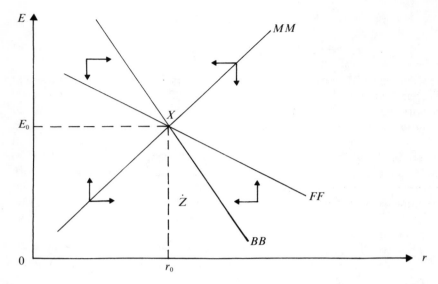

*Figure 7.1   Asset market equilibrium in the Portfolio Balance (Keynesian)
Model (PBKM)*

excess demand for bonds which, for a given supply, is eliminated by a rise
in the price of bonds and a fall in the rate of interest. The *FF* line,
representing the equilibrium in the market for foreign bonds has a negative slope, given by:

$$[dE/dr]_{FF} = Wf_1/(1-f)F^* < 0.$$

As the domestic rate of interest rises, the domestic demand for foreign
bonds falls as domestic residents substitute domestic for foreign bonds in
their portfolios. As foreign assets are sold, the foreign currency proceeds
are converted into home currency, thus bidding up the exchange rate (that
is a fall in E). Hence the *FF* line has a negative slope. It is reasonable to
assume that a change in the domestic rate of interest will have a larger
effect upon the domestic bond market than on the foreign bond market,
since the assets are gross substitutes, and hence the *BB* line is steeper than
the *FF* line.[2]

The intersection of the *MM, BB* and *FF* lines gives the short-run
equilibrium levels of the exchange rate and the domestic interest rate. In
fact, because of the wealth constraint, only two of the three market
equilibrium equations are independent, so the analysis can proceed using
just two of these loci. Before proceeding, however, it is necessary to

examine the local stability of the model. Stability requires that the domestic rate of interest rises in response to an excess supply of bonds or an excess demand for money. Formally:

$$dr/dt = \mu(m-M) \qquad\qquad dr/dt = \beta(B-b) \qquad\qquad\qquad (7.6)$$

where μ, $\beta > 0$. Given that $m_1 < 0$ and $b_1 > 0$, stability is assured. More intuitively, in Figure 7.1 all points to the right of the *BB* line are points of excess demand for domestic bonds and so the rate of interest needs to fall, as given by the horizontal arrows, and conversely for points to the left of the *BB* line. All points to the right (and above) the *FF* locus are points of excess supply of foreign assets, so the exchange rate needs to rise (a fall in *E*) to reduce the domestic currency value of the existing stock of foreign currency assets, as shown by the vertical arrows in Figure 7.1. Thus, starting from a disequilibrium position such as *Z*, in Figure 7.1, the system is seen to converge on the equilibrium at *X*.

The short-run comparative static effects of changes in the (exogenous) stocks of each of the domestically held assets is investigated in Figures 7.2 to 7.6. Consider a 'helicopter' increase in the supply of domestic money. At point *A* in Figure 7.2 there will now be an excess supply of money and an excess demand for both foreign and domestic bonds. The excess demand for domestic bonds drives up the price of domestic bonds, thereby lowering the rate of interest for each level of *E* and shifting the *BB* line to the left, to BB_1. The excess demand for foreign bonds results in domestic residents exchanging domestic currency for foreign currency, to purchase foreign bonds, thereby causing *E* to rise as the domestic currency falls in value. For each level of interest the exchange rate must be lower (*E* higher), so the *FF* line will shift up to the right, to FF_1. The new equilibrium will be established at *B*, which is above and to the left of *A*, where the exchange rate has depreciated and the interest rate has fallen.

The effect of an increase in the domestic bond supply, ignoring the effect of the open market sale on the money supply, is illustrated in Figure 7.3. In this case the interest rate will rise, but the exchange rate may rise or fall, depending upon the substitutability of domestic and foreign bonds. In both panels of Figure 7.3 the *BB* schedule shifts out to the right, to BB_1, since the higher supply of bonds will lower domestic bond prices and drive up the yield at each level of *E*. The higher level of wealth for each level of *r* will lead to the purchase of foreign currency by domestic residents as they attempt to purchase higher-yielding foreign bonds, which in turn will depreciate the domestic currency, leading to a rise in *E*. Hence the *FF* line will shift up to the right to FF_1 in both panels of Figure 7.3. The extent of the shift in the *FF* line is all important for the final effect on the exchange

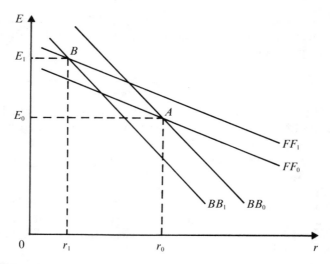

Figure 7.2   A pure monetary expansion in the PBKM

rate. If domestic and foreign assets are close substitutes, then the rise in r will cause substitution into domestic bonds which will dominate the wealth effect, leading to greater purchases of foreign bonds. In this case the shift in the *FF* line will be relatively small, as in panel A, and the net effect for the exchange rate will be an appreciation (a fall in E). If, on the other hand, domestic and foreign bonds are not very close substitutes, then the wealth effect will dominate, making the demand for foreign bonds stronger and hence giving rise to a larger shift of the *FF* line to the right, as shown in panel *B* of Figure 7.3. In this case the exchange rate is lower in the final equilibrium, at E_1.

Next consider an increase in the domestic holdings of foreign assets. This will lead to an excess supply of foreign assets (and hence foreign currency). The price of foreign currency will continue to fall until the new value of foreign bond holdings is exactly equal to the initial value, with wealth restored to its initial level. In this case the *FF* line will shift to the left, as in Figure 7.4, since the higher supply of foreign assets will only be willingly held at a lower price, and the *BB* line will also shift to the left since the fall in wealth will reduce the demand for domestic assets at each price, necessitating a fall in the interest rate at each level of E. Thus the rise in F^* leads to an appreciation of the exchange rate with r unchanged. This is illustrated in Figure 7.4 by a downward movement of the short-run equilibrium, from A to B.

As noted above, the authorities' monetary policy actions usually

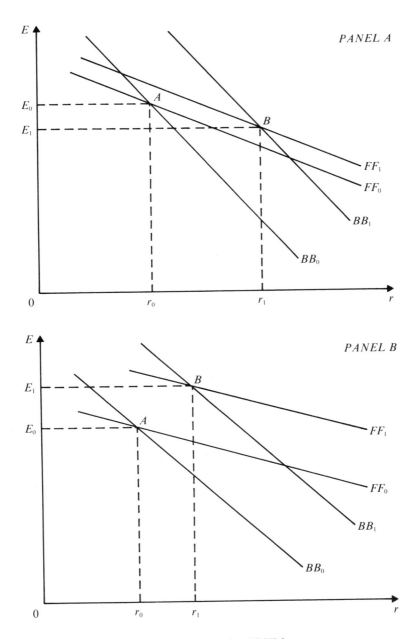

Figure 7.3   A pure bond expansion in the PBKM

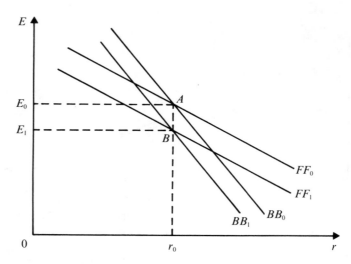

Figure 7.4   An increase in domestic residents' holdings of foreign debt in the PBKM

involve an exchange of domestic money for either domestic bonds or foreign bonds, or some combination of the two. Thus a net repurchase of government debt from the private sector means that $\triangle M = - \triangle B$ and a repurchase of foreign assets implies that $\triangle M = - E \triangle F$. Figure 7.5 shows these cases. Consider a net repurchase of domestic bonds by the authorities. In order to persuade domestic residents to sell their bonds back to the authorities, the latter will offer favourable prices, thereby lowering yields, which will in turn raise the demand for money. Hence the exchange of bonds for money will shift the *MM* line to the left in panel A, since, for any given value of *E*, *r* must be lower for the money stock to be willingly held. The *BB* locus will also shift to the left as, for a given level of *E*, a fall in the interest rate is necessary to persuade residents to part with bonds. Since the *FF* line is negatively sloped and flatter than the *BB* line, the new equilibrium position will be at point *B*, above and to the left of the initial equilibrium at point *A*. The exchange rate has therefore depreciated and the interest rate has fallen. The qualitative effects of the government exchanging money for foreign bonds are identical, although the quantitative effects are different. In panel B of Figure 7.5 the *MM* line moves to the left as before, while the *FF* line shifts up to the right, since the excess demand for foreign bonds will be reduced by a depreciation of the exchange rate for any level of *r*. Hence the new equilibrium will be above, and to the left, of the original equilibrium at *A*, as *BB* is downward-

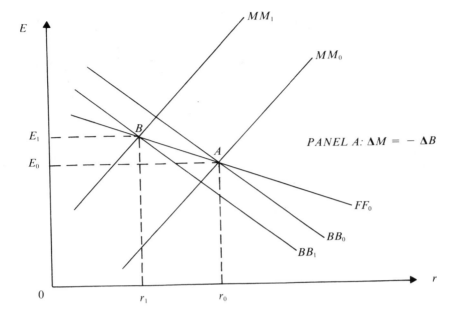

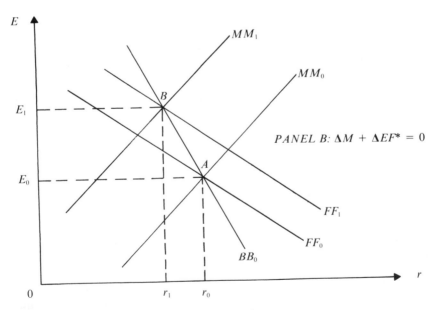

Figure 7.5   Debt repurchase in the PBKM

sloping. Because *BB* is steeper than *FF*, however, the rise in *E* is greater in panel B than in panel A. This result is entirely intuitive. Open market purchases of domestic assets affect *r* directly while open market purchases of foreign assets affect *E* directly. Thus the real impact of monetary policy on the real sector of the economy, via *r* and *E*, will depend upon the mix of the open market operations.

7.2.2   Exchange rate dynamics

In the portfolio balance model exchange rate dynamics require the specification of a wealth accumulation equation and a hypothesis about exchange rate expectations.

Wealth accumulation is assumed to occur only through the purchase of foreign currency assets, since domestic asset stocks are assumed fixed and the government budget in balance. Thus, with domestic output omitted for simplicity, the current account balance (in foreign currency) can be written as

$$dF^*/dt = \text{CAB} = T(E,W,i) + r^*F^* \qquad T_1 > 0,\ T_2, T_3 < 0 \qquad (7.7)$$

where T represents the trade balance which depends directly upon the (real) exchange rate and inversely upon the level of domestic non-bank private sector wealth, W, and an exogenous import shock parameter, i. The term r^*F^* represents net interest income from domestic holdings of foreign currency assets. If the economy has traditionally been a net capital exporter, so that r^*F^* is positive, then a trade deficit is needed to give current account balance and zero wealth accumulation in the long-run equilibrium.

Linearizing equation (7.7), with r^* assumed constant, gives a slope for $\dot{F}^* = 0$ of:

$$dE/dF^* = -(ET_2 + r^*)/(T_1 + T_2F^*) \gtrless 0 \qquad (7.8)$$

The denominator will be positive if the Marshall–Lerner condition holds,[3] although the numerator can be either positive or negative, depending upon the relative size of ET_2 and r^*. If ET_2 is large relative to r^* then the $\dot{F}^* = 0$ line has a positive slope. This implies that any rise is wealth is spent, in significant proportion, on foreign goods, which causes the trade balance to deteriorate and the exchange rate to depreciate. If, on the other hand, any increase in domestic residents wealth is only spent on domestic goods, then $T_2 = 0$, and the $\dot{F}^* = 0$ schedule has a negative slope. In fact the slope of the $\dot{F}^* = 0$ is not crucial for stability, providing that, if negatively sloped, the $\dot{F}^* = 0$ schedule is flatter than the $\dot{E} = 0$ schedule in the neighbourhood of the intersection (see Figure 7.6).

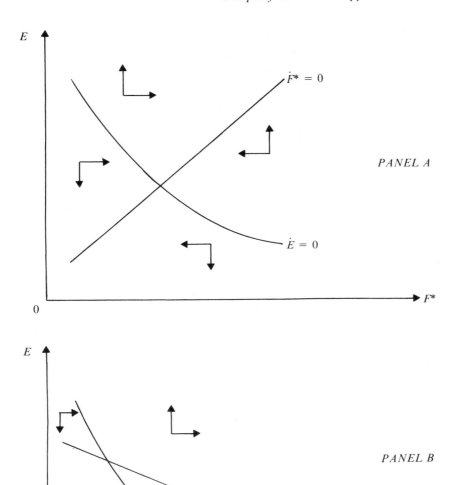

Figure 7.6   Equilibrium in the PBKM with perfect foresight

Agents are assumed to form their expectations of exchange rate changes according to the perfect foresight expectations hypothesis, in which case $\varepsilon \dot{e} = \dot{e}$. Since only two of equations (7.2) to (7.4) are independent owing to the wealth constraint, linearized versions of equations (7.2) and (7.4) give solutions for r and $\dot{e}$, as follows, assuming that r^* is constant:

$$\begin{bmatrix} EF^*/W \\ M/W \end{bmatrix} = \begin{bmatrix} f_1 & f_2 \\ m_1 & m_2 \end{bmatrix} \begin{bmatrix} r \\ \dot{e} \end{bmatrix} \tag{7.9}$$

which implies that

$$\begin{bmatrix} r \\ \dot{e} \end{bmatrix} = [f_1 m_2 - m_1 f_2]^{-1} \begin{bmatrix} m_2 & -f_2 \\ -m_1 & f_1 \end{bmatrix} \begin{bmatrix} EF^*/W \\ M/W \end{bmatrix} \tag{7.10}$$

so that $\dot{e}$ is given by

$$\dot{e} = \phi[(EF^*/W), (M/W)] \qquad \text{where } \phi_1 > 0, \phi_2 < 0 \tag{7.11}$$

Now setting $\dot{e} = 0$, since E and F^* enter (7.10) multiplicatively (in both EF^* and in W), changes in E and F^* which keep EF^* constant will also keep e constant. Hence the locus of points for which $\dot{e} = 0$ must be a rectangular hyperbola, given, say, as $EF^* = \kappa$, where κ is a constant. This is illustrated in Figure 7.6. From equation (7.11) a rise in E or F^* will lead to a depreciation of the exchange rate; that is a rise in E.

The linearized versions of (7.7) and (7.11) give the following second-order dynamic system:

$$\begin{bmatrix} \dot{e} \\ \dot{F}^* \end{bmatrix} = \begin{bmatrix} \phi_1(F^*/W) & \phi_1(E/W) \\ (T_1 + T_2 F^*) & (ET_2 + r^*) \end{bmatrix} \begin{bmatrix} E \\ F^* \end{bmatrix} + \begin{bmatrix} \phi_1(M/W) \\ T_2(M+B) + T_3 i \end{bmatrix} \tag{7.12}$$

Saddle path equilibrium requires that the determinant of the 2×2 matrix be negative. This is unambiguously the case if $ET_1 > r^*F^*$; that is, if the wealth effect on the trade balance exceeds the foreign interest rate effect. Figure 7.6 shows the plausible slopes of the $\dot{F}^* = 0$ line with their respective directions of movement given by the arrows.

The impact of a monetary shock and an exogenous trade balance shock can now be considered in the dynamic version of this portfolio balance model.

A monetary shock   Consider the case of an increase in the domestic money supply by way of an open market purchase of domestic bonds, so that $\triangle M = -\triangle B$. Figure 7.7 show that the long-run equilibrium impli-

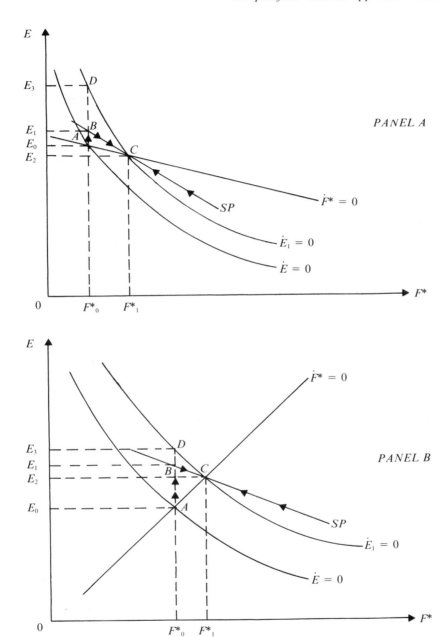

Figure 7.7   An open market purchase in the PBKM with perfect foresight

cations for the exchange rate differ according to the slope of the $\dot{F}^* = 0$ line. An unanticipated increase in the domestic money stock, due to an open market purchase, will shift the $\dot{e} = 0$ hyperbola up to the right. In Figure 7.7, panel A, where the $\dot{F}^*$ locus has a negative slope, the exchange rate initially depreciates from E_0 to E_1 and then appreciates down the saddle path to the new long-run equilibrium at E_2. The net effect on the exchange rate is therefore an appreciation, as the initial steep depreciation gives rise to a trade surplus as domestic residents accumulate foreign assets, thereby appreciating the exchange rate. There are two points to note about this result. First, it is rather different from that of the monetary and Mundell–Fleming models of the exchange rate, in that it shows that exchange rate may appreciate in response to a domestic monetary expansion. Moreover, in the short run the exchange rate actually moves in the opposite direction to that required to reach the long-run equilibrium. Secondly, notice that with static expectations, rather than perfect foresight expectations, the initial depreciation of the exchange rate would have been very much larger, with E rising to E_3. In this case perfect foresight expectations assist the adjustment of the foreign exchange market, because in face of the initial depreciation rational agents will realize that this will improve the trade balance and generate a future appreciation of the currency.

Panel B of Figure 7.7 shows an equivalent monetary expansion, with the $\dot{F}^* = 0$ line now having a positive slope, reflecting the point that higher domestic wealth requires a higher value of E to maintain current account balance as domestic residents use their higher wealth to buy foreign goods. The rise in the money supply causes an immediate depreciation of the exchange rate from E_0 to E_1, after which it partially appreciates back to E_2, as the trade balance improves from the initial depreciation. In this case the long-run equilibrium exchange rate is lower, at E_2, than in the initial equilibrium: a monetary expansion has depreciated the exchange rate. This result is consistent with the monetary and Mundell–Fleming models.

A trade balance shock   Consider a shock to the current account, through the shift parameter i, which represents an exogenous import shift parameter. From an initial balanced-trade position a fall in i will give rise to a trade balance surplus, hence requiring an appreciation of the exchange rate at all levels of F^* to maintain equilibrium. Thus the $\dot{F}^* = 0$ locus shifts down to the left, to $\dot{F}^*_1 = 0$ in Figure 7.8. From the initial equilibrium at A the exchange rate jumps immediately down to B on the stable manifold, which represents an appreciation of the exchange rate. E then continues to appreciate along the stable arm until the new long-run equilibrium is reached at point C. There is no short-run overshooting of

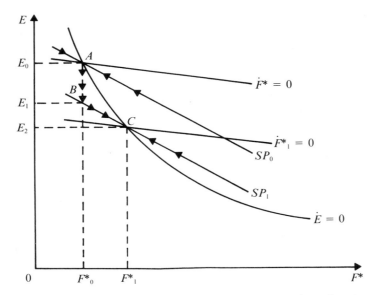

Figure 7.8   A fall in domestic imports in the PBKM with perfect foresight

the exchange rate in this case under perfect foresight or static expectations. If the $\dot{F}^* = 0$ line was to take a positive slope the long-run results would be unchanged.

7.3   The econometric evidence

Compared to the monetary approach of the exchange rate the portfolio balance approach has not been extensively tested. This is probably due to the fact that it is very difficult to find data on domestic residents' foreign currency assets, broken down by the currency denomination of the assets. Thus most empirical studies begin from the stock of foreign currency assets held by domestic residents and add the cumulated current account balances for each country.[4] This method therefore ignores any capital gains earned on foreign assets and assumes that only domestic residents hold domestic assets.

Broadly three kinds of empirical test of the portfolio balance model have been carried out. The first concentrates on solving the short-run portfolio balance model as a reduced form for the exchange rate, assuming static expectations, as, for example, in Branson *et al.* (1977, 1979). The second approach involves estimating a structural system of equations, like equations (7.1) to (7.4) above, as attempted by Kearney and MacDonald (1985, 1986) and Boughton (1984, 1987). These two kinds of test make up the next two sub-sections. The third test is more indirect and involves testing for the existence of a risk premium. This is a separate topic for discussion and is therefore left until Section 7.4.

7.3.1   Reduced form tests

Solving the asset market equilibrium equations (7.1)–(7.4) for domestic and foreign interest rates and the exchange rate, in terms of the asset stocks, the equilibrium exchange rate can be written as:

$$e = e(m, b, f^*) \tag{7.13}$$

where lower-case letters denote logarithms, asterisks denote foreign currency variables, and where b is the domestic stock of non-traded domestic bonds, f^* is the stock of foreign currency bonds held by domestic residents and m is the domestic money supply. Assuming an identical reduced form equation exists for the foreign country, the relevant reduced form for testing is:

$$e = e(m, m^*, b, b_0, f^*_0, f^*) \tag{7.14}$$

where m^* is the non-traded foreign money supply, b_0 are non-traded bonds held by foreign residents and f^*_0 are traded, foreign currency bonds held by foreign residents. Branson *et al.* (1977) estimate a log-linear version of (7.14) for the German Deutsche Mark–US dollar exchange rate, for the period August 1971 to December 1976. The actual form of the estimated equation is:

$$e_t = a_0 + a_1 m_t + a_2 m^*_t + a_3 f^*_{0t} + a_4 f^*_t + u_t \tag{7.15}$$

where the money supplies are defined as M1 and the stocks of traded foreign assets are proxied by cumulated current accounts. An obvious problem with this estimated model is the exclusion of non-traded assets, b and b_0, which means that omitted variables bias is likely to affect the estimates of the parameters a_i.

The ordinary least squares (OLS) estimates of Branson *et al.* (1977) are deemed supportive of the portfolio balance model, although once account is taken of acute first-order serial correlation only the coefficient on the US money supply is statistically significant. By specifying a simple reaction function, which purports to capture the simultaneity of the German money supply, equation (7.15) is re-estimated using two-stage least squares (2SLS). More satisfactory results are reported, although autocorrelation remains a major problem. Branson *et al.* (1979) estimate (7.15) for the longer period, August 1971 to December 1978, for the mark–US dollar exchange rate, but the results are similar to those obtained from the earlier period, with persistent serial correlation a major problem. Branson and Halttunen (1979) estimate equation (7.15) for five currencies (the yen, the French franc, the lira, the Swiss franc and the pound sterling) against the German mark for a variety of samples periods over the 1970s. The reported results are again only weakly supportive of the portfolio balance model since, although the results show correct and statistically significantly signed coefficients, the residuals from the equation are serially correlated, showing that factors unexplained by the model have a persistent effect on the exchange rate.

There are four problems with this set of tests of the portfolio balance model. Firstly, the use of cumulated current account balances to represent the stocks of foreign assets will include third-country items which are not strictly relevant to the determination of the bilateral exchange rate in question. Secondly, as noted above, the omission of the terms in non-traded bonds is likely to bias the estimated coefficients. Moreover, in practice, bonds are not the only internationally traded assets and so in principle equities should also be included. Thirdly, the price levels and the levels of real income are assumed to be constant and hence are also omitted from the estimated short-run equations. If the exchange rate is quickly affected by changes in the price level then perhaps this variable should also be included. More importantly perhaps, if the level of real income is an important element in the demand for assets then it should also appear as an additional explanatory variable in equation (7.15). A fourth limitation of the portfolio balance approach is that the relative riskiness of the assets is ignored. This is valid to the extent that the securities traded have similar risk characteristics, or to the extent that aggregation enables the conception of a common bundle of securities with very similar risk characteristics to be assumed.

The first limitation noted above is picked up by Bisignano and Hoover (1983) who argue that the portfolio balance approach should be implemented using only bilateral data for foreign assets. Moreover, to be consistent with the theoretical reduced form, b and b_0 should also be included, as also noted above. Using these modifications, Bisignano and Hoover estimate the portfolio balance reduced form of equation (7.14) for the Canadian dollar–US dollar, over the period March 1973 to December 1978, reporting moderately successful results. In particular, they show that the coefficients on domestic non-monetary assets are statistically significant.

Sarantis (1987) generalizes the portfolio balance model further by including equity capital stocks, prices and real incomes, *inter alia*, in the reduced form. Using an error-correction approach (Alogoskoufis and Smith, 1991), the model is tested for five sterling exchange rates (against the US dollar, the yen, the mark, the French franc and the lira) for the period 1973 Q1 to 1981 Q4. The results suggest that the extended asset market model provides a satisfactory explanation of sterling's behaviour over the sample period. In particular, UK asset holdings are shown to have a strong and significant influence on all bilateral sterling exchange rates. An expansion in equity holdings leads to an appreciation of the pound, while an expansion in bond holdings tends to depreciate the pound, except in the case of the US dollar, and an increase in the UK money supply, narrowly defined, leads also to a depreciation of the pound. External assets held by UK residents and money and external assets held by foreign residents showed less significant results.

More recently Sarantis and Stewart (1991) have applied cointegration techniques to the generalized portfolio balance model to four bilateral sterling exchange rates for the period 1973 Q1 to 1990 Q3. The US dollar–pound exchange rate does not give a cointegrating vector, but for the Deutsche Mark and the yen there is weak evidence of a cointegrating vector, although this is dependent upon the inclusion of relative prices among the explanatory variables. For the French franc–sterling exchange rate there is strong evidence for the existence of a cointegrating vector. Table 7.1 shows the cointegrating vector and the resulting error correction models for the Deutsche Mark–sterling and French franc–sterling exchange rates. In each case the models pass the various diagnostic tests[5] and the lagged residual terms are significant in the error correction models. The value of North Sea Oil reserves (NSO) is not significant in the error-correction equations, although it has some influence in the long-run equations, especially for the franc–pound rate. In each case foreign assets held by foreign residents, f^*_0, domestic bond holdings, b, and domestic equity holdings, k, tend to exert the strongest influence on both sterling exchange rates. Relative prices are correctly signed and moderately significant for the mark–pound rate and entirely insignificant for the franc–pound rate. These short-run effects contrast with the highly significant long-run effects of relative prices on all exchange rates. The estimates of the money supply effects were in the main wrongly signed or insignificant. These estimates show that an empirical model within the portfolio balance framework can provide a reasonable explanation for the behaviour of the pound sterling over the recent floating exchange rate period.

7.3.2   Structural tests of the portfolio balance model

A structural approach to testing the portfolio balance approach has been advocated by Boughton (1984, 1987) and by Kearney and MacDonald

Table 7.1   Cointegration and error correction results for the portfolio balance model

Cointegrating regression: DM/£

$e_t = 0.151 + 0.752(p^* - p)_t - 0.015m^*_t + 0.012m_t - 0.030k_t + 0.051b_t$
  (0.11) (3.84)   (0.23)   (0.10)   (1.17)   (2.83)
  $0.048f^*_{0t} + 0.537NSO_t$
  (4.07)   (1.30)

$R^2 = 0.926; DF = -4.402; ADF = -4.30\ (1); LM(4) = 2.04.$

Error correction model: DM/£

$\Delta e_t = 0.020 + 0.449\Delta(p - p^*)_t - 0.215\Delta m^*_{t-1} - 0.263\Delta m_t - 0.059k_{t-4}$
  (1.44) (1.20)   (1.69)   (2.01)   (1.85)
  $0.049b_t + 0.081b_{t-4} - 0.017f^*_{0t} + 0.269\Delta e_{t-2} - 0.417RES_{t-1}$
  (1.60)   (2.81)   (2.13)   (2.15)   (4.01)

$R^2 = 0.28: DW = 1.86; LM(4) = 2.01; LM_f(1) = 0.01; LM_n(2) = 1.79;$
$LM_h(1) = 0.01; ARCH(1) = 1.85; ARCH(4) = 5.99; LM_p(4) = 6.71.$

Cointegrating regression: Fr/£

$e_t = -0.095 + 0.982(p - p^*)_t - 0.034(m^* - m)_t - 0.033k_t + 0.066b_t$
  (0.09) (8.58)   (0.30)   (1.72)   (3.26)
  $+0.048f^*_{0t} + 2.123NSO_t$
  (1.57)   (5.29)

$R^2 = 0.639; DF = -4.232; ADF = -4.754; LM(4) = 6.60.$

Error correction model: Fr/£

$\Delta e_t = -0.011 - 0.059\Delta k_t + 0.085\Delta b_t + 0.072\Delta b_{t-4} - 0.045\Delta f^*_{0t}$
  (1.86) (2.04)   (2.93)   (2.70)   (1.70)
  $+0.354\Delta e_{t-1} - 0.428\ RES_{t-1}$
  (3.02)   (4.70)

$R^2 = 0.29; DW = 1.91; LM(4) = 1.58; LM_f(1) = 3.10; LM_n(2) = 0.45;$
$LM_h(1) = 2.03; ARCH(1) = 0.20; ARCH(4) = 0.92; LM_p(4) = 5.84.$

Source: Sarantis and Stewart (1991).

(1985, 1986). Although the approach of Kearney and MacDonald most closely follows the model developed in this chapter it yields less convincing empirical results. The authors define asset demand equations of the general form:

$$A_i/W = \beta_{i0} + \sum_i \beta_{ij} lnr_j \tag{7.16}$$

which are homogeneous in wealth and depend only upon the vector of nominal interest rates, like equations (7.1) to (7.4). The logarithms of interest rates are used because Smith and Brainard (1976) show that the simple levels of interest rates often produces absurd simulation results. Equation (7.16) implies the adding-up conditions

$\sum_i \beta_{i0} = 1$ and $\sum_i \beta_{ij} = 0$ where $j = 1, \ldots, n$.

Finally the model is completed by the specification of a partial adjustment process for the asset stocks

$$\triangle A_i = \sum_i \gamma_{ij}(A_{jt} - A_{jt-1}) \text{ where } \sum_i \gamma_{ij} = 1 \tag{7.17}$$

giving an estimating equation of:

$$\triangle A_i/W = \xi - \sum_i \gamma_{ij}(A_{jt-1}/W) + \sum \gamma_{ij}\beta_{ij}ln \; r_j \tag{7.18}$$

Wealth is defined to include four kinds of asset demand, broad money (A_1), bank loans (A_2), domestic bonds (A_3) and foreign assets held by the domestic non-bank private sector (A_4), which are converted into sterling by use of the US dollar–sterling exchange rate, and so four asset share equations, of the form of (7.18) are estimated simultaneously using the Theil–Goldberger mixed estimation procedure. This technique, by allowing prior restrictions to be made explicit at the outset, shows considerable improvement on the OLS estimates. In particular, nine of the sixteen interest rate coefficients have the correct sign, although some six coefficients remain wrongly signed. Kearney and MacDonald (1986) report six different simulations using this model. For example, a 1 per cent expansion in broad money leads to a fall in bond and bank lending rates while the exchange rate depreciates, as expected, and adjusts cyclically to its new equilibrium level. A more realistic simulation is to consider an open-market swap of domestic bonds for money. This gives rise to a higher interest rate and a lower bank lending rate, while the net effect on the exchange rate is a 5 per cent depreciation before commencing to converge cyclically.

The structural model of Boughton (1984, 1987) on the other hand, avoids the problems of estimating asset demand functions by specifying both asset demand and supply functions and then estimating equations for asset prices. Specifically, the money supply function depends upon the target level of the money supply and the real levels of domestic and foreign interest rates. Combining this with the standard demand for money function through a stock adjustment equation, Boughton (1984) derives an equation for the interest rate which depends upon the foreign real interest rate, the domestic level of output, expected inflation and the monetary target, which are all exogenous variables. The proportionate change in the exchange rate depends upon the excess demand for foreign assets plus the expected inflation differential between the home and the foreign country. Specifying equations for the demand and supply of foreign assets and postulating a stock adjustment process, *inter alia*, the change in the exchange rate can be expressed as a function of the nominal interest rate differential, the expected inflation differential and the cumulated balance of private capital flows, k. Since the nominal interest rate differential is endogenous, the interest rate differential is replaced by the estimates obtained from direct estimation of the interest rate equation.

The results reported in Boughton (1984) for the within-sample properties of the exchange rate are reproduced in Table 7.2. The results are good, with the exception of the pound sterling. There is no evidence of serial correlation in these equations although no effort is made to correct for it. Interest rate differentials are important in all cases except that of the pound and the coefficient on the cumulative private capital balance, k, is in the appropriate range, again apart from the pound sterling, and for the most part is significantly different from zero. The coefficients on the lagged

Table 7.2   Boughton's tests of the portfolio balance model

Currency	$r - r^*$	k_{-1}	$(EP^*/P)_{-1}$	R^2	F	h
US dollar	− 1.629	0.653	− 0.059	0.89	8.29	2.31
	(4.76)	(1.37)	(1.09)			(1.18)
Pound	− 0.294	− 0.237	− 0.033	0.90	4.18	1.68
	(1.50)	(2.61)	(0.61)			(1.01)
Yen	− 0.952	0.701	− 0.255	0.88	5.21	1.69
	(3.70)	(2.83)	(3.40)			(1.06)
French franc	− 1.011	0.177	− 0.090	0.94	6.07	2.14
	(3.33)	(1.85)	(1.01)			(0.63)
D-mark	− 1.055	0.197	− 0.225	0.85	4.74	2.13
	(2.89)	(2.59)	(2.78)			(0.58)

Notes
Estimated 1973 Q3–1983 Q3; *t*-values in parentheses; h is Durbin's *h*-test.
F statistics show that the equations are all significant at the 1% level, in terms of changes in the dependent variable.
The coefficients on expected inflation differentials are not reported by Boughton, since they are constrained to be equal to one plus the coefficients on $r - r^*$.

Source: Boughton (1984), p. 459.

real exchange rate are small, indicating that long adjustment processes are present.

Boughton also tests the out-of-sample properties of the model. This is done by re-estimating the model up to 1981 Q1 only and then forecasting the exchange rates through to the end of 1983. The root mean squared errors (RMSE) from these dynamic forecasts show that, with the exception of the pound sterling, this model outperforms both a nominal and a real random walk process of the exchange rate. Boughton (1987) compares the performance of this model with several other models of the exchange rate, including the monetary model, using monthly data from May 1973 to December 1984 for the US dollar, the yen and the Deutsche Mark. Only the Boughton stock-adjustment model consistently displays coefficient estimates that conform to prior expectations.

7.4   Risk premia

The key features of the portfolio balance approach are the existence of imperfect asset substitutability and the explicit consideration of the investor's stock of wealth. Since, by assumption, domestic and foreign non-money assets are not perfect substitutes, it follows that risk-averse agents will wish to hold a mixed portfolio of non-money assets, the proportions of particular assets held depending upon their relative risk and return characteristics. This implies that uncovered interest rate parity will not hold and instead is replaced with:

$$r - r^* - E\dot{e} = \rho \tag{7.19}$$

where ρ is the risk premium. The existence of risk premia permits an alternative, indirect, test of the portfolio balance model, since this is the only class of model to allow for imperfect asset substitutability. This section is therefore concerned with tests of the existence and importance of risk premia in foreign exchange markets. These tests have largely taken three forms: firstly, tests of the uncovered interest parity condition, which postulate the non-existence of a constant risk premia as part of the null hypothesis; secondly, tests which relate the risk premium to the relative stocks of assets outstanding or the current balance and hence measure the risk premium as the extent to which portfolio re-allocation influences uncovered interest rate parity; thirdly, tests which focus on time-varying risk premia, reflecting the fact that the premium may change over time even if the relative stocks of assets held do not. Each of these tests is considered in turn.

The first kind of tests (of uncovered interest parity) are suggested by equation (7.19). Assuming $\rho = 0$, equation (7.19) can be written in discrete time and parameterized to give:

$$e_t = a_0 e_{t+1} + a_1(r - r^*)_t + u_t \qquad (7.20)$$

where u_t is a random error term. Uncovered interest rate parity holds if $a_0 = -1$, $a_1 = +1$ and the error term is orthogonal with respect to the explanatory variable. Models of this type have been estimated by, *inter alia*, Cumby and Obstfeld (1981, 1984) and Davidson (1985), with the result that either the joint null hypothesis is rejected or the error orthogonality property is violated. Cumby and Obstfeld (1981) justify the rejection of the uncovered interest rate differential as evidence for the existence of a risk premium. It is, of course, not possible to say whether the rejection of uncovered interest rate parity is due to the existence of a risk premium, or to the failure of the rational expectations hypothesis,[6] or indeed, to some other factor. Thus these kinds of test provide only weak evidence in favour of the risk premium.

The second approach is to attempt to model the risk premium itself. There have been two broad methodologies used in this context. The first, due largely to Dooley and Isard (1982, 1983) and Frankel (1982a, 1983) emphasizes that the risk premium is related to the relative volume of domestic assets outstanding, while the second approach relates the risk premium to the current account balance (Currie and Hall, 1986, 1989; Hall 1987).

The former approach postulates that the risk premium required on domestic assets will rise as their relative *volume* outstanding increases, that is:

$$\rho = \rho(B/EF^*) \qquad \rho_1 > 0 \qquad (7.21)$$

Substituting equation (7.21) into (7.19), assuming rational expectations and inverting gives:

$$B/EF^* = \lambda(r - r^* - \dot{e}) \qquad (7.22)$$

where $\lambda = 1/\rho_1$. Invoking preferred habitat-type preferences, where domestic residents are assumed to hold a greater proportion of wealth in domestic assets, and assuming the world consists of only three countries, the home country (the UK), and two foreign countries (the USA and the rest of the world, RW), then in terms of the home country:

$$
\begin{aligned}
B_{uk} &= a_{uk} + \lambda(r - r^* - \triangle e)W_{uk} \\
B_{us} &= a_{us} + \lambda(r - r^* - \triangle e)W_{us} \\
B_{rw} &= a_{rw} + \lambda(r - r^* - \triangle e)W_{rw}
\end{aligned}
\qquad (7.23)
$$

where the rate of change in the exchange rate is measured in discrete time.

Because data are not available at a sufficiently disaggregate level these asset demand equations cannot be estimated directly. Frankel (1982a, 1983), however, aggregates these equations and divides by W, to obtain:

$$(B_{uk} + B_{us} + B_{rw})/W = a_{rw} + (a_{uk} - a_{rw})[W_{uk}/W] + (a_{us} - a_{rw})[W_{us}/W]$$
$$+ \lambda(r - r^* - \triangle e) \tag{7.24}$$

which can be inverted to give an equation for the risk premium as follows:

$$(r - r^* - \triangle e) = (a_{rw}/\lambda) + (1/\lambda)[(B_{uk} + B_{us} + B_{rw})/W] - [(a_{uk} - a_{rw})/\lambda]$$
$$\times [W_{uk}/W] + [(a_{us} - a_{rw})/\lambda][W_{us}/W] + v_t \tag{7.25}$$

where $(1/\lambda) > 0$, reflecting the presumption that an increase in the relative supply of UK bonds requires either an increase in the rate of interest or an expected appreciation of the exchange rate to maintain portfolio balance. The coefficient on UK wealth is negative because an increase in UK wealth increases the relative demand for UK assets, which implies a lower expected return on the assets if the outstanding bond stock is to be willingly held.

This version of the risk premium model has been estimated by Dooley and Isard (1982, 1983) and by Frankel (1982a, 1984). Dooley and Isard (1982) test the uniform preference version of the model, that is, when $a_{uk} = a_{us} = a_{rw}$, for the mark–US dollar exchange rate for the period 1973–8, using quarterly data, and find that the coefficients are insignificantly different from zero. Frankel (1982a) estimates a uniform preference and a preferred habitat model for the mark–US dollar exchange rate for the period January 1974 to October 1978, but finds no coefficients significantly different from zero. In another paper Frankel (1982b) extends the analysis by arguing that the parameters in the asset demand functions such as in equation (7.24) depend not only upon the degree of risk aversion, but also upon the variance–covariance matrix of expected returns. In terms of equation (7.24), $\lambda = \omega\Omega$, where Ω is the covariance matrix of exchange rate depreciation defined as: $\varepsilon(\triangle\sigma_{t+1} - \varepsilon\triangle\sigma_{t+1}) \times (\triangle\sigma_{t+1} - \varepsilon\triangle\sigma_{t+1})'$, σ is the vector of spot dollar rates against the five currencies concerned and ω is the coefficient of relative risk aversion. In vector notation equation (7.24) becomes:

$$x_t = \alpha + R_t/\omega\Omega \tag{7.26}$$

where x_t is the vector portfolio shares of each asset in total real wealth, α is the vector of consumption shares allocated to the five countries goods and R_t is a vector of the risk premia, as defined in (7.19), for each of the currencies against the dollar and measured as: $R_t = h_t - \lambda r^*_t - \triangle \sigma_{t+1}$, where h_t is a vector of the five 'domestic' interest rates. Frankel estimates (7.26) by maximum likelihood methods using monthly data for the 1970s and is unable to reject the null hypothesis of risk neutrality, given by $\omega = 0$. Changes in the composition of portfolios do not therefore seem to be able to explain very much of the actual fluctuations in differences in real returns. Frankel (1985) in fact demonstrates the very small size of the risk premium. He estimates that Ω is around 0.001 and assuming the coefficient of relative risk aversion, ω, is about two, the product, $\omega\Omega$, is about 0.002. Therefore if an increase in the relative supply of bonds, x_t, equal to 1 per cent of the portfolio is to be willingly held, it will have to increase the risk premium by about 0.002 per cent on a monthly basis, or a mere 0.024 per cent per annum.

An alternative approach to modelling the risk premium has been employed by Hall (1987) and Currie and Hall (1986, 1989). The approach is to derive an equilibrium relationship between the risk premium, measured as the uncovered interest rate differential, and the current account balance from an inter temporal, forward-looking model of the desired capital outflow. The model is tested using UK monthly data for the effective exchange rate index and the three months treasury bill rate (compared with the US rate) for the period 1973–84. The results reported in Currie and Hall (1989) show that the risk premium depends positively and significantly upon the current balance (excluding interest profits and dividends and transfers). The coefficient of 0.15 suggests that a sustained £1 billion increase in the current deficit is associated with a 0.015 rise in the risk premium measured on an annual basis. Interestingly Fisher *et al.* (1990) have used a similar equation with the risk premium modelled as a function of the ratio of the current balance to GDP, which outperforms other exchange rate equations used in other econometric models of the UK economy and a random walk model in out-of-sample forecast tests.

These recent successes in modelling the risk premiums, suggest that data limitations may go at least part of the way to explaining the failure of the portfolio allocation models of the risk premium. It was however, the failure of these tests to identify a significant risk premium that led to the third kind of test, that for time-varying risk premia.

Risk premia are assumed to vary with the proportion of different assets in the agent's portfolio. But, given that proportion, the risk premia may also vary over time, in which case it is referred to as a time-varying risk premium. One cause could be that the covariance of the exchange rate with the return on other assets varies over time, which is a measure of the degree to which portfolio diversification can contribute to the reduction in risk. The theoretical basis for such models is made by Fama and Farber

(1979), Lucas (1982) and Hodrick and Srivastava (1984), while at the empirical level testing these models is impossible owing to the intractable nature of the final equations. Thus all of the empirical work on time-varying risk premia is subject to the criticism that it is somewhat *ad hoc*. Although Hansen and Hodrick (1983) conclude their study of the risk premia by arguing the case for a latent variable model of the risk premia which they found to be important in at least two of the five currencies which they studied, many other authors have been more sceptical. Domowitz and Hakkio (1985), for example, use Engle's ARCH model (Engle, 1982) to test for the presence of a risk premium using monthly data for the period January 1977 to August 1987, and find that there is little support for the conditional variance of the exchange rate forecast error being an important sole determinant of the risk premium.

On the other hand, studies by Diebold and Pauly (1988) and Taylor (1988a) do find evidence of a time-varying risk premium. In particular, Taylor, using a Kalman filter technique to model the risk premium as a latent variable has found evidence for risk premia for the US dollar–pound, US dollar–Swiss franc and US dollar–yen exchange rates, over the period March 1976 to July 1986. The intuition is that domestic asset yield volatility raises the risk premia on domestic assets and hence causes a rise in the forward premium on sterling, and conversely for foreign asset yield volatility. The results, reported in Table 7.3, show that all of the estimated coefficients are of the expected sign and they are all significantly different from zero (marginally so for the Swiss case). Moreover, the estimated autoregressive coefficients, α_0, are all positive and significantly less than unity. The Wald tests, $W(2)$ and $W(3)$, are rejected strongly for each of the exchange rates concerned, which can be interpreted as offering strong support both for the presence of a time-varying risk premium and the dependence of that premium on domestic and foreign asset yield volatility. The Ljung-Box statistic reveals no sign of serial correlation in the innovations.

7.5   Conclusions

In this chapter the portfolio balance model of the exchange rate has been considered. The principal differences between this model and the monetary models are the assumption of imperfect asset substitutability and the explicit consideration of wealth effects. Theoretically, the portfolio balance model is the most general of all the exchange models considered in this book, although this greater generality is not easily translated into superior empirical results, partly, at least, owing to the limited data available on the ownership of asset stocks. In particular, the exchange rate may appreciate or depreciate in response to an unanticipated monetary

Table 7.3   Time-varying risk premia

Maximum likelihood estimates; sample period March 1976–July 1986

$$f_t - e_{t+1} = \rho_t + u_{t+1}$$
$$\rho_p = \alpha_0\rho_{t-1} + \alpha_1\bar{\omega}_t + \alpha_2\bar{\omega}^*_t + v_t$$

	α_0	α_1	α_2	$Q(33)$	$w(2)$	$w(3)$
$/£	0.2841	0.0818	−0.0177	31.7	74.4	80.7
	(0.107)	(0.011)	(0.004)			
$/Yen	0.1046	0.1037	−0.2158	32.2	24.8	28.4
	(0.052)	(0.042)	(0.052)			
$/Swiss franc	0.0884	0.3571	−0.4113	28.8	49.1	58.4
	(0.031)	(0.200)	(0.061)			

Notes
Standard errors in parentheses below coefficients.
$Q(i)$ is the Ljung-Box statistic applied to the innovations for up to i autocorrelations. $W(2)$ is the Wald Test for the H_o: $(\phi_1,\phi_2) = (0,0)$, distributed as $W(3)$ H_o: $(\phi_0,\phi_1,\phi_2) = (0, 0, 0)$. distributed as $\chi^2(3)$.
Critical values at 5% for chi-squared are: $\chi^2(2) = 5.991$ and $\chi^2(3) = 7.815$.

Source: Taylor (1988a), Table 2.

expansion, depending on the relative strengths of the wealth effects on the goods and assets markets. Indeed, as Driskill and McCafferty (1985) say, 'With wealth effects anything goes' (p. 339).

Econometric tests of the portfolio balance model have not in the main been very successful unless the model has been augmented by other variables. In particular, the need to consider a wider range of assets (Sarantis, 1987), partial adjustment of stock supplies and demands, (Boughton, 1984; Kearney and MacDonald, 1986) and some real-side variables such as relative prices (Sarantis and Stewart, 1991) seem to be important to obtaining a reasonably fitting estimated equation. The difficulty of directly testing this approach has led to a set of indirect tests of the existence of risk premia which, if discovered, would give indirect support to the portfolio balance hypothesis. The evidence surveyed in Section 7.4 suggests that risk premia can be detected either through an inter temporal forward-looking capital flows model or through *ad hoc* equations which model the risk premia as time-varying. These latter test results are liable to alternative interpretations. This matter will be raised again in Chapter 8.

Notes
1. In the Mundell–Fleming model the demand for money also depends upon the level of real income and the price level, both excluded in this model.

2. In the case where domestic and foreign bonds are perfect substitutes the *BB* and *FF* lines collapse to a single locus, with an infinite slope in (E,r) space.
3. See Chapter 3 for details.
4. Less any foreign currency assets held by central banks as reserves.
5. The statistics' all of which are distributed as chi-squared, are as follows: $LM(4)$ Lagrange multiplier test for 4th-order serial correlation; $LM_f(1)$, Ramsey's RESET test for functional form; $LM_n(2)$, Bera-Jarque Test for normality of residuals; $LM_h(1)$ Lagrange multiplier test for heteroscedasticity; $LM_p(4)$, Chow's post-sample predictive failure test; ARCH(1) is the Engle test for heteroscedasticity.
6. The use of survey data on exchange rate expectations does enable these distinct hypotheses to be unravelled. This evidence is surveyed by MacDonald and Taylor (1989), MacDonald and Taylor (1992a) and by Takagi (1991) and is reviewed in Chapter 8 of this volume.

8 Recent and future directions for research

8.1 Introduction

In this book the principal structural macroeconomic models of the exchange rate have been examined, together with some of the recent relevant empirical literature which purports to test these theories against the data. The conclusion from this extensive study is that none of the major structural models either adequately explains the long-run equilibrium exchange rate or its short-run dynamics, for all time periods and exchange rates. Some models seem to perform better than others in different time periods and with different bilateral exchange rates, but there is no generally accepted empirical model of the exchange rate. Recent research, therefore, has started to examine the reasons for this apparent failure of the models adequately to represent the data. This research programme has moved in two directions, the first looking at the short-run dynamics, often focusing on high-frequency exchange rate data, and the second, less well-developed, area focusing more upon the determinants of the long-run equilibrium exchange rate. This final chapter considers developments in both of these directions.

In terms of short-run exchange rate dynamics, recent research has looked at three areas: first, the use of survey data to test the validity of the rational expectations hypothesis in the context of the foreign exchange market; second, the possibility that exchange rates may best be modelled by non-linear deterministic processes; and third, short-run exchange rate behaviour when the exchange rate varies within a target zone. Section 8.2 reviews the recent empirical literature which utilizes survey data on market participants' expectations of the future exchange rate at various forecast horizons to test whether it conforms to the requirements of the rational expectations hypothesis. Clearly, if market participants' expectations do not use all available information, then structural models based upon rational expectations are likely to be flawed. Alternatively, if expectations are driven by charts, then economists clearly have little if anything to contribute in the short run and should concentrate on developing structural models which can adequately represent the long-run equilibrium exchange rate. Section 8.3 considers the second possibility noted above, that in the very short run exchange rate dynamics cannot be modelled as linear, deterministic processes. That is, either the models exhibit some non-linearities, or they are subject to stochastic shocks not currently identified in the data. This section therefore considers recent applications of non-linear, deterministic dynamic methods in theoretical exchange rate models and reviews the empirical literature in search of 'chaotic' dynamics in high-frequency exchange rate data. Section 8.4 uses a simple stochastic monetary model to show that the effects of target zones on exchange rate movements inside the band are stabilizing, even if the exchange rate target is not perceived as fully credible by agents in the market.

In the context of the long-run equilibrium exchange rate, economists are perhaps more likely to have some successes since economics is rather better at explaining long-run trends than very short-run speculative behaviour. Section 8.5 briefly considers two possible extensions to the supply side of existing structural models of the equilibrium exchange rate, due to Dornbusch (1987). The first is that current models do not allow for the effects of real capital accumulation on the exchange rate. These kinds of effects could perhaps be incorporated in some form of extended portfolio balance model, which would provide richer long-run dynamics. The second extension is to acknowledge that the simple assumptions of purchasing power parity (PPP) or fixed prices are at variance with real world experience, and to integrate some of the ideas about the determination of relative prices from the industrial economics literature into theories of exchange rate determination.

8.2   Exchange rate expectations and survey data

One area where many of the structural models of the exchange rate are inadequate is in their treatment of expectations. The basic problem is, of course, that expectations are not observable and therefore they have to be proxied by some rule of thumb. Economists have generally proxied exchange rate expectations by use of the forward rate or by the actual future spot exchange rate, although both proxies are inadequate. For example, if the forward rate is used then this assumes that there is no risk premium, which is against some of the empirical evidence presented in Chapter 7. Moreover, the existence of a risk premium itself is an interesting issue since this reflects the degree of substitutability between assets. If, on the other hand, the actual future exchange rate is used, this imposes rational expectations which, although attractive from the economic point of view, do not necessarily capture the way in which expectations are actually formed. Both proxies for the expected future exchange rate result in tests of a joint null hypothesis: that is, tests of the structural model and either a test of rational expectations or a zero-risk premium. The use of survey data on exchange rate expectations enables these joint hypotheses to be unravelled (Section 8.2.1). It also enables the importance of the use of technical analysis or chartism by market traders to be assessed (Section 8.2.2).

8.2.1   Survey data tests of the rational expectations hypothesis

There are two kinds of test of the rational expectations hypothesis using survey data. The first kind, surveyed by Takagi (1991), test for unbiasedness and orthogonality in the survey data, using simple regression analysis. The second type of test, due to Liu and Maddala (1992), extends these tests by using cointegration techniques.

Rational expectations are assumed to have two properties: unbiasedness and orthogonality. These properties can be tested using survey data on exchange rate expectations. A test of unbiasedness would be to estimate the following model:

$$e_{t+j} = a_1 + a_2 E_t e_{t+j} + u_t \qquad (8.1)$$

where $E_t e_{t+j}$ is measured by the survey expectations series, u_t is a random error term and unbiasedness implies the joint null hypothesis, $a_1 = 0$ and $a_2 = 1$. Dominguez (1986) tested this hypothesis for US dollar–pound, US dollar–mark and US dollar–yen exchange rates, using Money Market Services (MMS)[1] data, for the period 1983–5, and almost unanimously rejected the null for one-week, one-month and three-month expectations for all currencies. Ito (1990), using Japanese Centre for International Finance (JCIF)[2] data over the period 1985–7, could not reject the null hypothesis except for the six-month expectation. The difference between these two sets of results may be due to the behaviour of the US dollar in the earlier period, when it continued to appreciate on a sustained basis, despite expectations to the contrary.

The orthogonality property is another important property of rational expectations. If expectations are efficient, in that they incorporate all available information, their predictable powers cannot be improved by including any variable which is in the current information set. Hence prediction errors are uncorrelated with any variable in the set of known information. This condition can be tested by running the following regression:

$$E_t e_{t+j} - e_{t+j} = b_1 + b_2 X_t + v_t \qquad (8.2)$$

where the dependent variable is the prediction error, X_t is a set of known information at time t and v_t is a random error term. The orthogonality hypothesis is $b_1 = b_2 = 0$. Tests of this type have been carried out by Dominguez (1986), Froot and Frankel (1989), MacDonald and Torrance

(1989) and Ito (1990). Although these studies differ by what variables they include in X_t, the results are all very similar, with the joint null hypothesis almost unanimously rejected, particularly for the time horizons longer than three months.[3] These results suggest that the expected exchange rates, as reported in the survey data, did not fully incorporate all available information and are thus inconsistent with the rational expectations hypothesis.[4]

If the rational expectations hypothesis can be rejected, is there any other expectations schema which is consistent with the survey data? Frankel and Froot (1987), again using survey data, have tested extrapolative, adaptive and regressive expectations formation structures. Interestingly, their results demonstrate a difference between short-run and long-run expectations for all expectations mechanisms, but particularly for the extrapolative and regressive mechanisms. The extrapolative expectations mechanism can be represented as:

$$E_t e_{t+j} - e_t = \gamma(e_t - e_{t-j}) \tag{8.3}$$

The sign of γ is of great importance. If $\gamma > 0$, the past movement of the exchange rate is followed by an expectation of currency movement in the same direction; that is, a 'bandwagon' effect. On the other hand, if $\gamma < 0$, then the past currency movement is followed by a movement in the opposite direction. Frankel and Froot found that for the short-run horizons of one or two weeks to one month the sign of γ was positive, but for the long-run horizons of six and 12 months the sign of γ was negative. This clearly reflects a difference in behaviour between short-run and long-run expectations. The regressive expectations hypothesis can be represented as:

$$E_t e_{t+j} - e_t = \eta(\bar{e}_t - e_t) \tag{8.4}$$

where $\bar{e}_t$ is the long-run equilibrium exchange rate, proxied by purchasing power parity (PPP) or moving averages of the actual exchange rate series. If $\eta > 0$, then the exchange rate is expected to move toward its long-run equilibrium level, whereas if $\eta < 0$, the exchange rate moves away from its long-run equilibrium level. Once again the results showed a different kind of behaviour in the short run as compared to the long run. For expectations of one week to one month, η was found to be negative, indicative of short-run instability, whereas for long-run expectations of six and 12 months, η was found to be positive. To try to rationalize the difference between short-term and long-term expectations, prevalent in both regressive and extrapolative cases, Froot and Frankel (1990) argued that market participants may be using two types of forecasting techniques. It may be that for the short-run forecasts the predominant method is technical analysis or chartism, whereas for the longer-run forecasts the economic fundamentals are most important: that is, relative prices, relative output and interest rate differentials.

Liu and Maddala (1992) used the cointegration methodology and weekly survey data from MMS on the pound sterling, the Swiss franc, German mark and Japanese yen, all against the US dollar for the period 24 October 1984 to 19 May 1989, to test the rational expectations hypothesis in these foreign exchange markets. Since both the exchange rate series and the expectations series were integrated of order one,[5] if the difference between e_t and $E_t e_{t+j}$ is found to be I(0) then e_t and $E_t e_{t+j}$ are cointegrated. Liu and Maddala found all spot exchange rate and expectations series to be cointegrated. For the rational expectations hypothesis to be accepted, however, it is also required that the residuals be random. The Box-Pierce Q-statistics showed no significant serial correlation in the weekly residuals, thus the rational expectations hypothesis cannot be rejected using weekly data. Liu and Maddala ran identical tests on monthly expectations and spot exchange rate data, but on this data set the Q-statistics indicated non-randomness in the residuals and thus rejected the rational expectations hypothesis.

The results of Liu and Maddala differ from those of Frankel and Froot (1987) in that one-week ahead expectations are found to be consistent with rational expectations, rather than against the hypothesis. This could be due to the different sample data set – in particular Liu and Maddala's data set does not include the whole period of dollar overvaluation, which may have affected market participants' expectations of the future value of the dollar – or it could be due to the methodology used. Given the existence of unit roots in the data, the cointegration method is to be preferred. At horizons of one month or more, however, the results of Frankel and Froot are confirmed and the rational expectations hypothesis is rejected.

8.2.2   Chartism

Given the rejection of the rationality of exchange rate expectations, from the work of Frankel and Froot (1987), Froot and Frankel (1989), Allen and Taylor (1989, 1990) conducted a survey of chief foreign exchange dealers in the London foreign exchange market to discover the means by which expectations were generated. They found that a high proportion of foreign exchange dealers use some form of chart analysis in forming their trading decisions, particularly at the short horizons. At the shortest horizons, intra-day to one week, over 90 per cent of their survey respondents reported using some form of chartism and around 60 per cent judged charts to be at least as important as fundamentals at this horizon. At the longest horizons, one year or longer, considered in their survey, Allen and Taylor found that nearly 30 per cent of the chief dealers reported relying on pure fundamental analysis and 85 per cent judged fundamentals to be more important than chart analysis at this forecast horizon. Furthermore, only 8 per cent of respondents believed the two approaches to be mutually exclusive, with the majority regarding the methods as complementary to a greater or lesser degree.

In addition, Allen and Taylor (1990) find that the accuracy of a number of individual chart analysts' one-week-ahead Deutsche Mark and US dollar–yen exchange rate forecasts is such that they consistently outperform a range of alternative forecasting procedures, including the random walk model, vector autoregressions and time series (ARIMA) models. This evidence suggests that empirical models of the exchange rate based on the pure fundamentals of economic theory will be unsuccessful in predicting short-run exchange rate movements. It also suggests that exchange rate expectations are not formed in a way that is consistent with the rational expectations hypothesis. In fact, for most of the participants in the survey, Allen and Taylor (1990) failed to reject the null hypothesis of static expectations against four alternative (adaptive, regressive, extrapolative and bandwagon) expectations hypotheses. Of particular note is that bandwagon expectations were never identified, thus ruling out chartism as a cause of instability in the foreign exchange markets, in the sense that the chartists' expectations do not systematically overreact to changes in the current exchange rate.

The results of Allen and Taylor to the effect that chartism is the prevalent method in generating weekly expectations is consistent with the findings of Froot and Frankel (1990) but very much against the findings of Liu and Maddala (1992). The evidence to date suggests that survey data may be consistent with almost any type of expectations hypothesis in the short run (up to one week), except bandwagon expectations, but at horizons of greater than one week the one type of expectations hypothesis which does not gain any support is the rational expectations hypothesis, upon which many of the structural exchange rate models developed in this book rely.

8.3   Chaos and non-linear dynamics

This section briefly considers non-linear dynamic models in the context of the exchange rate. According to Scheinkman (1990) from the viewpoint of economic dynamics there are two related properties of non-linear systems of interest: 'The first one is that such systems can generate the quasiperiodic or even erratic behaviour that characterizes some economic time series .... The second is that such non-linear systems can generate sensitive dependency to initial conditions, i.e. small initial differences can be magnified by the dynamics' (p. 45). This section is sub-divided into theoretical models of non-linear dynamics generating chaos and empirical studies trying to find evidence of chaos in time series data on the exchange rate. Section 8.3.1 considers two non-linear (and chaotic) theoretical models of the exchange rate due to De Grauwe and Vansanten (1990) and De Grauwe and Dewachter (1990). Section 8.3.2 considers the principal empirical tests for the presence of chaos and some test results for chaos in exchange rate time series data, due to Vassilicos (1990), Tata (1991), and Tata and Vassilicos (1991). The mathematics of simple empirical tests for chaos are outlined in the Appendix to this chapter.

8.3.1   A theoretical model of the exchange rate with non-linear dynamics
In two recent papers, De Grauwe and Vansanten (1990) and De Grauwe and Dewachter (1990) have developed non-linear dynamic models of the portfolio balance and monetary approaches to the exchange rate. The dynamic properties of these models are similar in that both can generate chaotic dynamics for the exchange rate time path. In this section the monetary model is outlined and the results compared with those of the portfolio balance model.

The monetary model, as in the models discussed in Chapter 4, consists of four basic relationships: a money market equilibrium equation, uncovered interest rate parity, purchasing power parity and an exchange rate expectations formation mechanism, as given by equations (8.5) to (8.9) respectively:

$$M_t = Y_t^a P_t (1 + r_t)^{-c} \qquad (8.5)$$

$$\varepsilon_t(E_{t+1}/E_t) = (1 + r_t)/(1 + r^*_t) \qquad (8.6)$$

$$E_t = P_t/P_t^* \qquad (8.7)$$

$$\varepsilon_t(E_{t+1})/E_t = [\varepsilon_{ct}(E_{t+1})/E_t]^{m_t}[\varepsilon_{ft}(E_{t+1})/E_t]^{1-m_t} \qquad (8.8)$$

where M is the money supply, Y is domestic output (exogenous), P is the domestic price level, r is the nominal interest rate, E is the spot exchange rate, ε is the expectations operator, where the subscripts c and f denote expectations held by chartists and fundamentalists respectively, a and c are constant parameters, m_t is a time-varying parameter and asterisks denote foreign currency variables. The model dynamics are completed by adding equations for the adjustment of the price level to PPP and by specifying processes for the expectations held by chartist and fundamentalists. The domestic price level adjusts to PPP according to:

$$P_t/P_{t-1} = (E_t/E_t)^k \qquad \text{where } k \geq 0 \tag{8.9}$$

Chartist expectations are assumed to be extrapolative and measured as a moving average process of the form:

$$\varepsilon_{ct}(E_{t+1})/E_t = (E_t/E_{t-1})^d(E_{t-1}/E_{t-2})^e(E_{t-2}/E_{t-3})^f \tag{8.10}$$

where d, e, and f are weights of the moving average process. The fundamentalists use the rule:

$$e_{ft}(E_{t+1})/E_t = (E_t/E_t)^h \tag{8.11}$$

which says that fundamentalists expect the rate to move back towards its equilibrium rate in the next period at speed h. Finally, the weights given to fundamentalists and chartists are assumed to be endogenous and to depend on the deviation of the market rate from the fundamental rate. The specification used is:

$$m_t = n/[1 + b(E_{t-1} - E_{t-1})^2] \tag{8.12}$$

where $0 < n < 1$ and $b > 0$. Higher values of n denote a greater weight given to the chartists and a lower value given to fundamentalists.

The model is solved for the endogenous variables P and E, which give two dynamic equations of the form:

$$P_t = Z_{1t}P_t^{ch(1-m_t)}[E_t^{-h(1-m_t)}\varepsilon_{ct}(E_{t+1}/E_t)^{m_t}]^c \tag{8.13}$$

$$E_t = [(G_1G_2)^{-1}E_{t-1}^{-f_1}E_{t-2}^{-f_2}E_{t-3}^{-f_3}E_{t-4}^{-f_4}]^{(1/f_1)} \tag{8.14}$$

where

$$f_0 = (cdm_t - ch(1-m_t))(1+k) - k$$
$$f_1 = (1+k)cm_t(e-d) - (cdm_{t-1} - ch(1-m_{t-1}))$$
$$f_2 = (1+k)cm_t(f-e) - c(e-d)m_{t-1}$$
$$f_3 = -fcm_t(1+k) - c(f-e)m_{t-1}$$
$$f_4 = cfm_{t-1}$$
$$G_1 = Z_{1t}^{(1+k)}/Z_{1t-1}$$
$$G_2 = P_t^{(1-ch(1-m_t))(1+k)}/P_{t-1}^{(1-ch(1-m_t))}$$

$$Z_1 = M_t Y_t^{-a}(1 + r_t^*)^c P_t^{*-c(1-m)}$$

Thus the exchange rate is determined by its own past values, the lagged values of prices and the composite exogenous variable, Z_1. As equations (8.13) and (8.14) show, the solution is a complex system of non-linear difference equations for which no analytic solutions can be derived. The dynamic properties of the model can thus only be obtained by simulation. The model is therefore simulated over a period of 7000 observations, with fixed parameter values[6] except for those underlying the behaviour of the speculators, n and b.

The results from these simulations show that the exchange rate may exhibit four different kinds of dynamic behaviour, depending upon the values for n. For values of $n < 0.5$ stable solutions emerge, but as n rises increasingly unstable behaviour emerges. For example, for $0.55 < n < 0.72$, the dynamics display periodicity, but for $0.74 < n < 0.80$ chaotic dynamics are observed and for $n > 0.80$ explosive solutions are the most likely outcome. This implies that as a greater weight is attached to chartist expectations the greater the instability of the model.[7] The possibility of chaotic dynamics, that is dynamics which look random but actually have a structure, raises important issues for modelling the exchange rate. Firstly, models which exhibit chaotic dynamics are sensitive to the initial conditions and to very small changes in the parameter values. This makes the exchange rate impossible to forecast using traditional modelling techniques and, if valid, could account for the poor out-of-sample forecasting performance of the structural exchange rate models. Secondly, transitory shocks can have permanent effects on the time path of the exchange rate, thereby adding to the volatility of the exchange rate over time. Furthermore, in De Grauwe and Vansanten (1990), a similar simulation exercise using a portfolio balance model of the exchange rate suggests that sterilized intervention in the foreign exchange market by the monetary authorities can serve to reduce the extent of instability in the market. This seems to contradict recent empirical evidence which has suggested that sterilized intervention is not a significant determinant of the exchange rate on account of the small scale of official intervention compared to private-sector stocks and flows of foreign exchange and the failure of a large number of econometric studies (see Almekinders and Eijffinger, 1991, for a survey) to identify intervention as significant unless it is associated with other 'news'.

Simulation exercises are not, in general, particularly satisfactory, for two reasons. First, since any simulation is finite in length, it is impossible to discriminate between chaos and solutions with a periodicity equal to the length of the simulation plus one. Another problem is that the exchange rate data produced in these simulations may bear no resemblance at all to actual exchange rate data. De Grauwe and Dewatcher have undertaken steps to limit both of these objections. By simulating the model over 7000 periods De Grauwe and Dewachter should have minimized the finite horizon problem. Second, they demonstrate that the exchange rate data yielded by the simulations contain a unit root and are hence consistent with actual exchange rate data! An alternative test is to examine actual, high-frequency exchange rate data and test for the presence of non-linearities. This is the subject of the next section.

8.3.2   Empirical tests for chaos in exchange rate time series data
Recent empirical work has focused upon three kinds of test for the presence of chaotic dynamics in exchange rate time series data. These tests are the Liapunov exponent test, the 'correlation dimension', and the residual and shuffle tests. The mathematics underlying these tests is outlined in the appendix to this chapter. In this section only the empirical findings are considered.

Vassilicos (1990) and Tata and Vassilicos (1991) use tick-by-tick data on the US dollar–Deutsche Mark exchange rate advertised on Reuter's FXFX page. The data set includes both ask and bid prices, although only ask prices are used to avoid any smoothing of the data. The data set spans only a week in calendar time, running from Sunday 9 April 1989 to Saturday 15 April 1989, giving 20 408 data points. Tata and Vassilicos (1991) report that no evidence of chaos could be found in the data with the largest Liapunov exponent not significantly different from zero. Moreover, as the sample size fell, to bias the test in favour of chaotic behaviour, with as few as 5000 sample observations still no evidence of chaos could be found.

Tata (1991) tests the US dollar–Swiss franc spot exchange rate for evidence of chaotic behaviour, using ask prices from tick-by-tick data over the period from Sunday 9 April 1989 to Saturday 29 April 1989, giving 34 466 data points, of which for computational reasons only 32 200 observations were used. The shuffle test indicates that the dimension estimates were higher after scrambling, but this is only a necessary and not a sufficient condition for chaos. Tata also used the BDS test (see Appendix 8.1) to check for randomness in the US dollar–Swiss franc exchange rate data. After pre-whitening the time series using an AR(2) filter, the residuals were tested for chaos. The largest computed value of the BDS statistic (critical value 1.96) was 0.763, which does not reject the null hypothesis of randomness at 5 per cent, indicating no evidence of chaos.

On the other hand, Kugler and Lenz (1990) have analysed time series on the US dollar–Deutsche Mark, US dollar–Swiss franc, US dollar–French

franc and US dollar–yen exchange rates and found significant non-linearities for all cases and showed, using the BDS test statistic, that the null
hypothesis can be rejected at 1 per cent. These results may be highly
misleading, however, since only 572 data points are used. There are two
reasons for this. First, there is no method to verify that a process has an
infinite correlation dimension using finite amounts of data. Certainly 572
observations would seem to be insufficient, with natural scientists typically
using 5000 to 10 000 data points to detect low-dimensional chaotic
systems. The second problem is the possibility of bias in small data sets.
Even with as many as 2000 observations, Ramsey and Yuan (1989) have
showed a bias in favour of finding chaos, even where there is none.

Even the tick-by-tick data, used by Tata (1991) and Tata and Vassilicos
(1991) are not without their problems. Tick-by-tick data capture bid–ask
bounces and other dependencies which are caused by the micro-market
structure, such as the sequential execution of limit orders on the books of
the specialist as the market structure moves through those limit prices.
These artificial dependencies will be picked up by any good test of non-
linear dynamics and this is why in both studies only ask prices are used.
The preferred solution must be to increase the sampling interval in order
to average out these 'artificial' dependencies, but in order to obtain more
observations the researcher must look at longer histories, which runs into
the problem of regime changes which may in turn impart non-stationarity
to the data. Thus the requirements of long sampling intervals, to avoid
micro-market structure dependencies, and short histories, to avoid non-
stationarity, impose severe limitations on testing for chaos in exchange
rate data. The best evidence to date suggests that high-frequency exchange
rate data do not exhibit chaotic behaviour.

8.4   Target zones

The third recent approach to modelling exchange rate dynamics is to
acknowledge that in the real world exchange rates do not float freely, but
rather that the authorities have some notion of a target band within which
the exchange rate can fluctuate in the short term. The exchange rate
mechanism of the European Monetary System would be a good example
of a target zone regime with explicit bands, although the reference zones
established need not be publicly announced, nor strongly defended. The
crucial issue in modelling exchange rate dynamics under a target zone
regime is the formation of expectations. The basic idea is that because the
movement in the exchange rate is limited by the existence of explicit or
implicit bands the behaviour of the exchange rate within the band will be
different to that if there were no band. This section draws heavily on the
seminal paper by Krugman (1991) which considers only a simple monet-

ary model, although Miller and Weller (1991) examine target zones in the context of a model with sticky prices.

Following Krugman (1991) a simple graphical approach can be developed based upon a very simple monetary model of the exchange rate. The exchange rate is assumed to be equal to

$$e = m + v + \gamma E(de)/dt \tag{8.16}$$

where e is the log of the spot exchange rate, m is the domestic money supply, v is a shift term representing velocity shocks and the last term is the expected rate of depreciation. The money supply is assumed to be passive in that m is only changed in order to maintain the exchange rate within the zone. Specifically, m is reduced by the authorities to prevent e from exceeding some maximum value $\bar{e}$, and increased to prevent e from falling below some minimum value $\underline{e}$. As long as e lies between $\bar{e}$ and $\underline{e}$ the money supply remains unchanged. The velocity term, v, is assumed to be the only source of exchange rate dynamics and to follow a random walk. Figure 8.1 plots the exchange rate against velocity; the target zone is indicated by the dotted lines that define a band that bounds the exchange rate between $\bar{e}$ and $\underline{e}$.

If m is held constant and v follows a random walk then $E(de/dt) = 0$. Thus inside the exchange rate bands $e = m + v$ and behaves like a freely floating exchange rate. If $m = 0$ and $v = 0$ the model will be at the origin

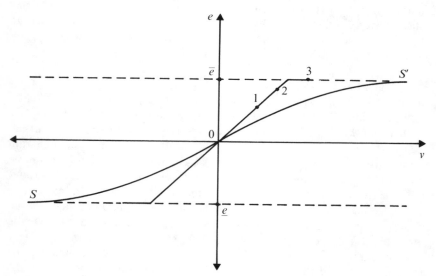

Figure 8.1   Exchange rate movement in a target zone model

(point 0) in Figure 8.1. If *v* increases then with a fixed money supply the exchange rate must increase in direct proportion to *v* until *e* reaches the edge of the band, when the money supply will be adjusted to prevent the exchange rate from moving outside the band. If this so-called naive view were correct then the exchange rate would move up the solid 45-degree line in Figure 8.1. To see that this view is not correct consider the situation starting at a point just inside the band, at say point 2. Starting at point 2, if *v* falls a little, the exchange rate would slip down the 45-degree line to a point like 1. If *v* rises a little however, the exchange rate will not rise by an equal amount, because the monetary authority will act to defend the target zone, so the exchange rate will move to a point like 3. On this argument, towards the top of the band a fall in *v* will reduce *e* by more than a rise in *v* will increase *e*. Since *v* is random, the expected rate of change of *e* is negative, that is, as *e* approaches the top of the band its rate of increase slows. Because expected depreciation enters the basic exchange rate equation (8.16), the exchange rate itself is dragged down from point 2 to a somewhat lower point. The same must be true at the bottom of the band, when the expected rate of fall in *e* declines the level of *e* is pulled up to a point above that on the solid, 45-degree line. Thus the 45-degree line becomes bent at the edges of the zone and so the actual relationship between *e* and *v* becomes the S-shaped curve, S0S', in Figure 8.1.[8]

There are two important characteristics of the S-curve in Figure 8.1. First, the exchange rate lies below the 45-degree line in the upper half of the figure and above it in the lower half; by (8.16) this must mean that the expected rate of change of *e* is negative in the upper part of the figure and positive in the lower part. This is only possible, given that *m* is constant and *v* is random, because of the curvature of the S-line. Because the S is concave in the upper half of Figure 8.1, even though the expected rate of change in *v* is zero, the expected rate of change of *e* is negative; and conversely in the lower part. The second characteristic of the S-curve is that it shows that the effect of the target zone on exchange rates is stabilising. Without the band then the exchange rate would simply move up and down the 45-degree line. Because the S-curve is flatter then the 45-degree line shocks to velocity have a smaller effect on the exchange rate, and thus, the exchange rate itself has less variation than under a free float. This reduction in volatility occurs while the exchange rate is inside the band although no effort is made by the authorities to stabilize it.

Figure 8.2 shows the implications for monetary policy of the target zone. Suppose that initially the market is at point 1 and for a while there are positive shocks to *v*. The model will move along the original S-curve until point 2 is reached at the edge of the band. Any further increase in *v* will be offset by reductions in the money supply, so that the exchange rate

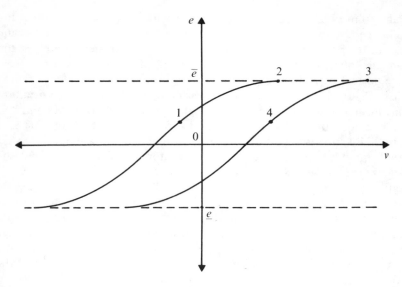

Figure 8.2   Monetary policy in a target zone model

will remain constant and the model would move along the upper band limit to point 3. Suppose that v is now affected by negative shocks. This will have the effect of moving e inside the band, so the authorities would not wish to prevent this from happening, and the market will therefore move back down a new S-curve to a point like 4. This analysis shows that there are in fact a family of S-curves. The market stays on any one curve as long as v remains within the range where e lies inside the band. The money supply shifts whenever the edge of the band is reached, placing the market on a new curve.

The final issue to consider in this section is that of credibility. Suppose agents in the foreign exchange market do not know whether the monetary authorities are prepared to defend the band. When the exchange rate reaches the limit of the band either the monetary authorities will show their willingness to defend the band, or they will not and the market will discover that it is operating under a freely floating exchange rate system after all. In Figure 8.3 the 45-degree line shows combinations of e and v under a freely floating exchange rate system. The flatter S-curve shows the combination of e and v when the target zone is perceived as perfectly credible. With imperfect credibility of the target zone agents will attach a non-zero probability to each of these outcomes giving rise to a steeper (average) S-curve. Suppose the exchange rate hits the band at point 1, where the value of v is given as v_0. If the target zone is defended the

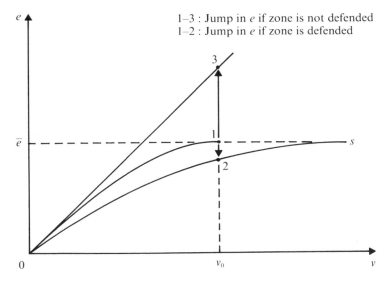

Figure 8.3   Credibility in the target zone model

exchange rate jumps down onto the flatter S-curve at point 2, while if it is not defended the exchange rate jumps up to a point on the 45-degree line. The important point is that even if the target zone is not perceived as fully credible it will still have a stabilizing effect on exchange rate at least until the band limit is reached.

8.5   New directions for structural models

Sections 8.2, 8.3 and 8.4 have focused on recent developments in modelling short-run exchange rate dynamics. This section is concerned with recent suggestions for modelling the long-run equilibrium exchange rate. There have been two recent proposals of note: the inclusion of real capital assets in the portfolio balance structure and the effects of hysteresis on industrial structure, both due to Dornbusch (1987). These proposals are briefly considered in turn.

8.5.1   Real capital assets and portfolio balance

The standard portfolio balance model remains oversimplified even if account is taken of current account balances and risk premia. The omission lies in the exclusion of real capital from portfolios and in disregarding the effect over time of investment on the capital stock and thus on the supply side of the economy. To fully integrate real capital flows into the analysis complicates the analysis considerably. In particular, among the many sources of ambiguity is the effect of a demand expansion on the stock market. An expansion in demand will bring about both an increase in output and an increase in interest rates. The net effect on the valuation of the stock market is therefore not unambiguous with the higher output increasing optimism, while higher interest rates push down bond prices, thereby fostering a movement out of equities into gilts and lowering equity prices. Thus non-bank private sector wealth may rise or fall and this will therefore lead to a rise or fall in spending and money demand.

A second important consideration is the substitutability of money and debt and debt and capital. This is relevant for the extent of yield changes and hence for the direction and magnitude of exchange rate changes. For example, if current account deficits were associated with excessive domestic private investment over savings, thereby enhancing the productive capacity of the economy, the exchange rate would not be expected to depreciate in the long run. On the other hand, if the current deficit were associated with a consumption-financing fiscal deficit then the prospect of greater domestic inflation is likely to be linked to a long-term depreciation of the exchange rate.

8.5.2   Relative prices and industrial organization

Traditionally macroeconomists have made one of two assumptions about relative prices. As noted in Chapter 2, the Classical approach was to invoke purchasing power parity (PPP) so that domestic prices were completely insulated from foreign price changes. A fall in foreign prices would be completely offset by an appreciation of the home currency, leaving relative prices unchanged. The simple Keynesian model of Chapter 3, on the other hand, assumes domestic wages and prices are fixed in national currency terms, so that exchange rate movements change relative prices one-for-one. Both of these assumptions are unrealistic and are perhaps no longer a firm foundation upon which to base models of the exchange rate. Pentecost (1992), for example, shows that the UK experienced falling (local currency) non-oil import prices despite a real depreciation of the effective exchange rate throughout much of the 1980s. Dornbusch (1987) argues for a newer approach which recognizes the sluggishness of wages, but builds on that a theory of equilibrium price determination along the lines of the industrial organization literature.

By way of illustration, due to Dornbusch (1987), consider an imperfectly competitive world in which firms are price-setters. Firms attempt to maximize profits, subject to the strategic assumptions about the determinants of the demand facing each firm and the responses of all other firms in the market. The impact of a change in the exchange rate on equilibrium prices will depend upon a number of factors: whether goods are perfect substitutes or differentiated products; whether the market structure is characterized by monopoly, oligopoly or imperfect competition; the relative number of domestic and foreign firms; and the functional form of the market demand curve. For the case of homogeneous products, the industry price falls following an exchange rate appreciation, with the fall being larger the more competitive the market and the larger the share of foreign firms. For the case of differentiated products, an appreciation leads to a rise in the relative price of domestic goods, while imported varieties decline in price both absolutely and relatively. Dornbusch also notes an interesting case where an appreciation may give rise to a more than proportionate fall in market price. This could arise where the favourable cost-shock to the foreign firm is substantial enough to make foreign sales overly profitable, resulting in an expansion in supply to the home market with a consequent fall in domestic currency prices.

Although this brief digression into industrial organization has not resulted in any firm conclusions, it should be apparent that it opens up a large area of future theoretical and empirical work at the interface of open economy macroeconomics and industrial organization. Perhaps the biggest challenge for future researchers is to translate these complex issues into testable empirical hypotheses, given the frequently unreliable and aggregate nature of most macroeconomic data.

Notes

1. MMS (Money Market Services) New York and London. The data set is: November 1982–October 1984 bi-weekly; two-week and three-month expectations; October 1984–present, weekly; a sample of about 30 professional traders; UK pound, Deutsche Mark, yen, Swiss franc against the US dollar; one-week and one-month expectations.
2. JCIF (Japanese Centre for International Finance), Tokyo. The data set is: May 1985–present; semi-monthly; a sample of 44 market participants; yen–US dollar; one-month, three-month and six-month expectations.
3. Dominguez, Froot and Frankel include the forward discount, Ito uses the lagged exchange rate and MacDonald and Torrance use the nominal interest rate differential as the X variable.
4. Lewis (1989), however, points out that systematic forecast errors can be consistent with the behaviour of rational agents who are learning about new processes determining the fundamentals.
5. The tests used are the Augmented Dickey Fuller (ADF) Test (see appendix to Chapter 2) and Phillip's Z_t and Z_α tests (Phillips, 1987).
6. These values are: $a = 0.5$, $c = 0.8$, $d = 0.6$, $e = 0.3$, $f = 0.1$ and $h = k = 0.45$.
7. This does not seem to square with Allen and Taylor's survey of London FX dealers whose expectations were not inconsistent with a static generating mechanism.
8. Krugman shows that it is not possible to approach the edge of the band on an S-curve that actually crosses the edge. The only possible curves are those just tangent to the edge. This phenomenon is known as 'smooth pasting'.

Appendix: Some mathematics and tests of non-linear and chaotic dynamics
There are four different tests of empirical chaos which dominate the
literature. In this appendix little attention is paid to theoretical rigour, for
which the reader is referred to the mathematics literature. It is hoped,
however, that this annex will make the empirical literature accessible. For
a non-technical introduction to the concept of chaos and applications in
economics, Baumol and Benhabib (1989), Frank and Stengos (1988),
Hsieh (1991) and May (1976) are recommended.

Liapunov functions and exponents
Consider the general, autonomous non-linear system:

$$x_{it} = f_i(x_{1t}, x_{2t}, \ldots, x_{nt}) \tag{A8.1}$$

where $f_i = x^e_i$ for all $x_{it} = x^e_t$ for all i. Suppose there exits a continuous
scalar function:

$$V(x_1 - x^e_1, x_2 - x^e_2, \ldots, x_n - x^e_n)$$

such that:

(i) $V > 0$ if at least one of the quantities $x_1 - x^e_1, x_2 - x^e_2 \ldots, x_n - x^e_n$ is
      different from zero and $V = 0$ if, and only if, $x_i - x^e_i$ for all i.
(ii) $V \to +\infty$ as $\| x - x^e \| \to +\infty$
(iii) $\triangle V < 0$ if at least one of the quantities $x_1 - x^e_1, x_2 - x^e_2, \ldots,$
      $x_n - x^e_n$ is different from zero or $\triangle V = 0$ if, and only if,
      $x_1 - x^e_1 = 0$ for all i,

then $(x^e_1, x^e_2, \ldots, x^e_n)$ is globally stable.
     What this theorem says is that, if the point whose coordinates are $x_1(t)$,
$x_2(t), \ldots, x_n(t)$ approaches $(x^e_1, x^e_2, \ldots, x^e_n)$ as t increases then the
equilibrium is stable. Thus the existence of the Liapunov function, V, is a
necessary and sufficient condition for stability. This theorem can also be
used to prove instability, since if (i) and (ii) hold, but $\triangle V > 0$, then the
equilibrium is unstable. In other words, when $\triangle V < 0$, the system contracts; when $\triangle V > 0$, the system is stretched. It is this stretching and
contracting which characterize chaotic dynamics.
     The presence of at least one positive Liapunov exponent, λ, is taken to
be the definition of chaos. In vector notation (A8.1) becomes $dX/
dt = F(X)$ and if $X(t) = X^*(t) + D(t)$, where $X^*(t)$ is a particular trajectory
which solves $dX/dt = F(X)$ and $D(t)$ is an arbitrary small, but positive
initial displacement from the start of $X^*(t)$, then:

$$dD/dt = (\partial F/\partial X)|_{x=x^*} + 0(D^2) \tag{A8.2}$$

where the $\partial F/\partial X$ is an $n \times n$ Jacobian matrix with time-dependent elements and where $0(D_2)$ collects the terms in second-order smalls. On dropping these second-order terms, a linear-homogeneous equation system emerges with a solution of the general form:

$$D(t) = A(t).D(0) \tag{A8.3}$$

where $A(t)$ is also an $n \times n$ matrix. Under fairly general conditions, for a given value of $D(0)$, the following limit exists:

$$\lambda_i = \lim_{t \to \infty} t^{-1} ln|D_i(t)|, \; i = 1,2, \ldots , n. \tag{A8.4}$$

The λ_i are the Liapunov exponents for the trajectory $X^*(t)$ and the disturbance $D(0)$. There are as many Liapunov exponents as there are degrees of freedom, with the larger the value of λ the faster the rate of separation. For the estimation of Liapunov exponents there is an algorithm developed by Wolf *et al.* (1985), which is used by Tata (1991) and Tata and Vassilicos (1991).

Correlation dimension
An observed time series x_t is used to create a set of 'M-histories' as $x_t^M = (x_t, x_{t+1}, x_{t+2}, \ldots , x_{t+m-1})$. This converts the series of scalars into slightly shorter series of vectors with overlapping entries. The correlation integral, calculated from the m-histories, is defined as:

$$C^M(\varepsilon) = \{\text{the number of pairs } i \neq j \text{ with distance } ||x^m_i - x^m_j|| \leq \varepsilon\}/T^2$$

where $T \to \infty$. In practice, of course, T is given by the length of the data series. The correlation dimension, D, is simply how the correlation integral scales as ε shrinks; that is, $C^M(\varepsilon) \sim \varepsilon^D$, that is:

$$D^M = \lim_{\varepsilon \to 0} \{ln C^M(\varepsilon)/ln\varepsilon\} \tag{A8.5}$$

As a practical matter, if as M increases so does D^M then the system is regarded as being high-dimensional or stochastic. If, however, D^M settles down, or saturates at some level D, then D is the estimated dimension of the system. If the estimated value of D is not an integer then the system under investigation is referred to as 'fractal'.

Residual and shuffle tests

Because many economic time series, especially exchange rates, are generated by near unit root processes (Nelson and Plosser, 1982), correlation dimension and Liapunov exponent tests are not to be relied upon as primary evidence for chaos, since a unit root process generating x_t, will result in the variance of the innovations in x_t being very close to zero. Consequently, successive draws from this process will be close together for a wide range of values for ε. Only very small values of ε can avoid this problem. Brock (1986) proposed the residual test to overcome this problem. It is based on an important property of chaotic equations; that is, that they are invariant to linear transformations. If a linear transformation is performed on chaotic data, then the original data and the transformed data should have the same correlation dimension and Liapunov exponents. Formally, let $\{X_t; t = 1, 2, \ldots, \infty\}$ be a deterministic chaotic time series. Then fit the linear model:

$$X_t + \psi_1 X_t + \psi_2 X_t + \ldots + \psi_n X_t = U_t, \text{ where } t = n + 1, n + 2, \ldots$$
(A8.6)

and U_t is the residual at t and ψ_i are the estimated coefficients. Then the correlation dimension estimates and the largest Liapunov exponent of $\{X\}$ and $\{U\}$ are the same. Thus, if the calculated dimension and Liapunov exponents are substantially different, the hypothesis of a deterministic chaos law is suspect. This test is able to distinguish between lower-dimensional processes, which are in fact unit root processes, and real chaotic processes.

Scheinkman and LeBaron (1989) have proposed a similar type of test called the shuffle test. Suppose the original data series has been pre-whitened, so it does not possess any non-linear structure and comes from an independently, identically distributed (iid) data-generating process. Shuffling the series by sampling with replacement would create a new series with a similar dimension estimate to the original series. If, however, the series still possessed non-linear structure, the shuffling process would destroy it.

An alternative approach to addressing the question of statistical inference has been proposed by Brock *et al.* (1987), who have developed a family of test statistics based on correlation integral. The so-called BDS test statistics test the null hypothesis of an iid. process against non-linear dependent alternatives.

References

Abauf, N. and Jorion, P. (1990), 'Purchasing Power Parity in the Long Run', *The Journal of Finance*, **45**, pp. 157–73.

Alexander, S.S. (1952), 'Effects of a Devaluation on the Trade Balance', *International Monetary Fund Staff Papers*, **2**, pp. 263–78.

Alexander, S.S. (1959), 'Effects of a Devaluation: A Simplified Synthesis of Elasticities and Absorption Approaches', *American Economic Review*, **49**, pp. 23–42.

Allen, H. and Taylor, M.P. (1989), 'Charts and Fundamentals in the Foreign Exchange Market', Bank of England Discussion Paper, No. 40, August.

Allen, H. and Taylor, M.P. (1990), 'Charts, Noise and Fundamentals in the London Foreign Exchange Market', *The Economic Journal*, **100**, Supplement, pp. 49–59.

Allen, P.R. and Kenen, P.B. (1978), *The Balance of Payments, Exchange Rates and Economic Policy: A Survey and Synthesis of Recent Developments*, Athens: Centre of Planning and Economic Research.

Almekinders, G.J. and Eijffinger, S.C.W. (1991), 'Empirical Evidence on Foreign Exchange Market Intervention: Where Do We Stand?', *Weltwirtschaftliches Archiv*, **126**, pp. 645–77.

Alogoskoufis, G. and Smith, R. (1991), 'On Error Correction Models: Specification, Interpretation, Estimation', *Journal of Economic Surveys*, **5**, pp. 97–128.

Backus, D. (1984), 'Empirical Models of the Exchange Rate: Separating the Wheat from the Chaff', *Canadian Journal of Economics*, **17**, pp. 824–46.

Baillie, R.T. and McMahon, P.C. (1989), *The Foreign Exchange Market: Theory and Econometric Evidence*, Cambridge: Cambridge University Press.

Baillie, R.T. and Pecchenino, R.A. (1991), 'The Search for Equilibrium Relationships in International Finance: The Case of the Monetary Model', *Journal of International Money and Finance*, **10**, pp. 582–93.

Baillie, R.T. and Selover, D.D. (1987), 'Cointegration and Models of Exchange Rate Determination', *International Journal of Forecasting*, **3**, pp. 43–52.

Balassa, B. (1964), 'The Purchasing Power Parity Doctrine: A Reappraisal', *Journal of Political Economy*, **72**, pp. 584–96.

Barr, D.G. (1989), 'Exchange Rate Dynamics: An Empirical Analysis', in

R. MacDonald and M.P. Taylor (eds), *Exchange Rates and Open Economy Macroeconomics*, pp. 111–29, Oxford: Blackwell.

Barro, R.J. (1977), 'Unanticipated Money Growth and Unemployment in the United States', *Journal of Political Economy*, **86**, pp. 101–15.

Baumol, W.J. (1970), *Economic Dynamics*, 3rd edition, New York: Macmillan.

Baumol, W.J. and Benhabib, J. (1989), 'Chaos: Significance, Mechanism, and Economic Applications', *Journal of Economic Perspectives*, **3**, pp. 77–105.

Bergstrand, J. and Bundt, T. (1990), 'Currency Substitution and Monetary Autonomy: the Foreign demand for US Demand Deposits', *Journal of International Money and Finance*, **9**, pp. 325–34.

Bickerdike, C.F. (1920), 'The Instability of Foreign Exchange', *Economic Journal*, **30**, pp. 118–22.

Bilson, J.F.O. (1978a), 'Rational Expectations and the Exchange Rate', in J.A. Frenkel and H.G. Johnson (eds), *The Economics of the Exchange Rate*, Reading, Mass.: Addison-Wesley.

Bilson, J.F.O. (1978b), 'The Monetary Approach to the Exchange Rate – Some Empirical Evidence', *International Monetary Fund Staff Papers*, **25**, pp. 48–75.

Bilson, J.F.O. (1979), 'Recent Developments in Monetary Models of Exchange Rate Determination', *International Monetary Fund Staff Papers*, **26**, pp. 201–3.

Bisignano, J. and Hoover, K.D. (1983), 'Some Suggested Improvements to a Simple Portfolio Balance Model of Exchange Rate Determination with Special Reference to the US Dollar/Canadian Dollar Exchange Rate', *Weltwirtschaftliches Archiv*, **119**, pp. 19–37.

Blanchard, O.J. (1979), 'Speculative Bubbles, Crashes and Rational Expectations', *Economics Letters*, **3**, pp. 387–9.

Blaug, M. (1968), *Economic Theory in Retrospect*, 2nd edition, London: Heinemann.

Boothe, P.M. and Glassman, D. (1987), 'Off the Mark: Lessons for Exchange Rate Modelling', *Oxford Economic Papers*, **39**, pp. 443–57.

Boothe, P.M. and Poloz, S.S. (1988), 'Unstable Money Demand and the Monetary Model of the Exchange Rate', *Canadian Journal of Economics*, **21**, pp. 785–98.

Boughton, J.M. (1984), 'Exchange Rate Movements and Adjustment in Financial Markets: Quarterly Estimates for Major Currencies', *International Monetary Fund Staff Papers*, **31**, pp.445–68.

Boughton, J.M. (1987), 'Tests of the Performance of Reduced-Form Exchange Rate Models', *Journal of International Economics*, **23**, pp. 41–56.

Branson, W.H. (1968), *Financial Capital Flows in the US Balance of Payments*, Amsterdam: North Holland.

Branson, W.H. and Buiter, W. (1983), 'Monetary and Fiscal Policy with Flexible Exchange Rates', in J.S. Bhandari and B.H. Putnam (eds), *Economic Interdependence and Flexible Exchange Rates*, pp. 251–85, Cambridge, Mass.: MIT Press.

Branson, W.H. and Halttunen, H. (1979), 'Asset Market Determination of Exchange Rates: Initial Empirical and Policy Results' in J.P. Martin and A. Smith (eds), *Trade and Payments Adjustment under Flexible Exchange Rates*, pp. 55–85, London: Macmillan.

Branson, W.H., Halttunen, H. and Masson, P. (1977), 'Exchange Rates in the Short Run: The Dollar–Deutschemark Rate', *European Economic Review*, **10**, pp. 303–24.

Branson, W.H., Halttunen, H. and Masson, P. (1979), 'Exchange Rates in the Short Run: Some Further Results', *European Economic Review*, **12**, pp. 395–402.

Branson, W.H. and Henderson, D.W. (1985), 'The Specification and Influence of Asset Markets', in R.W. Jones and P.B. Kenen (eds), *Handbook of International Economics*, vol. II, Amsterdam: North Holland.

Brock, W.A. (1986), 'Distinguishing Random and Deterministic Systems: Abridged Version', *Journal of Economic Theory*, **40**, pp. 168–95.

Brock, W., Dechert, W. and Scheinkman, J. (1987), 'A Test for Independence Based on the Correlation Dimension', SSRI Working Paper No. 8702, Economics, University of Wisconsin–Madison.

Buiter, W. and Miller, M.H. (1981), 'Monetary Policy and International Competitiveness: The Problems of Adjustment', *Oxford Economic Papers*, Supplement, **33**, pp. 143–75.

Calvo, G.A. and Rodriguez, C.A. (1977), 'A Model of Exchange Rate Determination Under Currency Substitution and Rational Expectations', *Journal of Political Economy*, **85**, pp. 261–78.

Cassel, G. (1916), 'The Present Situation of Foreign Exchange', *Economic Journal*, **26**, pp. 62–5.

Cassel, G. (1918), 'Abnormal Deviations in International Exchanges', *Economic Journal*, **28**, pp. 413–5.

Cassel, G. (1921), *The World's Monetary Problems*, London: Constable

Cassel, G. (1922), *Money and Foreign Exchanges After 1914*, London: Constable.

Cassel, G. (1928), *Post-war Monetary Stabilisation*, New York: Columbia University.

Cassel, G. (1930), *Money and Foreign Exchange after 1919*, London: Macmillan.

Charemza, W.W. and Deadman, D.F. (1992), *New Directions in Econometric Practice*, Aldershot: Edward Elgar.

Chiang, A.C. (1974), *Fundamental Methods of Mathematical Economics*, 2nd edition, London: McGraw-Hill.

Clements, K.W. (1981), 'The Monetary Approach to Exchange Rate Determination: A Geometric Analysis', *Weltwirtschaftliches Archiv*, **20**, pp. 20–29.

Cochrane, J.H. (1991), 'A Critique of the Application of Unit Root Tests', *Journal of Economic Dynamics and Control*, **15**, pp. 275–84.

Copeland, L.S. (1984), 'The Pound Sterling/US Dollar Exchange Rate and the "News" ', *Economics Letters*, **16**, pp. 109–13.

Corbae, D. and Ouliaris, S. (1988), 'Cointegration Tests of Purchasing Power Parity', *Review of Economics and Statistics*, **55**, pp. 508–11.

Cuddington, J.T. (1983), 'Currency Substitution, Capital Mobility and Money Demand', *Journal of International Money and Finance*, **2**, pp. 111–33.

Cumby, R.E. and Obstfeld, M. (1981), 'A Note on Exchange Rate Expectations and Nominal Interest Differentials: A Test of the Fisher Hypothesis', *Journal of Finance*, **36**, pp. 697–703.

Cumby, R.E. and Obstfeld, M. (1984), 'International Interest Rate and Price Level Linkages Under Flexible Exchange Rates: A Review of Recent Evidence', in J.F.O. Bilson and R. Marston (eds), *Exchange Rate Theory and Practice*, Chicago: University of Chicago Press.

Currie, D.A. and Hall, S.G. (1986), 'The Exchange Rate and the Balance of Payments', *National Institute Economic Review*, February, pp. 521–9.

Currie, D.A. and Hall, S.G. (1989), 'A Stock–Flow Model of the Determination of the UK Effective Exchange Rate', in R. MacDonald and M.P. Taylor (eds), *Exchange Rates and Open Economy Macroeconomics*, Oxford: Blackwell, pp 130–41.

Cuthbertson, K., Hall, S.G. and Taylor, M.P. (1992), *Applied Econometric Techniques*, Hemel Hempstead: Philip Allan.

Davidson, J.E.H. (1985), 'Econometric Modelling of the Sterling Effective Exchange Rate', *Review of Economic Studies*, **52**, pp. 231–50.

Davutyan, N. and Pippenger, J. (1985), 'Purchasing Power Parity Did Not Collapse', *American Economic Review*, **84**, pp. 1151–8.

De Grauwe, P. and Dewachter, H, (1990), 'A Chaotic Monetary Model of the Exchange Rate', CEPR Discussion Paper, No, 466, October.

De Grauwe, P. and Vansanten, K. (1990), 'Deterministic Chaos in the Foreign Exchange Market', CEPR Discussion Paper, No. 370, January.

Demery, D. (1984), 'Exchange Rate Dynamics', *European Economic Review*, **24**, pp. 151–9.

Devereux, M.B. and Purvis, D.D. (1990), 'Fiscal Policy and the Real Exchange Rate', *European Economic Review*, **34**, pp. 1201–11.

Diebold, F.X. and Pauly, P. (1988), 'Endogenous Risk in a Portfolio-Balance Rational Expectations Model of the Deutschemark–Dollar Rate', *European Economic Review*, **32**, pp. 27–53.

Dominguez, K. (1986), 'Are Foreign Exchange Forecasts Rational? New Evidence from Survey Data', *Economics Letters*, **21**, pp. 277–81.

Domowitz, I. and Hakkio, C.S. (1985), 'Conditional Variance and the Risk Premium in the Foreign Exchange Market', *Journal of International Economics*, **18**, pp. 47–66.

Dooley, M.P. and Isard, P. (1982), 'A Portfolio Balance Rational Expectations Model of the Dollar–Mark Exchange Rate', *Journal of International Economics*, **12**, pp. 257–76.

Dooley, M.P. and Isard, P. (1983), 'The Portfolio-Balance Model of Exchange Rates and Some Structural Estimates of the Risk Premium', *International Monetary Fund Staff Papers*, **30**, pp. 683–702.

Dornbusch, R. (1976a), 'Expectations and Exchange Rate Dynamics', *Journal of Political Economy*, **84**, pp. 1161–76.

Dornbusch, R. (1976b), 'Exchange Rate Expectations and Monetary Policy', *Journal of International Economics*, **6**, pp. 231–44.

Dornbusch, R. (1987), 'Exchange Rate Economics: 1986', *Economic Journal*, **97**, pp. 1–8.

Dornbusch, R. and Fischer, S. (1980), 'Exchange Rates and the Current Account', *American Economic Review*, **70**, pp. 960–71.

Driskill, R.A. (1981), 'Exchange Rate Dynamics: an Empirical Investigation', *Journal of Political Economy*, **89**, pp. 357–71.

Driskill, R.A. and McCafferty, S. (1985), 'Exchange Rate Dynamics With Wealth Effects: Some Theoretical Ambiguities', *Journal of International Economics*, **19**, pp. 329–40.

Edison, H.J. (1985a), 'Purchasing Power Parity: A Quantitative Reassessment of the 1920's Experience', *Journal of International Money and Finance*, **4**, pp. 361–72.

Edison, H.J. (1985b), 'The Rise and Fall of Sterling: Testing Alternative Models of Exchange Rate Determination', *Applied Economics*, **17**, pp. 1003–21.

Edwards, S. (1982), 'Exchange Rates and "News": A Multi-currency Approach', *Journal of International Money and Finance*, **1**, pp. 211–24.

Enders, W. (1988), 'ARIMA and Cointegration Tests of PPP Under Fixed and Flexible Exchange Rate Regimes', *Review of Economics and Statistics*, **55**, pp. 504–8.

Engle, R.F. (1982), 'Autoregressive Conditional Heteroscedasticity with

Estimates of United Kingdom Inflation', *Econometrica*, **50**, pp. 987–1007.

Engle, R.F. and Granger, C.W.J. (1987), 'Cointegration and Error Correction: Representation, Estimation and Testing', *Econometrica*, **55**, pp. 251–76.

Engle, R.F. and Yoo, S. (1987), 'Forecasting and Testing in Co-Integrated Systems', *Journal of Econometrics*, **15**, pp. 143–58.

Evans, G.W. (1986), 'A Test For Speculative Bubbles and the Dollar–Sterling Exchange Rate: 1981–84', *American Economic Review*, **76**, pp. 621–36.

Fair, R.C. (1970), 'The Estimation of Simultaneous Equations Models with Lagged Endogenous Variables and First Order Serially Correlated Errors', *Econometrica*, **38**, pp. 507–16.

Fama, E.F. and Farber, A. (1979), 'Money, Banks and Foreign Exchange', *American Economic Review*, **69**, pp. 639–49.

Finn, M. (1986), 'Forecasting the Exchange Rate: A Monetary or Random Walk Phenomenon?', *Journal of International Money and Finance*, **5**, pp. 181–94.

Fisher, E. O'N. and Park, J.Y. (1991), 'Testing Purchasing Power Parity Under the Null Hypothesis of Cointegration', *Economic Journal*, **101**, pp. 1476–84.

Fisher, P.G., Tanna, S.K., Turner, D.S., Wallis, K.F. and Whitley, J.D. (1990), 'Econometric Evaluation of the Exchange Rate in Models of the UK Economy', *Economic Journal*, **100**, pp. 1230–44.

Fleming, J.M. (1962), 'Domestic Financial Policies Under Fixed and Under Floating Exchange Rates', *International Monetary Fund Staff Papers*, **3**, pp. 369–80.

Flood, R.P. and Garber, P.M. (1980), 'Market Fundamentals Versus Price Level Bubbles: The First Tests', *Journal of Political Economy*, **88**, pp. 745–70.

Flood, R.P. and Hodrick, R.J. (1990), 'On Testing for Speculative Bubbles', *Journal of Economic Perspectives*, **4**, Spring, pp. 85–101.

Frank, M. and Stengos, T. (1988), 'Chaotic Dynamics in Economic Time Series', *Journal of Economic Surveys*, **2**, pp. 103–33.

Frankel, J.A. (1979), 'On the Mark: A Theory of Floating Exchange Rates Based On Real Interest Differentials', *American Economic Review*, **69**, pp. 601–22.

Frankel, J.A. (1982a), 'In Search of the Exchange Rate Risk Premium: A Six-Currency Test Assuming Mean-Variance Optimisation', *Journal of International Money and Finance*, **1**, pp. 255–74.

Frankel, J.A. (1982b), 'The Mystery of the Multiplying Marks: A Modification of the Monetary Model', *Review of Economics and Statistics*, **64**, pp. 515–19.

Frankel, J.A. (1983), 'Monetary and Portfolio Balance Models Exchange Rate Determination', in J.S. Bhandari, B.H. Putnam, and J.H. Levin (eds), *Economic Interdependence and Flexible Exchange Rates*, Cambridge, Mass.: MIT Press.

Frankel, J.A. (1984), 'Tests of Monetary and Portfolio Balance Models of Exchange Rate Determination', in J.F.O. Bilson and R.C. Marston (eds), *Exchange Rate Theory and Practice*, pp. 239–60, Chicago: University of Chicago Press.

Frankel, J.A. (1985), 'The Dazzling Dollar', *Brookings Papers on Economic Activity*, **1**, pp. 199–217.

Frankel, J.A. (1986), 'International Capital Mobility and Crowding-out in the US Economy: Imperfect Integration of Financial or of Goods Markets?' in R.W. Hafer (ed), *How Open Is the US Economy?* pp. 33–67, Lexington Mass.: Lexington.

Frenkel, J.A. and Froot, K.A. (1987), 'Using Survey Data to Test Propositions Regarding Exchange Rate Expectations', *American Economic Review*, **77**, pp. 133–53.

Frenkel, J.A. (1976), 'A Monetary Approach to the Exchange Rate: Doctrinal Aspects and Empirical Evidence', *Scandinavian Journal of Economics*, **78**, pp. 200–24.

Frenkel, J.A. (1978), 'Purchasing Power Parity: Doctrinal Perspective and Empirical Evidence from the 1920's', *Journal of International Economics*, **8**, pp. 169–91.

Frenkel, J.A. (1981a), 'The Collapse of Purchasing Power Parity During the 1970's', *European Economic Review*, **16**, pp. 145–65.

Frenkel, J.A. (1981b), 'Flexible Exchange Rates, Prices and the Role of "News": Lessons from the 1970's', *Journal of Political Economy*, **89**, pp. 665–705.

Frenkel, J.A. and Rodriguez, C.A. (1982), 'Exchange Rate Dynamics and the Overshooting Hypothesis', *International Monetary Fund Staff Papers*, **29**, pp. 1–29.

Frisch, R. (1936), 'On the Notion of Equilibrium and Disequilibrium', *Review of Economic Studies*, **3**, pp. 100–5.

Froot, K.A. and Frankel, J.A. (1989), 'Forward Discount Bias: Is It An Exchange Rate Risk Premium?', *Quarterly Journal of Economics*, **104**, pp. 139–61.

Froot, K.A. and Frankel, J.A. (1990), 'Exchange Rate Forecasting Techniques, Survey Data and Implications for the Foreign Exchange Market', IMF Working Paper 90/43, Washington: International Monetary Fund.

Fuller, W.A. (1976), *Introduction to Statistical Time Series*, New York: John Wiley.

Gailliot, H.J. (1970), 'Purchasing Power Parity as an Explanation of Long-Term Changes in Exchange Rates', *Journal of Money Credit and Banking*, **2**, pp. 348–57.

Gandolfo, G. (1980), *Economic Dynamics: Methods and Models*, 2nd revised edition, Amsterdam: New Holland.

Goldstein, M. and Khan, M.S. (1978), 'The Supply and Demand for Exports: A Simultaneous Approach', *Review of Economics and Statistics*, **60**, pp. 275–86.

Goldstein, M. and Khan, M.S. (1985), 'Income and Price Effects in Foreign Trade', in R.W. Jones and P.B. Kenen (eds), *Handbook of International Economics*, vol. II, Amsterdam: North Holland.

Goodhart, C.A.E. (1989), *Money, Information and Uncertainty*, 2nd edition, Basingstoke: Macmillan.

Granger, C.W.J. (1986), 'Developments in the Study of Cointegrated Economic Variables', *Oxford Bulletin of Economics and Statistics*, **48**, pp. 213–28.

Gylfason, T. (1978), 'The Effect of Exchange Rate Changes on the Balance of Trade in Ten Industrial Countries', unpublished, Washington: IMF.

Gylfason, T. (1987), 'Does Exchange Rate Policy Matter?', *European Economic Review*, **30**, pp. 375–81.

Haberler, G. (1949), 'The Market for Foreign Exchange and the Stability of the Balance of Payments: A Theoretical Analysis', *Kyklos*, **3**, pp. 193–218.

Hakkio, C.S. and Rush, M. (1991), 'Cointegration: How Short is the Long Run?', *Journal of International Money and Finance*, **10**, pp. 571–81.

Hall, S.G. (1986), 'An Application of the Engle and Granger Two–Step Estimation Procedure to United Kingdom Wage Data', *Oxford Bulletin of Economics and Statistics*, **48**, pp. 229–40.

Hall, S.G. (1987), 'A Forward Looking Model of the Exchange Rate', *Journal of Applied Econometrics*, **2**, pp. 47–60.

Hansen, L.P. and Hodrick, R.J. (1983), 'Risk-Averse Speculation in the Forward Foreign Exchange Market: An Econometric Analysis of Linear Models', in J.A. Frenkel (ed.), *Exchange Rates and International Macroeconomics*, Chicago: University of Chicago Press.

Harris, L. (1981), *Monetary Theory*, New York: McGraw-Hill.

Harrod, R.F. (1948), *Towards a Dynamic Economics*, London: Macmillan.

Hausman, J.A. (1978), 'Specification tests in Econometrics', *Econometrica*, **46**, pp. 1251–72.

Hawtrey, R.G. (1919), *Currency and Credit*, London: Longmans, Green & Co.

Hayek, F.A. (1976), 'Choice in Currency: A Way to Stop Inflation', Occasional Paper, No. 48, London: Institute of Economic Affairs.

Hayek, F.A. (1978), *Denationalisation of Money*, 2nd edition, London: Institute of Economic Affairs.

Haynes, S, and Stone, J. (1981), 'On the Mark: Comment', *American Economic Review*, **71**, pp. 1060–67.

Helmers, F.L.C.H. (1988), 'Real Exchange Rate Indexes', in R. Dornbusch and F.L.C.H. Helmers (eds), *The Open Economy: Tools for Policymakers in Developing Countries*, Oxford: Oxford University Press.

Hendry, D.F. and Mizon, G. (1978), 'Serial Correlation as a Convenient Simplification, Not a Nuisance', *Economic Journal*, vol. 88, pp. 808–17.

Hendry, D.F., Pagan, A. and Sargan, J.D. (1984), 'Dynamic Specification', in Z. Grilliches and M.D. Intrilligator (eds), *Handbook of Econometrics*, vol. 2, Amsterdam: North Holland.

Hicks, J.R. (1939), *Value and Capital*, Oxford: Oxford University Press.

Hicks, J.R, (1967), *Capital and Growth*, Oxford: Oxford University Press.

Hodrick, R.J. (1978), 'An Empirical Analysis of the Monetary Approach to the Determination of the Exchange Rate', in J.A. Frenkel and H.G. Johnson (eds), *The Economics of Exchange Rates*, pp. 97–128, Reading Mass.: Addison–Wesley.

Hodrick, R.J. and Srivastava, S. (1984), 'An Investigation of Risk and Return in Forward Exchange', *Journal of International Money and Finance*, **3**, pp. 3–50.

Hoffman, D.L. and Schlagenhauf, D.E. (1983), 'Rational Expectations and Monetary Models of the Exchange Rate Determination', *Journal of Monetary Economics*, **11**, pp. 247–60.

Holden, K. and Thompson, J. (1992), 'Co-integration: An Introductory Survey', *British Review of Economic Issues*, **14**, pp. 1–55.

Hsieh, D.A. (1991), 'Chaos and Non-linear Dynamics: Application to Financial Markets', *Journal of Finance*, **46**, December, pp. 1839–77.

Huang, R.D. (1981), 'The Monetary Approach to the Exchange Rate in an Efficient Foreign Exchange Market: Test Based on Volatility', *Journal of Finance*, **36**, pp. 31–41.

Humphrey, T.M. (1980), 'Denis H. Robertson and the Monetary Approach to Exchange Rate', *Federal Reserve Bank of Richmond Economic Review*, May/June, pp. 19–26.

Hylleberg, S., Engle, R.F., Granger, C.W.J. and Yoo, B.S. (1990), 'Seasonal Integration and Cointegration', *Journal of Econometrics*, **44**, pp. 215–38.

Isard, P. (1977), 'How Far Can We Push the "Law of One Price"?', *American Economic Review*, **67**, pp. 942–8.

Isard, P. (1983), 'An Accounting Framework and Some Issues in Modeling How Exchange Rates Respond to News', in J.A. Frenkel (ed), *Exchange*

Rates and International Macroeconomics, Chicago: Chicago University Press, pp. 19–65.

Ito, T. (1990), 'Foreign Exchange Rate Expectations: Micro Survey Data', *American Economic Review*, **80**, pp. 434–49.

Johansen, S. (1988), 'Statistical Analysis of Cointegration Vectors', *Journal of Economic Dynamics and Control*, **12**, pp. 231–54.

Johansen, S. and Juselius, K. (1990), 'Maximum Likelihood Estimation and Inference on Cointegration – With Applications to the Demand for Money', *Oxford Bulletin of Economics and Statistics*, **52**, pp. 169–210.

Junge, G. (1984), 'Purchasing Power Parity in the 1920's and 1970's', *European Economic Review*, **26**, pp. 73–82.

Kearney, C. and MacDonald, R. (1985), 'Asset Markets and the Exchange Rate: A Structural Model of the Sterling–Dollar Rate 1972–82', *Journal of Economic Studies*, **12**, pp. 3–60.

Kearney, C. and MacDonald, R. (1986), 'A Structural Portfolio Balance Model of the Sterling–Dollar Exchange Rate', *Weltwirtschaftliches Archiv*, **122**, pp. 478–96.

Keynes, J.M. (1924), *A Tract on Monetary Reform*, London: Macmillan.

Keynes, J.M. (1930), *A Treatise on Money*, London: Macmillan.

Keynes, J.M. (1936), *The General Theory of Employment, Interest and Money*, London: Macmillan.

Kim, Y. (1990), 'Purchasing Power Parity in the Long Run: A Cointegration Approach', *Journal of Money, Credit and Banking*, **22**, pp. 491–503.

Kouri, P.J.K. (1976), 'The Exchange Rate and the Balance of Payments in the Short Run and in the Long Run: A Monetary Approach', *Scandinavian Journal of Economics*, **78**, pp. 280–308.

Krugman, P.R. (1991), 'Target Zones and Exchange Rate Dynamics', *Quarterly Journal of Economics*, **106**, pp. 669–82.

Kugler, P, and Lenz, C. (1990), 'Sind Wechselkursschwankungen Zufällig Oder Chaotisch?', *Schweizerische Zeitschrift für Volkswirtschaft und Statistik*, **2**, pp. 113–28.

Laursen, S. and Metzler, L.A. (1950), 'Flexible Exchange Rates and the Theory of Employment', *Review of Economics and Statistics*, **32**, pp. 281–99.

Layton, A.P. and Stark, J.P. (1990), 'Co-integration as an Empirical Test of Purchasing Power Parity', *Journal of Macroeconomics*, **12**, pp. 125–36.

Lerner, A.P. (1944), *The Economics of Control*, New York: Macmillan.

LeRoy, S. and Porter, R. (1981), 'The Present value Relation: Test Based on Implied Variance Bounds', *Econometrica*, **49**, pp. 555–74.

Leventakis, J.A. (1987), 'Exchange Rate Models: Do They Work?', *Weltwirtschaftliches Archiv*, **123**, pp. 363–76.

Lewis, K.K. (1989), 'Changing Beliefs and Systematic Rational Forecast Errors with Evidence from Foreign Exchange', *American Economic Review*, **79**, pp. 621–36.

Liu, P.C. and Maddala, G.S. (1992), 'Using Survey Data to Test Market Efficiency in the Foreign Exchange Markets', *Empirical Economics*, **17**, pp. 303–14.

Lucas, R.E. (1982), 'Interest Rates and Currency Prices in a Two-Country World', *Journal of Monetary Economics*, **10**, pp. 255–60.

MacDonald, R. (1983), 'Some Tests of the Rational Expectations Hypothesis for the Foreign Exchange Market', *Scottish Journal of Political Economy*, **30**, pp. 235–50.

MacDonald, R. (1988), *Floating Exchange Rates: Theory and Evidence*, London: Unwin Hyman.

MacDonald, R. (1991), 'Long Run Purchasing Power Parity: Is It For Real?', Dundee Discussion Papers in Economics, No. 29, November. (Forthcoming in *Review of Economics and Statistics*).

MacDonald, R. and Taylor, M.P. (1989), 'Economic Analysis of Foreign Exchange Markets: An Expository Survey', in R. MacDonald and M.P. Taylor (eds), *Exchange Rates and Open Economy Macroeconomics*, Oxford: Basil Blackwell.

MacDonald, R. and Taylor, M.P. (1992a), 'Exchange Rate Economics: A Survey', *International Monetary Fund Staff Papers*, **39**, March, pp. 1–57.

MacDonald, R and Taylor, M.P. (1992b), 'The Monetary Model of the Exchange Rate: Long-Run Relationships and Short-Run Dynamics', Discussion Papers in Financial Markets, No. 6, March, University of Dundee.

MacDonald, R. and Torrance, T.S. (1989), 'Some Survey-based Tests of Uncovered Interest Parity', in R. MacDonald and M.P. Taylor (eds), *Exchange Rates and Open Economy Macroeconomics*, Oxford: Basil Blackwell.

Machlup, F. (1955), 'Relative Prices and Aggregate Spending in the Analysis of Devaluation', *American Economic Review*, **45**, pp. 225–78.

Machlup, F. (1956), 'The Terms-of-Trade Effects of Devaluation upon Real Income and the Balance of Trade', *Kyklos*, **3**, pp. 417–50.

Machlup, F. (1959), 'Statics and Dynamics: Kaleidoscopic Words', *Southern Economic Journal*, **26**, pp. 91–110.

Manzur, M. (1990), 'An International Comparison of Prices and Exchange Rates: A New Test of Purchasing Power Parity', *Journal of International Money and Finance*, **9**, pp. 75–91.

Mark, N.C. (1990), 'Real and Nominal Exchange Rates in the Long Run: An Empirical Investigation', *Journal of International Economics*, **28**, pp. 115–36.

Markowitz, H. (1952), 'Portfolio Selection', *Journal of Finance*, **7**, pp. 77–91.

Marshall, A. (1923), *Money, Credit and Commerce*, London: Macmillan.

May, R.M. (1976), 'Simple Mathematical Models With Very Complicated Dynamics', *Nature*, **261**, June, pp. 459–67.

McCallum, B.T. (1976), 'Rational Expectations and the Estimation of Econometric Models: An Alternative Procedure', *International Economic Review*, **17**, pp. 484–90.

McKinnon, R.I. (1969), 'Portfolio Balance and International Payments Adjustment', in R.A. Mundell and A.K. Swoboda (eds), *Monetary Problems of the International Economy*, Chicago: University of Chicago Press.

McKinnon, R.I. (1982), 'Currency Substitution and Instability in the World Dollar Standard', *American Economic Review*, **72**, pp. 329–33.

McKinnon, R.I. and Oates, W. (1966), *The Implications of International Economic Integration for Monetary, Fiscal and Exchange Rate Policy*, Princeton Studies in International Finance, No. 16, Princeton.

McNown, R. and Wallace, M. (1989), 'Co-integration Test for Long-Run Equilibrium in The Monetary Exchange Rate Model', *Economics Letters*, **31**, pp. 263–7.

Meese, R.A. (1986), 'Testing for Bubbles in Exchange Markets: The Case of Sparkling Rates', *Journal of Political Economy*, **94**, pp. 345–73.

Meese, R.A. and Rogoff, K. (1983a), 'Empirical Exchange Rate Models of the Seventies: Do They Fit Out-of-Sample?', *Journal of International Economics*, **14**, pp. 3–24.

Meese, R.A. and Rogoff, K. (1983b), 'The Out-of-Sample Failure of Empirical Exchange Rate Models: Sampling Error or Misspecification?', in J.A. Frankel (ed.), *Exchange Rates and International Macroeconomics*, pp. 67–105, Chicago: University of Chicago Press.

Meese, R.A. and Rose, A.K. (1989), 'An Empirical Assessment of the Non-Linearities in Models of Exchange Rate Determination', Federal Reserve System, *International Finance Discussion Papers*, No. 367.

Metzler, L.A. (1942), 'Underemployment Equilibrium and International Trade', *Econometrica*, **10**, pp. 97–112.

Miles, M.A. (1978), 'Currency Substitution, Flexible Exchange Rates and Monetary Independence', *American Economic Review*, **68**, pp. 428–36.

Miles, M.A. (1981), 'Currency Substitution: Some Further Results and Conclusions', *Southern Economic Journal*, **438**, pp. 78–86.

Miller, M.H. and Weller, P. (1990), 'Currency Bubbles which Affect Fundamentals: A Qualitative Theorem', *Economic Journal*, **100**, Supplement, pp. 170–9.

Miller, M. and Weller, P. (1991), 'Exchange Rate Bands with Price Inertia', *Economic Journal*, **101**, pp. 1380–99.

Mundell, R.A. (1963), 'Capital Mobility and Stabilisation Policy Under Fixed and Flexible Exchange Rates', *Canadian Journal of Economics and Political Science*, **27**, pp. 475–85.

Mussa, M. (1976), 'The Exchange Rate, The Balance of Payments and Monetary and Fiscal Policy Under a Regime of Controlled Floating', *Scandinavian Journal of Economics*, **78**, pp. 229–48.

Myhrman, J. (1976), 'Experiences of Flexible Exchange Rates in Earlier Periods: Theories, Evidence and a New View', *Scandinavian Journal of Economics*, **78**, pp. 169–96.

Nelson, C.R. and Plosser, C.I. (1982), 'Trends and Random Walks in Macroeconomic Time Series: Some Evidence and Implications', *Journal of Monetary Economics*, **10**, pp. 139–62.

Niehans, J. (1977), 'Exchange Rate Dynamics with Stock/Flow Interaction', *Journal of Political Economy*, **85**, pp. 1245–57.

Niehans, J. (1984), *International Monetary Economics*, Deddington: Philip Allan.

Officer, L.H. (1974), 'Purchasing Power Parity and Factor Price Equalisation', *Kyklos*, **27**, pp. 868–78.

Officer, L.H. (1976a), 'The Purchasing Power Parity Theory of Exchange Rates: A Review Article', *International Monetary Fund Staff Papers*, **23**, pp. 1–60.

Officer, L.H. (1976b), 'The Productivity Bias in Purchasing Power Parity: An Econometric Investigation', *International Monetary Fund Staff Papers*, **23**, pp. 515–79.

Papell, D.H. (1984), 'Activist Monetary Policy and Exchange Rate Overshooting: The Deutschemark/Dollar Rate', *Journal of International Money and Finance*, **3**, pp. 293–310.

Papell, D.H. (1985), 'Activist Monetary Policy, Imperfect Capital Mobility and The Overshooting Hypothesis', *Journal of International Economics*, **18**, pp. 219–40.

Papell, D.H. (1988), 'Expectations and Exchange Rate Dynamics After a Decade of Floating', *Journal of International Economics*, **25**, pp. 303–17.

Park, J.Y. (1990), 'Testing Unit Roots and Cointegration by Variable Addition', in T.B. Formby and G.F. Rhodes (eds), *Cointegration, Spurious Regression and Unit Roots: Advances in Econometrics*, Greenwich, Connecticut and London: JAI Press.

Pentecost, E.J. (1984), 'Exchange Rate Determination and Macroeconomic Policy', unpublished PhD thesis, University of London.

Pentecost, E.J. (1991), 'Econometric Approaches to Empirical Models of Exchange Rate Determination', *Journal of Economic Surveys*, **5**, pp. 71–96.

Pentecost, E.J. (1992), 'The UK Non-oil Trade Balance and External Adjustment', in C.R. Milner and N. Snowden (eds), *Current Account Imbalances and External Adjustment in the 1990s*. Basingstoke: Macmillan.

Pentecost, E.J. and Mizen, P.D. (1992), 'Evaluating the Empirical Evidence for Currency Substitution: A Case Study of the Demand for Sterling in Europe', mimeo, Loughborough University.

Phillips, P.C.B. (1987), 'Time Series Regression With a Unit Root', *Econometrica*, **55**, pp. 460–72.

Pigou, A.C. (1920), 'Some Problems of Foreign Exchanges', *Economic Journal*, **30**, pp. 460–72.

Putnam, B.H. and Woodbury, J.R. (1979), 'Exchange Rate Stability and Monetary Policy', *Review of Business and Economic Research*, **15**, pp. 1–10.

Radaelli, G. (1988), 'Testable Restrictions and the Forecasting Performance of Exchange Rate Determination Models', Chase Manhattan Bank, Working Papers in Financial Economics, No. 4.

Ramsey, J.B. and Yuan, H-J. (1989), 'Bias and Error Bias in Dimension Calculations and Evaluations in Some Simple Models', *Physics Letters A*, **134**, pp. 287–97.

Ricardo, D. (1821), *On the Principles of Political Economy and Taxation*, Cambridge: Cambridge University Press.

Robertson, D.H. (1928), *Money*, Cambridge: Cambridge University Press.

Robinson, J. (1937), 'The Foreign Exchanges', in her *Collected Economic Papers*, vol. IV, Oxford: Basil Blackwell.

Samuelson, P.A. (1947), *Foundations of Economic Analysis*, Cambridge Mass.: Harvard University Press.

Sarantis, N. (1987), 'A Dynamic Asset Market Model for the Exchange Rate of the Pound Sterling', *Weltwirtschaftliches Archiv*, **124**, pp. 24–37.

Sarantis, N. and Stewart, C. (1991), 'Monetary and Portfolio Balance Models for Sterling Exchange Rates: A Cointegration Approach', mimeo, Kingston Polytechnic.

Sargan, J.D. (1958), 'The Estimation of Economic Relationships Using Instrumental Variables', *Econometrica*, **36**, pp. 393–413.

Scheinkman, J.A. (1990), 'Nonlinearities in Economic Dynamics', *Economic Journal*, **100**, Supplement, pp. 33–48.

Scheinkman, J.A. and LeBaron, B. (1989), 'Nonlinear Dynamics and Stock Returns', *Journal of Business*, July, pp. 311–37.

Schinasi, G.J. and Swamy, P.A.V.B. (1987), 'The Out-Of-Sample Forecasting Performance of Exchange Rate Models When Coefficients are Allowed to Change', Federal Reserve System, *International Finance Discussion Papers*, No. 301.

Schumpeter, J.A. (1952), *History of Economic Analysis*, London: Allen and Unwin.

Smith, G. and Brainard, W.C. (1976), 'The Value of A Priori Information in Estimating a Financial Model', *Journal of Finance*, **31**, pp. 1299–1322.

Smith, P.N. and Wickens, M.R. (1986), 'An Empirical Investigation into the Causes of Failure of the Monetary Model of the Exchange Rate', *Journal of Applied Econometrics*, **1**, pp. 143–62.

Somanath, V.S. (1986), 'Efficient Exchange Rate Forecasts: Lagged Models Better than the Random Walk', *Journal of International Money and Finance*, **5**, pp. 195–220.

Spinelli, F. (1983), 'Currency Substitution, Flexible Exchange Rates and the Case for International Monetary Cooperation', *International Monetary Fund Staff Papers*, **30**, pp. 755–83.

Takagi, S. (1991), 'Exchange Rate Expectations: A Survey of Survey Studies', *International Monetary Fund Staff Papers*, **38**, pp. 156–83.

Tata, F. (1991), 'Is the Foreign Exchange Market Characterized by Non-linearity?', LSE Financial Markets Group Discussion Paper Series, No. 118, April.

Tata, F. and Vassilicos, C. (1991), 'Is There Chaos in Economic Time Series? A Study of the Stock and Foreign Exchange Markets', LSE Financial Markets Group Discussion Paper Series, No. 120, July.

Taylor, M.P. (1988a), 'A DYMIMIC Model of Forward Exchange Risk, With Estimates For Three Major Exchange Rates', *The Manchester School*, **56**, pp. 55–68.

Taylor, M.P. (1988b), 'An Empirical Examination of Long-Run Purchasing Power Parity Using Cointegration Techniques', *Applied Economics*, **20**, pp. 1369–82.

Taylor, M.P. and McMahon, P.C. (1988), 'Long-Run Purchasing Power Parity in the 1920's', *European Economic Review*, **32**, pp. 179–97.

Tobin, J. (1958), 'Liquidity Preference As Behaviour Towards Risk', *Review of Economic Studies*, **25**, pp. 65–86.

Tobin, J. (1969), 'A General Equilibrium Approach to Monetary Theory', *Journal of Money Credit and Banking*, **1**, pp. 15–29.

Tsiang, S.C. (1959), 'The Theory of Forward Exchange and Effects of Government Intervention in the Foreign Exchange Market', *International Monetary Fund Staff Papers*, **7**, pp. 75–106.

Tsiang, S.C. (1961), 'The Role of Money in Trade-Balance Stability: Synthesis of the Elasticity and Absorption Approaches', *American Economic Review*, **51**, pp. 912–36.

Vassilicos, J.C. (1990), 'Are Financial Markets Chaotic? A Preliminary Study of the Foreign Exchange Market', LSE Financial Markets Group Discussion Paper Series, No. 86.

Vaubel, R. (1984), 'The Government's Money Monopoly: Externalities or Natural Monopoly?', *Kyklos*, **37**, pp. 27–58.

Viner, J. (1937), *Studies in the Theory of International Trade*, New York: Harper & Bros.

Visser, H. (1991), *Modern Monetary Theory: A Critical Survey of Recent Developments*, Aldershot: Edward Elgar.

West, K.D. (1987), 'A Specification Test for Speculative Bubbles', *Quarterly Journal of Economics*, **102**, August, pp. 553–80.

Williamson, J. and Milner, C.R. (1991), *The World Economy*, London: Harvester Wheatsheaf.

Wolf, A., Swift, J.B., Swinney, H.L. and Vastano, J.A. (1985), 'Determining Liapunov Exponents from a Time Series', *Physica D*, **16**, pp. 285–317.

Wolff, C.C.P. (1985), 'Time Varying Parameters and the Out-of-Sample Forecasting Performance of Structural Exchange Rate Models', mimeo, London Business School.

Woo, W.T. (1985), 'The Monetary Approach to Exchange Rate Determination Under Rational Expectations', *Journal of International Economics*, **18**, pp. 1–16.

Yeager, L.B. (1968), *The International Monetary Mechanism*, New York: Holt, Rinehart and Winston.

Zellner, A. (1962), 'An Efficient Method of Estimating Seemingly Unrelated Regressions and Tests of Aggregation Bias', *Journal of the American Statistical Association*, **57**, pp. 348–68.

Zervoyianni, A. (1988), 'Exchange Rate Overshooting, Currency Substitution and Monetary Policy', *The Manchester School*, **56**, pp. 247–67.

Author index

Subject index